Forging Multilingual Spaces

PEFC
PEFC/16-33-111
CATG-PEFC-052
www.pefc.org

BILINGUAL EDUCATION AND BILINGUALISM
Series Editors: Professor Nancy H. Hornberger, *University of Pennsylvania, Philadelphia, USA* and Professor Colin Baker, *University of Wales, Bangor, Wales, Great Britain*

Recent Books in the Series

Language Learning and Teacher Education: A Sociocultural Approach
Margaret R. Hawkins (ed.)
Bilingual Education in South America
Anne-Marie de Mejía (ed.)
Teacher Collaboration and Talk in Multilingual Classrooms
Angela Creese
Words and Worlds: World Languages Review
F. Martí, P. Ortega, I. Idiazabal, A. Barreña, P. Juaristi, C. Junyent, B. Uranga and E. Amorrortu
Language and Aging in Multilingual Contexts
Kees de Bot and Sinfree Makoni
Foundations of Bilingual Education and Bilingualism (4th edn)
Colin Baker
Bilingual Minds: Emotional Experience, Expression and Representation
Aneta Pavlenko (ed.)
Raising Bilingual-Biliterate Children in Monolingual Cultures
Stephen J. Caldas
Language, Space and Power: A Critical Look at Bilingual Education
Samina Hadi-Tabassum
Developing Minority Language Resources
Guadalupe Valdés, Joshua A. Fishman, Rebecca Chávez and William Pérez
Language Loyalty, Language Planning and Language Revitalization: Recent Writings and Reflections from Joshua A. Fishman
Nancy H. Hornberger and Martin Pütz (eds)
Language Loyalty, Continuity and Change: Joshua A. Fishman's Contributions to International Sociolinguistics
Ofelia Garcia, Rakhmiel Peltz and Harold Schiffman
Bilingual Education: An Introductory Reader
Ofelia García and Colin Baker (eds)
Disinventing and Reconstituting Languages
Sinfree Makoni and Alastair Pennycook (eds)
Language and Identity in a Dual Immersion School
Kim Potowski
Bilingual Education in China: Practices, Policies and Concepts
Anwei Feng (ed.)
English Learners Left Behind: Standardized Testing as Language Policy
Kate Menken
Pathways to Multilingualism: Evolving Perspectives on Immersion Education
Tara Williams Fortune and Diane J. Tedick (eds)
Biliteracy and Globalization: English Language Education in India
Viniti Vaish
Advocating for English Learners: Selected Essays
James Crawford

For more details of these or any other of our publications, please contact:
Multilingual Matters, St Nicholas House, 31-34 High Street,
Bristol, BS1 2AW, England
http://www.multilingual-matters.com

BILINGUAL EDUCATION AND BILINGUALISM 68
Series Editors: Nancy H. Hornberger and Colin Baker

Forging Multilingual Spaces

Integrated Perspectives on Majority and Minority Bilingual Education

Edited by

Christine Hélot and Anne-Marie de Mejía

MULTILINGUAL MATTERS
Bristol • Buffalo • Toronto

Library of Congress Cataloging in Publication Data
Forging Multilingual Spaces: Integrated Perspectives on Majority and Minority Bilingual Education. Edited by Christine Helot and Anne-Marie de Mejia.
Bilingual Education and Bilingualism: 68
Includes bibliographical references and index.
1. Education, Bilingual–Cross-cultural studies. 2. Linguistic minorities–Education–Cross-cultural studies. I. Hélot, Christine. II. De Mejía, Anne-Marie
LC3715.F67 2008
370.117–dc22 2008000300

British Library Cataloguing in Publication Data
A catalogue entry for this book is available from the British Library.

ISBN-13: 978-1-84769-076-0 (hbk)
ISBN-13: 978-1-84769-075-3 (pbk)

Multilingual Matters
UK: St Nicholas House, 31-34 High Street, Bristol BS1 2AW.
USA: UTP, 2250 Military Road, Tonawanda, NY 14150, USA.
Canada: UTP, 5201 Dufferin Street, North York, Ontario M3H 5T8, Canada.

The policy of Multilingual Matters/Channel View Publications is to use papers that are natural, renewable and recyclable products, made from wood grown in sustainable forests. In the manufacturing process of our books, and to further support our policy, preference is given to printers that have FSC and PEFC Chain of Custody certification. The FSC and/or PEFC logos will appear on those books where full certification has been granted to the printer concerned.

Typeset by Datapage International Ltd.
Printed and bound in Great Britain by MPG Books Ltd.

Contents

The Contributors

Jim Anderson is Lecturer in Modern Languages in Education in the Department of Educational Studies at Goldsmiths, University of London. He has many years' experience of working in London comprehensive schools where a wide range of languages have been taught. His research interests lie in the field of bilingualism and new media literacies. Jim is coordinator of the Flexible PGCE in Community Languages (Arabic, Mandarin Chinese, Panjabi and Urdu) at Goldsmiths, which won a 2007 European Award for Languages. He has recently directed a project, funded by the Nuffield Foundation, to create curriculum guides for Arabic, Mandarin, Panjabi, Tamil and Urdu. These were published by CILT, the National Centre for Languages, in 2007.

Cristina Banfi is currently in charge of the Department of Language Planning for the Ministry of Education of the City of Buenos Aires. She holds a Teacher of English degree from INES en LV 'J.R. Fernandez', an MPhil in Linguistics from the University of Cambridge and a PhD, also in Linguistics, from University College London. She has taught at university level in the UK, the USA and Argentina, at teacher training colleges, and at schools at primary and secondary school levels. She has published many articles and edited a journal. She has organised several conferences and has an active participation in professional associations.

Cristina Escobar Urmeneta is Professor of Foreign Language Pedagogy in the Faculty of Education at the Universitat Autònoma de Barcelona. She has conducted research in the teaching and learning of foreign languages in multilingual environments. More specifically, she has specialised in Portfolio Assessment and in Content and Language Integrated Learning (CLIL) in inclusive classrooms. She has extensive experience as a pre-service and in-service teacher educator and has written numerous articles on foreign language teaching and learning.

Ofelia García is Professor at Columbia University's Teachers College in the Department of International and Transcultural Studies. García has been Dean of the School of Education in the Brooklyn Campus of Long Island University and Professor of Bilingual Education at The City College of New York. Her latest books include *Imagining Multilingual Schools* (with Skutnabb-Kangas & Torres-Guzmán), *A Reader in Bilingual Education* (with Colin Baker) and *Language Loyalty, Continuity and Change: Joshua Fishman's Contributions to International Sociolinguistics* (with Peltz &

Schiffman). She is a Fellow of the Stellenbosch Institute for Advanced Study (STIAS) in South Africa, and has been a Fulbright Scholar, and a Spencer Fellow of the US National Academy of Education.

Eve Gregory is Professor of Language and Culture in Education at Goldsmiths College, University of London. Her research interests are in bilingualism and early literacy, home–school relations and ethnography. She has written widely in these fields. Her most recent book is *Learning to Read in a New Language: Making Sense of Words and Worlds*, published by Sage (2008). She has directed and co-directed a number of funded research projects into children's home language and literacy learning in bilingual contexts.

Rainer Enrique Hamel is Professor of Linguistics in the Department of Anthropology at Universidad Autónoma Metropolitana (UAM) in Mexico City. He is a member of the Mexican Academy of Science and the Director of the inter-institutional Research Programme 'Indigenous Communities and Intercultural Bilingual Education'. His areas of research include sociolinguistics, applied linguistics, bilingualism and bilingual education, language politics and planning, and discourse analysis. He has published several books and over 70 articles and book chapters in five different languages. Over the past years he has worked as a visiting researcher and professor in the Universities of Campinas and Belem, Brazil, Stanford and UC Santa Barbara, USA, and Frankfurt and Mannheim, Germany, as well as in other countries.

Christine Hélot is Professor of English at the University of Strasbourg in the teacher education department (IUFM d'Alsace). Prior to this post, she was a Lecturer in Applied Linguistics at the National University of Ireland. She is the author of several books in French on bilingualism in the family and in school contexts and on intercultural education. She has also published many articles on bilingualism and bilingual education in France, language policy, language awareness, linguistic diversity, teacher education and children's literature. She is a member of the editorial board of the *Bilingual Family Newsletter* and the journal *Language Policy.*

Charmian Kenner is Lecturer in Educational Studies at Goldsmiths College, University of London, where her research focuses on bilingualism, literacy and family learning. She has recently led ESRC-funded studies on early biliteracy, intergenerational learning between young children and grandparents and bilingual learning. Her books include *Home Pages: Literacy Links for Bilingual Children* (2000) and *Becoming Literate* (2004), both published by Trentham.

Anne-Marie de Mejía is currently Associate Professor at the Centre for Research and Teacher Development at Universidad de los Andes, Bogotá, Colombia. Prior to this, she worked for many years at Universidad del Valle in Cali, Colombia. Her areas of research include bilingual classroom interaction, bilingual teacher education and teacher empowerment. She has worked with the Colombian Ministry of Education on the research and development of bilingual programmes in Colombia. Her latest books include *Power, Prestige and Bilingualism* (2002, Multilingual Matters), *Bilingual Education in South America* (2005, Multilingual Matters) and *Empowerment. Empoderamiento y Construcción de Currículos Bilingües* (2006, Universidad del Valle) with Harvey Tejada and Sol Colmenares.

María Emilia Montes Rodríguez studied journalism at the Universidad Javeriana in Bogotá and has an MA in Ethnolinguistics from the Universidad de Los Andes. In 1994, she received her Doctorate in 'Linguistique Théorique et Formelle' from the Université de Paris VII-Jussieu. Much of her research work has been devoted to the grammatical description of Tikuna, an isolated Amazon language. She has also been involved in educational consultancy work in indigenous education in Colombia, Brasil and Peru, and has participated in education and development programmes for indigenous teachers. She has published articles and books in the areas of grammar, ethnolinguistics, ethnoeducation and sociolinguistics. Since 1998 she has been working at the Universidad Nacional de Colombia, Facultad de Ciencias Humanas en Bogotá. She has also worked at the Universidad del Valle in Cali and Universidad de Los Andes.

Muiris Ó Laoire is a senior lecturer at the Institute of Technology Tralee, Ireland and works on a consultative basis on the Review of Languages at the National Council for Curriculum and Assessment (NCCA) Dublin. He is co-editor of *Teagasc na Gaeilge* (Ireland) and *The Celtic Journal of Language Learning* (USA). He is author of textbooks, academic books and several articles on sociolinguistics and language pedagogy. He is a past president of IRAAL, the Irish Association of Applied Linguistics, the Irish affiliate of AILA.

Silvia Rettaroli is a teacher of English and has been a teacher educator for the last 25 years. She has also worked as school manager at bilingual schools, where she has developed a number of professional development projects. During the 1990s she worked as Foreign Languages Co-coordinator in the Research and Educational Development Unit of the Ministry of Education of Argentina and was in charge of designing the national matrix for the Argentine Teacher Education curricula. Her main areas of interest are professional development and bilingual education research.

Virginia Unamuno Kaschapava is Professor of Language Pedagogy at the Universitat Autònoma de Barcelona. Her main research interests are sociolinguistics and discourse analysis applied to language education in multilingual contexts. In the last few years she has focused her attention on the development and implementation of linguistic reception schemes in Catalan schools. She has published widely in these fields.

Chapter 1

Introduction: Different Spaces – Different Languages. Integrated Perspectives on Bilingual Education in Majority and Minority Settings

CHRISTINE HÉLOT and ANNE-MARIE DE MEJÍA

In many parts of the world there exists a traditional divide between policy, practice and research into bilingualism and bilingual education programmes for majority language speakers, and modalities offered for minority language speakers. As a result, policymakers, teachers and researchers who are involved with bilingual programmes in international languages often have little contact with researchers and practitioners who are concerned with bilingual education programmes in minority communities. This separation leads to a necessarily limited view of the progress of research on bilingualism and bilingual education, and means that linguistic and pedagogical insights and perceptions from each tradition are often not available to inform future general developments in the field.

Furthermore, while bilingualism in internationally prestigious languages is generally considered worthy of investment of considerable sums of money, as it provides access to a highly 'visible', socially accepted form of bilingualism, leading to the possibility of employment in the global marketplace, bilingualism in minority languages leads, in many cases, to an 'invisible' form of bilingualism in which the native language is undervalued and associated with underdevelopment, poverty and backwardness. Thus, on the one hand, bilingualism may well bring advantages, prestige and power (de Mejía, 2002), but on the other, it can give rise to problems and disadvantages, 'disempowering' individuals who happen to speak languages considered of limited value in the global marketplace (Cummins, 2000). This double vision of bilingualism has been referred to by Barriga Villanueva (2007: 14) as a phenomenon of 'claroscuros'. She characterises the two sides of bilingualism in the following manner, 'the luminous side is related to a high level of culture, of personal prestige ...; the dark side ... is that which is related to the power and domination of a hegemonic language'.

The discourse commonly used to refer to bilingual education generally reinforces these types of dichotomies. As Hornberger (1989: 273, 2003a) recognises in her postulation of a continua model of biliteracy, rather than concern ourselves with 'polar opposites, ... we need to take account of all dimensions represented by the continua'. In other words, we need to go beyond these dichotomies so that we can represent the nature of bilingualism and multilingualism more appropriately in relation to the complex, shifting realities of the world today. Ofelia García (2005: personal communication) acknowledges, with regard to the situation in the USA, 'The old paradigms of bilingual education do not work anymore. Bilingual situations today are fluid.' The implication is that if we continue to use a naturalised discourse which focuses on dichotomies, barriers will continue to exist and the lack of a shared discourse will be exploited to create division, so that bilingualism in minority languages will continue to be seen as a disadvantage.

In a colloquium organised on this topic at the Fifth International Symposium on Bilingualism in Barcelona in 2005, participants from eight different countries were asked to rethink bilingual education in a way which broke away from dichotomous oppositions, and to critically examine some of the more recent policies and practices in relation to the development of bi/multilingualism in schools. While the main aim of the colloquium was to confront reflections on how to bridge the gap between elite and minority bilingualism, another objective was to gather together researchers who have studied bilingual education from different points of view. Some researchers were more familiar with programmes for indigenous groups (Hamel), others with programmes for national minority groups (O'Laoire, Escoba Urmeneta and Unamuno), others with programmes for migrant minority groups (Anderson, Kenner, Gregory and García) and others again with programmes for dominant language groups (Hélot, de Mejía, Montes Rodríguez, Banfi and Rettaroli).

In the Barcelona colloquium there was testimony to the success of teacher initiatives at grassroots level in countries such as the USA, Ireland, France and England; however, responses at government level were seen as less encouraging. Participants acknowledged the need for the development of more powerful strategies at macro level and highlighted the responsibility of academics in promoting change. There was also a call for the creation of spaces in school programmes, which would allow for bilingual children's voices to be heard in a collaborative learning situation, rather than existing in isolation, in separate streams or in 'pull-out' situations. Charmian Kenner (2005, personal communication) suggested that, 'the needs of L1 and L2 speakers should be met in the same shared space', in a sensitive manner. Both Dual Language Programmes and Language Awareness Programmes were seen as possible ways forward for developing this kind of 'meeting-place' of different languages and cultures. Thus, the possibility of integrating a language awareness component into bilingual education professional development courses was proposed as a means of helping bilingual teachers come to terms with the challenges of recognising and promoting language and cultural diversity in the classroom. Indeed, it should be acknowledged that today pupils attending bilingual education programmes may speak a different language from the two languages used to learn in school. It is somewhat ironic that bilingual education should exclude the home languages of some pupils in the same way as monolingual education does. This implies that bilingual educators need to rethink their attitudes and representations towards languages and move from a strictly bilingual framework to a multilingual one.

It should be stressed that the editors of this book do not wish to deny the importance of context in analysing bilingual or multilingual education. Our aim is, in fact, to find new ways of revisiting bilingual education typologies and, hopefully, to redirect bi/multilingual education policy. While it is clear for the authors in this book that the present linguistic and cultural diversity of our classrooms questions existing bilingual programmes, the ways in which the relationships between minority and majority languages are treated in national policies (or supranational policies at the European level) can inform researchers looking for new models of language education; models which focus on practices that highlight the value of bi/multilingualism in any language and which take into account the social practices of languages, and not just national education agendas. In other words, as we stated initially, what we want to address in this book is the traditional divide which exists in most countries between language education for the monolingual majority in dominant languages and compensatory education in the national language for the bilingual minorities. We also wish to argue for the recognition of a necessary complementarity between foreign language education and the education of language minority students, based on the principle of integration across linguistic communities.

Beyond the contextual and structural characteristics of bilingual education developed in the countries represented in this book, we wish to understand the ways in which all these programmes are being questioned by researchers and practitioners who are redefining the goals of language education (and bilingual education) in order to adapt to the growing linguistic and cultural diversity of classrooms and pupils. While Fishman (1976, 1977, 1982) believed in the notion of 'enrichment' bilingual education as a model which offers the greatest potential benefit, not only to language minority speakers but to the national society as a whole, and consequently that it should be extended beyond its elitist origin from the majority group to the minority group, we would argue today that minority language settings can also teach us a lot about language learning in majority contexts. As researchers in the field of language biographies have shown, multilingual students have a more developed awareness of the relationship between language and identity and language and power. They also show greater metalinguistic resources when learning languages in formal contexts. In other words, as García *et al.* (2006: 10) explains, 'immigrants, exiles, refugees and other "transnationals" have resources, namely their ability to have "double vision", or to be "in the middle", so as to be able to have a critical orientation towards the many places in which they have lived'. Thus, an integrated vision of bilingual education does not mean applying the same goals and programmes to minority students as to majority students, but educating minority and majority students together, as in the Dual Language Immersion schools in the USA or the peace schools in Israel (www.handinhand.org.il).

Looking at the eight countries described in this book, it is clear that within each sociolinguistic setting, different languages are allocated different spaces in the respective curricula (or no space at all). They are taught according to different modalities, assigned more or less time, more or less space, more or less value. Thus, most education systems reflect the divided vision prevalent in society that some languages are worth more than others. Schools everywhere reflect societal characteristics, societal needs, societal views and, above all, societal power constellations. Programmes that pose little threat to the established power structure are the ones that generally get implemented in schools, yet reflective practitioners and researchers are continually challenging institutional racism in schools and devising potentially empowering pedagogical alternatives (Cummins, 2000).

The contributors to this volume give examples of such programmes, while at the same time focusing on the inter-relationships between language and the wider social and political environment, contesting traditional relations of power. For example, some of the authors point to the gap between bilingualism developed in the home context and bilingualism developed at school and how educational language policies deny the former and invest heavily in the latter. This is another type of dichotomy which needs to be reframed conceptually and envisaged as a continuum, rather than being examined in isolation. It needs to be understood within a framework where all dimensions of bilingualism are linked to one another. Due to the fact that some home bilingualism is supported in school and some is not, depending on the status of the language concerned, Hornberger and Skilton Sylvester's continua of biliteracy model (2003) is particularly useful in this respect, because it was developed within an ecological perspective which makes transparent the ideologies that pervades language policies and language choice.

As Heller and Martin Jones (2002: 30 quoted by Creese & Martin, 2003: 164) point out, an ecological approach makes clear 'what kinds of language practices are valued and considered good, normal, appropriate or correct in particular classrooms and schools, and who are likely to be the winners or losers in the ideological orientations'.

What we would like to show in this book is how it is possible to approach language education from a more ecological point of view, that is to say where all languages are envisaged as learning resources for those who speak them, as well as for the monolingual majorities. Thus, we contend that any language should be seen as a linguistic and cultural resource to learn another language, including the school language, helping to promote mutual understanding and opening to others. We agree with Ruiz (1984) and Hornberger (1991: 226) who maintain that, 'The primary identifying characteristics for enrichment bilingual education is that the program structure incorporates a recognition that the minority language is not only a right of its speakers but a potential resource for majority language speakers'.

Most of the papers in this collection are co-authored because the researchers needed to collaborate with colleagues in order to be able to jointly examine the diverse forms of bilingual education in their own sociolinguistic and political context. They examine points of contact between minority and majority bilingual or multilingual provision in eight different national scenarios, discussing ways in which the unequal balance of power across different languages and literacies is either reinforced, or challenged by policymakers and educators, and examining reasons for this. The emphasis is on asking whether it is possible to find 'various modes of interplay' (Hélot, 2005: 5) between prestigious bilingualism and the bilingualism of minorities, and whether this approach can help to envisage new models of language education in school settings.

This volume is divided into two sections. The focus of the first section is entitled 'Bilingualism in the Americas' and includes discussion of the situation in one North American nation, the USA, and three Latin American countries: Colombia, Argentina and Mexico. The second section is concerned with the situation in Europe and includes contributions from France, Ireland, Catalonia and England.

Part 1: The Americas

Our characterisation of the situation of bilingual education in four national scenarios in the Americas is intended, on one hand, to complement the discussion of developments in Europe in Part 2 of this collection of papers. It is also a convenient label to group together countries, which although sociolinguistically diverse in nature, are marked by their differing relationships with the Spanish language at international and intranational level. Mexico, Colombia and Argentina all recognise Spanish either as their official language or as the first language of the majority of their population,[1] while in the USA there are more than 30 million speakers of the language, according to the Census carried out in 2000 (Hamel, 2003).

However, it must also be recognised that this apparent homogeneity with respect to the Spanish language conceals a wide range of diversity. In the USA alone, the Hispanic (Latino) community form a,

> very heterogeneous medley of races and nationalities (...) Latinos include native born US citizens (predominantly Chicanos – Mexican-American – and Nuyoricans – 'mainland' Puerto Ricans) and Latin American immigrants of all racial and national combinations. (Flores, 1993: 199)

Not only is the Latino community a diverse community, but there is also evidence of a highly complex linguistic situation with multiple varieties of Spanish spoken and the emergence of a language continuum with varying levels of proficiency and with distinctive characteristics, such as a tendency to replace the subjunctive and conditional forms with the indicative, due to the high degree of contact with English (Gutierrez & Fairclough, 2006).

However, in spite of this situation, traditionally the teaching of Spanish as a foreign language in the USA has been based on the teaching of a standard form of the language and the rejection of local varieties. Yet, as Gutierrez and Fairclough (2006: 174) argue, sociolinguistic studies of language heterogeneity have begun to challenge such concepts as 'the standard language', and thus, 'the goal should be for students to communicate both with Spanish speakers in the United States and around the world (so they) should also (be) able to communicate using the predominant local or regional vernacular norms'.

Even though Spanish is challenging English in certain parts of the USA where a number of towns have predominantly Spanish-speaking populations (Graddol, 2006), the use of this language in bilingual education in the USA has been mainly confined to transitional bilingual programmes (TBE) aimed at integrating minority students into the monolingual English-speaking mainstream. Initially, these were envisaged as 'early exit' programmes, based on a deficit perspective, positioning bilingual children as 'handicapped'. Later, there was the emergence of TBE 'late exit', or language maintenance programmes, where children's bilingualism was seen as a resource rather than a problem (Abbate-Vaughn, 2004).

More recently, two-way bilingual education, or 'dual language programmes', have continued this vision of additive bilingualism, helping students from linguistic minority and linguistic majority backgrounds to develop two languages, as well as promoting 'positive cross-cultural proficiency and understanding in all students' (Abbate-Vaughn, 2004: 31).

These programmes ideally involve balanced numbers of students from each language background, and have been instrumental in offering both Anglophone and Latino students the possibility of learning Spanish and English in a bilingual environment, particularly at elementary level (Freeman, 1998). However, as noted by Torres-Karna and de Kanter (2004: 351–352), the undoubted success of this initiative in developing Spanish–English bilingualism among these populations should not blind us to the intrinsic difficulties involved in providing appropriate educational provision for 'low socioeconomic status language minority students with language majority students from middle-class professional homes'.

The other three Latin American nations that form part of our collection, Mexico, Colombia and Argentina, were subjected to an official policy of compulsory Castilianisation, which characterised the situation of the colonies under Spanish rule in the 15th and 16th centuries. However, in 1550, Carlos V also allowed for the use of vernacular languages in certain areas; in particular, Nahuatl in Mexico, as well as Quechua for the Andean region and Tupi-Guarani for the central South American area (today Paraguay) (Hamel, 2006). Thus, a certain degree of multilingualism was favoured in certain majority languages, though as time progressed the two former colonial languages, Spanish and Portuguese, were increasingly consolidated as the main languages of communication and unification within the newly emergent nation states in Latin America in the 19th century.

Furthermore, during the 20th century, as these two languages developed into international languages, indigenous languages found themselves increasingly under threat throughout the region (Hamel, 2006). As Barriga Villanueva (2007: 16) observes in the case of Mexico, since colonisation 'there has been a continuous pendular movement between two main poles: indigenous languages and Spanish, although in reality the pendulum has swung more towards Castilianisation, and with this, the displacement of the Indo-Mexican languages'. In the case of the National Programme of Intercultural Bilingual Education (PNEIB) set up in Argentina in 2004, which aims at revitalising indigenous knowledge, language and identity, 'curricular contents are, for the most part, not delivered in the pupils' native language, but rather in Spanish' (Banfi & Rettaroli, this volume).

In the course of these developments, the Spanish language gained independence from the Castilian variety, and language academies were set up to preserve the distinct varieties of the language in the different

Latin American nations (Hamel, 2006). However, more recently, it has been noted that the Spanish language is, itself, under threat in various Latin American nations. In Colombia, for example, the Colombian Language Academy has expressed concern about the rapid spread of English, particularly among the upper and middle classes by means of the elite bilingual school system, and its negative effect on the perceived status and importance of Spanish as a language appropriate for the development of scientific discourse (Patiño, 2005).

In a recent survey of bilingual education in the Andean region of South America, King (2005: 2) distinguishes between

> enrichment models (of bilingual education) which promote language development for the elite; and ... transitional (or nominally maintenance) models for indigenous sectors which, in the long term, promote subtractive bilingualism.

She argues that these two different models lead to different 'imagined communities' (Norton, 2000, cited in King, 2005: 2). While parents and staff in enrichment model schools hope that students will become fluent in a high status language, such as English or French, so that they are able to move in international circles, those working with indigenous minority language groups 'tend to emphasize mastery of Spanish and transition to the dominant language and national culture' (King, 2005: 3). Hamel (2006) sees the latter as part of a wider strategy of language policy and education for indigenous peoples involving the suppression of indigenous languages and the assimilation of their speakers in the process of building a unified nation state.

In similar fashion, this time from a broader Latin American perspective, Hamel (this volume) identifies a first space (or domain) with the intercultural bilingual education programmes offered to indigenous pupils at public schools, which are characterised by a lack of pedagogical and human resources. He sees a second space as that belonging to elite bilingual schools where the emphasis is on the teaching and learning of prestigious international languages. Although, as Hamel observes, there is generally very little contact between the two types of communities and their schools, he does envisage the possibility of reciprocal processes of mutual exchange and learning across the systems, leading to the fostering of the growth of multilingual spheres and the development of pluricultural nation states that value cultural and linguistic diversity.

De Mejía and Montes Rodríguez are also concerned about similar issues in relation to the Colombian context. They note that while,

> discussion in majority language contexts has concentrated particularly on pedagogical and administrative aspects involved in the implementation of bilingual programmes ..., in minority language

> contexts, there has been an emphasis on the non-neutrality of languages and an overemphasis on political and anthropological issues. (De Mejía & Montes Rodríguez, this volume)

They propose a dialogue between the actors in these different spaces, particularly in relation to the linguistic, cultural and contextual issues that have been successfully addressed in ethnoeducation programmes,[2] and the pedagogical initiatives related to efficient processes of the teaching and learning of languages developed in bilingual education in majority language contexts.

The relationship of different languages with different spaces, foregrounded in the title of this book, brings to mind the concept of 'third spaces' (Bhabha, 1994) which has been in use in recent years in the fields of cultural studies and applied linguistics. These intermediate spaces between relatively stable and homogeneous norms in 'first' and 'second' spaces have been seen as essentially problematic because they constitute neither one thing nor another but are heterogeneous in nature. They also presuppose the presence of relatively fixed outer norms. However, it may be argued that these spaces can transcend their component sources through a dialectical process to make a new, expanded space which permits the possibility of stimulation and renewal, as well as threat (CELTEAL, 2005). Thus, for example, in a bilingual education context, it may be asked how students construct learning experiences that are meaningful for themselves out of what they receive from their teachers and others. Another question that arises has to do with how particular teachers and learners in specific classroom settings adopt or adapt teaching methodologies, materials, established bilingual models and rules governing classroom language use in relation to the demands of their particular context.

These are some of the issues addressed by García in her discussion of the relationship between the teaching of Spanish and the use of Spanish in teaching in the US school context in this volume. She considers that there is evidence that enlightened bilingual teachers can go beyond the established norms of elite foreign language programmes and those which characterise transitional bilingual education programmes for minority language speakers in order to enable children's plurilingual and pluriliteracy practices. However, this implies that they need to be able to 'work in the gap' (and) 'to hold a heteroglossic view of how language is negotiated' (García, this volume), rather than continue to support the monoglossic language ideologies that the author considers characteristic of language in education polities in the USA.

In her analysis of data from a dual (Spanish–English) language classroom, García characterises this 'unconscious' reaction of individual teachers against externally imposed structures developed in the dual language model of bilingual education as the 'Trojan Horse' of the language separation model. She notes that although the teacher in the class observed was very concerned to maintain the standard separation of the two languages, the actual language practices of the bilingual learners, which reflected their heterogeneous levels of language proficiency, combined with the collaborative nature of workshop literacy activities militated against the strict separation of English and Spanish decreed in the tenets of the dual language programme. Thus, the bilingual 'space' spontaneously created by the participants in the interaction reflected the communication needs and potential of the students far more appropriately than could have been achieved in a separatist approach to language use.

This focus on individual initiatives 'place(s) the classroom practitioner at the heart' (Ricento & Hornberger, 1996: 417), facilitating processes of educational and social change and institutional transformations from the grass roots, a 'bottom-up' perspective. García (1993: 36) sees teachers as prime agents in these processes. Thus, she maintains that, '(the teacher) must stop being an instructor, accepting of orders, of curriculum planned, of material given, and must claim her role as an educator'. This echoes Cummins' recognition of teachers as powerful actors in shaping school contexts. As he says,

> Legislative and policy reforms may be necessary conditions for effective change but they are not sufficient ... The social organisation and bureaucratic constraints within the school reflect not only broader policy and societal factors, but also the extent to which individual educators accept or challenge the social organisation of the school ... (Cummins, 1986/2001: 657)

Consequently, we need to ask how far these essentially individual actions of particular teachers in particular classroom situations should be seen within wider changes in policy and pedagogy. How far is it necessary that bottom-up, grassroots initiatives, such as that documented by Garcia, mesh with top-down developments in policy to achieve noticeable effects?

In this respect, de Mejía and Montes (this volume) recognise the positive results of some productive individual experimentation in ethnoeducation programmes in minority language contexts in Colombia. Yet, they also acknowledge that there is a strong case to be made for a policy of 'positive discrimination' towards this type of bilingual/multilingual programme in order to 'compensate for the linguistic fragility of minority contexts' (de Mejía & Montes, this volume). The responsibility given to individual bilingual indigenous teachers to 'innovate, research and transform contents and practices' (de Mejía and Montes, this volume) has, in many cases, proved to be too heavy a burden and has resulted in a lack of visible results. Thus, the authors argue it is important to develop a national bilingual education policy to ensure State commitment to implementing the principles enshrined in the country's political constitution.

Perhaps though, rather than juxtaposing individual versus society or state, we should be thinking of a more inclusive, a more additive vision, where macro and micro levels are addressed in a more integrated fashion. As Hornberger (2003b: 301), commenting on an article by Skilton-Sylvester (2003), reminds us, 'macro-level policies and ideologies are so entangled with teachers' policies and ideologies at the micro level that educators need to be involved at both levels, if a truly additive perspective is to be possible'.

In this sense, the chapter by Banfi and Rettaroli is important, as the authors focus their attention specifically on the profiles of teachers working in the different types of bilingual programmes in Argentina. These include: Intercultural Bilingual Education Programmes for Indigenous Children, Bilingual Education Programmes for Deaf Children, Bilingual Education in State Schools, Bilingual Education Programmes in Language Contact Situations and Bilingual Education Programmes in Elite Schools. The researchers come to the conclusion, along with many other writers on bilingual education provision (Baker, 1995; Lindholm-Leary, 2005), that the lack of teacher background in bilingualism and bilingual education can result in difficulties in the effective implementation of bilingual programmes at both majority and minority level. The authors make a case for 'cross-programme cooperation and collaboration in teacher development activities' (Banfi & Rettaroli, this volume). They argue that for this to happen it is important that all the different modalities of bilingual provision present in the country be officially recognised as such. Thus, the authors maintain that 'an explicit acknowledgement of the existence of bilingual education as an encompassing term would be helpful in providing common ground and theoretical support for all these different programmes'.

Echoing Hamel (this volume), Banfi and Rettaroli (this volume) recognise that due to the fact that the origin of many of these programmes is mutually exclusive and also that neither teacher nor student populations overlap, there is a 'total lack of contact ... (which) generate(s) mutual mistrust and prejudice'. In order for this to be overcome, the authors advocate that all actors in bilingual programmes (teachers, headteachers, school supervisors, education authorities) should be familiar with five basic areas of knowledge: the languages and cultures involved in the programme; the content to be taught; pedagogical knowledge; and knowledge about bilingualism and bilingual education.

The issue of terminology referred to in relation to educational programmes in Argentina is worth raising here, as it sheds light on the ideologies that underpin the label 'bilingual education' in different parts of the continent. Banfi and Rettaroli (this volume) note that 'although the label "bilingual school/programme" is widely applied in common parlance to a number of different types of programmes, it is only this modality (i.e. Intercultural Bilingual Education Programmes for Indigenous Children) that is granted official recognition, as exemplified in the recently approved Law of National Education in Argentina (2006)'. Until the South Atlantic Conflict in 1982, the prestigious English–Spanish schools were referred to as 'British-type' schools (ESSARP, 1995), rather than bilingual institutions.

This recognition of bilingual education provision for students from minority indigenous communities is similar to pronouncements in Colombia. Article 10 of the Political Constitution (1991) states that,

> Spanish is the official language of Colombia. The languages and dialects of the ethnic groups are also official in their territories. The teaching given in communities with their own linguistic traditions will be bilingual.

However, Barriga Villanueva sounds a note of caution in this respect. She reminds us, in the case of Mexico, that,

> Official and academic discourse has sometimes propagated a false idea of bilingualism as the 'mastery of two languages'. If this were so, there would not be room for the negation of ethnic identity and the danger of the extinction of some languages. (Barriga Villanueva, 2007: 24)

In contrast to the explicit recognition of bilingual teaching and learning as a right for indigenous groups in Argentina and in Colombia, García notes the gradual elimination of the term 'bilingual' in US legal discourse over the past five years, as a result of the pressure from the 'English Only' movement. As well as the fact that California, Massachusetts and Arizona have declared bilingual education illegal, the Bilingual Education Act itself has been supplanted by the 'No Child Left Behind Act' (2001) and the Office of Bilingual Education and Minority Languages Affairs has been renamed the 'Office of English Language Acquisition, Language Enhancement and Academic Achievement for Limited English Proficient Students'. Perhaps it is significant that the only bilingual modality that is currently seen as successful in the US context is entitled 'Dual Language' rather than 'Bilingual Education'.

In spite of the fact that the Americas is the second poorest part of the world, after Europe, in terms of native languages (García *et al.*, 2006), in general it may be said that interest in bilingualism and bilingual education is gaining momentum, even though, in the case of the USA, this may be referred to as 'dual language' provision. In Latin America, this interest has been evidenced in the creation of an international symposium series on bilingualism and bilingual education (Buenos Aires, 2004; Bogotá, 2006) aimed at an exchange of knowledge among those working in majority and minority language contexts in the region. Researchers and academics from different traditions have begun to recognise the importance of each other's contributions to developments in the field. Thus, the way is open for a widening vision, which takes into account the changing linguistic and cultural constellations of a globalised world in flux, as well as the increasing complexity of local interests and priorities.

Part 2: Europe

The presentation of the four European countries (autonomous region in the case of Catalonia) described in this second part of our book reflects the wide variety of sociolinguistic contexts present in Europe and how educational language policies can only be understood within a historical and political perspective. It is not our aim here to compare these different settings[3] but rather to envisage them as a multiple springboard to rethink bilingual education within the present development of multilingualism in each of the countries concerned. We would like to argue, based on the authors' analyses, that for the most part, bilingual education has been framed within a monolingual habitus, and we propose to examine here whether and how it is possible to go beyond this monolingual framework and envisage language education as more inclusive, more integrative and more coherent.

In other words, through the critical re-examination of various dichotomies, we ask whether it is possible to bridge the gap between the different forms of bilingualism (and plurilingualism[4]), because we wish to question the negative attitudes towards the bilingualism of minority language speakers, and more specifically towards the often denied, or at best ignored, bilingualism of immigrant populations. Can we develop truly integrated and inclusive language policies that will challenge monolingual monocultural perspectives and envisage plurilingualism from a plurilingual point of view? Can we envisage new relationships between languages at the societal level and translate these into more open education policies which will break down barriers between the different categories of languages? Can we translate these policies at the classroom level so that educators ensure that students from linguistically diverse backgrounds have the right to maintain their home language(s) with the support of the school system. In short, can we move towards a more integrated multilingual society? These are some of the questions we will be concerned with in this section.

The researchers from the four countries represented here are all trying to grapple with these questions, within the limits of curricula and syllabi designed at the national or regional level and as a product of national histories. They are dealing with linguistically pluralist societies where different languages are in contact, and where the relationships between the various languages are complex. Here again, traditional dichotomies, such as that established between dominant and dominated languages, do not work any longer. Indeed, the presence of many languages resulting from processes of immigration has changed the traditional hierarchies, pushing endogenous minority languages up the ladder and maintaining the exogenous languages of mostly non-European migrants on the margins. It is as if some minority languages are now seen as belonging to the nation, as being part of its heritage, and others, because they have come with economic migrants, are envisaged, like their speakers, as outsiders. For example, regional languages in France have seen a shift in their status in education, no doubt helped by the European recommendations to protect linguistic and cultural diversity, but the fact that they are now being recognised as part of French heritage means that some other languages are not. Yet one could easily argue that the languages of immigration are also part of the history of France (Cerquiglini, 2003). As long as the history of colonisation is ignored, however, the languages of migrants will continue to be viewed with suspicion, as if they were the sign of a threatening heterogeneity, in a society which would prefer to see itself as homogenous and united around its national language.

Let us present briefly each of the countries described in the following chapters. Ireland is an officially bilingual country (Irish and English) where the minorisation of the Irish language is the result of a long history of colonisation. Ireland has a relatively long history of immersion bilingual education through the medium of Irish. Catalonia is an autonomous region of Spain which is also bilingual, with two official languages, Catalan and Spanish. Catalan was forbidden for 40 years, so that education through Catalan as the official language of schooling has been the main agent of revitalisation of the language. After a long history of legislating against its regional languages, France is just beginning to acknowledge the multiplicity of languages present within its hexagonal borders and the discourse of the European Union on the protection of linguistic and cultural diversity is questioning its institutional monolingualism. England, as opposed to France, is a country which sees itself very much as multicultural, and as early as 1975 the well known Bullock report insisted on the recognition in schools of the importance of home languages. However, as explained by Anderson, Kenner and Gregory (this volume), multicultural policies did not automatically translate into multicultural practices in schools, and ensuing policy documents continued to be based on monolingual assumptions.

Both Catalonia and Ireland have seen a recent and substantial influx of immigrants from all over the world. As a result, their school population has changed considerably in a very short space of time, creating new learning needs. The general consensus in this respect is that newcomers should learn the dominant language as quickly as possible (English in Ireland and Catalan in Catalonia). In England and France, where there is a much older tradition of immigration because as colonial powers these two countries built their postwar wealth on the migrants' labour force, the immigrant population has been expected either to assimilate, integrate or eventually to return to their native country. The main difference between the UK and France is that in the UK communities can be recognised and have special rights, whereas in France the constitution does not recognise minority groups and, in theory, all citizens are equal.

Common to the four countries presented here is the new wave of immigration,[5] no longer related to former colonies but mostly to war-torn and poverty-stricken countries. These new immigrants have brought with them a far greater variety of languages and cultures and their children have had very different experiences of schooling, not to mention life experiences. In the current climate of restrictive immigration policies, and a prevalent political discourse which reinforces the importance of the national language as a prerequisite to obtaining legal status, it is interesting to consider the educational policies implemented for newly arrived immigrants, in relation to the recognition (or not) of their bilingual or plurilingual competence. Thus, the questions we can ask here are threefold:

- Would Ireland and Catalonia, as bilingual countries who have fought for the revitalisation of their language, base their language education policy on a reflection anchored on the value of bilingualism in any language?
- In the case of France and England, what has been learnt from the 50 years of experience with the schooling of immigrant children and from the research carried out on this topic? After half a century of research, are we able to propose more inclusive policies which integrate mother tongue teaching in the mainstream classroom and which promote linguistic tolerance and openness to others?
- Can inclusive linguistic policies develop out of national contexts? What kind of impact can we expect policies from supranational institutions like the Council of Europe and the European Union to have on national agendas? Can we expect the same exclusionary phenomenon at the European level and discover a Eurocentric bias in favour of European languages?

In relation to immigrant minority languages in Europe, researchers in many countries are working alongside European institutions and a substantial number of publications, conventions and recommendations are currently available. Dealing with the educational management of linguistic diversity in the increasingly multicultural and multilingual context of European nation states, the comprehensive volume by Extra and Yagmur (2004) on urban multilingualism in Europe provides important information on the status of immigrant communities and their languages in a variety of contexts. It also presents detailed perspectives on multilingualism in six major European cities and addresses the question of transmission in home and school contexts of the 20 most prominent languages.

In a previous volume, Extra and Gorter (2001) have challenged the limitations of the European Charter for Regional and Minority Languages (1992) and proposed including, rather than excluding, immigrant[6] languages. Their introduction presents a useful comparative perspective on regional and immigrant minority languages in Europe. They point, in particular, to the lack of connection in the sociolinguistic, educational and political domain between the status of regional minority languages and immigrant minority languages. They also show that the linguistic reality in Europe is of the utmost complexity, with roughly 150 languages spoken by pupils in schools in Hamburg, and more than 350 languages in London, for example. They point to the fact that all these languages and varieties exist at the same time and in the same space, constructing what Fraser (1994) calls 'a multiple public sphere', where national cultures and languages and languages of special groups do not simply coexist but where a continuous process of border crossing takes place among all these dimensions.

Other researchers in Europe have contributed to the field as well; for example, Byram and Leman (1990) in Belgium, Gogolin (1994) in Germany, Akinci *et al.* (2004) in France, Lüdi and Py (1996) in Switzerland, Nussbaum (2003) in Catalonia, Martin *et al.* (2004) in England, as well as the authors included in Part 2 of this volume. Their work often goes beyond a merely educational perspective and includes sociolinguistic analysis, demographic data, philosophical reflection on ethnicity and identity, as well as the perspective of language rights.

We will not give a complete review here of European perspectives on language rights (see Extra & Yagmur, 2004, and O'Riagain & Lüdi, 2003) but would like to mention some policy documents which refer explicitly to immigrant minority languages. These include the directive from the Council of Europe (1977) to promote mother tongue teaching for the children of migrant workers, the declaration of the European Cultural Foundation entitled 'Moving away from a monolingual habitus'[7] (Declaration of Oegstgeest, 2001) and the Guide for the Development of Language Policies in Europe (Beacco & Byram, 2003). The Council of Europe language policy division[8] (in Strasbourg, France) has been particularly active in producing several policy guides and studies towards plurilingual education, in encouraging the development of language education policy profiles for each country and in publishing pedagogical instruments such as *The Common European Framework of Reference for Languages* (2001) and the European Language Portfolio (2000). Furthermore, The European Centre for Modern Languages[9] in Graz (Austria) concentrates on implementing these policies through cooperation between different partners working on pedagogical programmes meant to improve the learning and teaching of languages.

While one might think there is a certain emphasis on reflection meant to improve the teaching of European languages, a special section of the language policy division of the Council of Europe deals with 'minorities and migrants' and offers two very interesting studies, one by Gogolin (2002) on linguistic diversity and new minorities in Europe[10] and one on 'Bilingual Education: Some Policy Issues' by O'Riagain and Lüdi (2003).[11] It is indeed noteworthy that the document on bilingual education has been placed in the section 'minorities and migrants', when most bilingual education programmes being developed in Europe at present concern European languages. However, the authors note the following,

> The goal of bilingual language education is not necessarily societal bilingualism. The Council of Europe and the EU promote linguistic diversification. The goal of bilingual education can, therefore be to develop diverse, dynamic and plurilingual repertoires with particular (partial) competences in different languages as a starting point for lifelong learning. (O'Riagain & Lüdi, 2003: 5)

Thus, it is important to understand that, according to the authors of the text, such a goal implies that school-supported bilingual education is not meant only to give monolingual children a better chance on the labour market, but is aimed at maintaining linguistic diversity *and* preserving the linguistic rights of minorities. It is clear here that the objectives of the Council of Europe stress the development of plurilingualism for all pupils and this is important for immigrant minority languages because the notion of plurilingual competence[12] can help to legitimise their competence in their home language. Moreover, as Gogolin (2002) explains, contrary to widely held beliefs, immigrant minority languages are here to stay. The vitality of these languages is evident, even if the language of the majority comes to dominate because the function and practices of language use change in minority situations. Thus, instead of language loss, we should talk of language change, and language education policies and practices should take these changes into account.

Aware that these multilingual public spheres will be a long-term phenomenon in Europe, the European Commission launched a new framework strategy for multilingualism (Eurydice, 2004) in 2005, and some of its policies deal specifically with the integration of immigrant children in schools in Europe. The report published on its website[13] in 2004 gives a clear outline of the situation and challenges facing each country in the European Union. As stated in the conclusion of the report, 'A second challenge is to ensure that immigrants are successfully integrated within their host societies. How can one implement appropriate arrangements to facilitate the integration of immigrant persons while also remaining fully mindful of their origins and attentive to requirements deriving from them?' (Eurydice, 2004: 67). Some final recommendations are made about languages of immigration, which should be seen as a foothold in the host education system and the mother tongue as a bridge between two cultures. It is also proposed that intercultural education be taught not only across the curriculum but this should be seen as an integral aspect of how schools function. Teacher education is briefly mentioned, demanding that teachers mobilise new skills (Bourne, 2003). The report closes with the following statement, 'Educational policy makers in European countries are faced with the difficult task of transforming the intercultural diversity now characteristic of schools into an asset for everyone concerned, whether immigrant or native pupils, teachers or parents' (Eurydice, 2004: 71).

Policy work at the European level does not preclude the work of international organisations like UNESCO, for example, which has also decreed principles relating to minority language speakers. As early as 1953, an often quoted UNESCO declaration considered it axiomatic that the best medium for teaching is the mother tongue of the pupil. More recently, *The Universal Declaration on Cultural Diversity* (UNESCO, 2001)[14] insists as part of its action plan for implementation that linguistic diversity should be encouraged 'while respecting the mother tongue-at all level of education wherever possible, and that the learning of several languages should be fostered from the earliest age' (Point 6). This declaration has been followed by a position paper on *Education in a Multilingual World* in 2003 and a new legal instrument, *the Convention on the Protection and Promotion of the Diversity of Cultural Expressions,*[15] which came into force on 18 March 2007.

However, despite these substantial efforts at policy level to move forward on the issue of immigrant minority languages, what the four chapters which follow show quite clearly is that these languages are still marginalised in the respective countries described. In Ireland, while Irish–English bilingualism is still strongly promoted, little or no account is being taken of the home or heritage languages of new immigrant students. In Catalonia, the main agenda is about the promotion of

Catalan and improving the level of competence in international languages; the linguistic needs of immigrants should be catered for in schools, but the sole aim is the integration of immigrant pupils into the mainstream. There is no mention of intercultural education and of the wealth that linguistic and cultural diversity can bring to a classroom. In France the promotion of plurilingualism, of bilingual education in regional languages and European languages, is part of a larger plan to improve foreign language learning, but bilingual education is based on a largely monolingual and elitist vision of bilingualism, neglecting the bilingualism of immigrant children developed in the home or community context. In England, children's bilingual abilities are marginalised in mainstream school settings, community language schools operate in 'borrowed spaces', and even if the National Language Strategy promotes language learning from age seven onwards, and in theory includes languages spoken by minority communities, in reality, many more schools offer French rather than community languages. It is the same in France, where, in theory, some immigrant languages have been included in the primary curriculum, but they are de facto in competition with dominant European languages, especially English.

What is very clear from the four case studies presented below is the huge gap between the European and national discourse at policy level and the practices in schools around multilingualism. Yet, some of the authors report on research and projects which show that it is possible to translate policies into pedagogical practices, but these 'good practices' might not coincide with national priorities. For example, in France, the teaching of one foreign language at primary level is compulsory from Grade 2 onwards, and the emphasis on learning one language means it is very difficult to implement more inclusive approaches to language education, such as language awareness.

In Catalonia, as in France, policy documents clearly refer to the priority of the national language and the presence of immigration languages can be seen as a threat to social cohesion. In France the harmonious integration of foreign pupils depends first and foremost on their learning of the French language, just as in Catalonia where Catalan is supposed to play a key role in the integration of migrant students in Catalan society. In Catalonia, the arrival of immigrant minorities has reopened the debate about Catalan being part of the ethnic heritage of the province and immigrant languages are seen as contributing to increasing its fragility. The situation is very different in Ireland where the Irish language has always been in a precarious situation, so that 'the uneasy relationship between Irish and English has been replicated in the tacit, quiet subtractive bilingualism taking place among new Irish immigrant communities' (O'Laoire, this volume). But in Ireland as well, the emphasis has been on providing English language classes without acknowledging the bi- or multilingualism of the learners.

In a sense, it is as if school systems were unable to think about language learning outside of a monolingual framework, as if immigrant children only needed the language of schooling to learn school subjects and everything learnt in the home context or prior to schooling in the host country did not count.[16] As Beacco and Byram explain in the preface to Gogolin's (2002: 6) text: 'Their plurilingualism is not sufficiently recognised and their potential as language learners can be stifled by the organisation of language learning dominated by concern for monolingual speakers. Yet these young people are a model for plurilingualism.' Of course, schools also mirror the way immigrants are perceived in general as people needing employment rather than in terms of providing a much needed work force,[17] thus the languages of immigrant children are envisaged as a problem rather than as a resource; they are seen as lacking value and status and these attitudes work against their integration in schools, even when they are officially part of the list of languages on offer in the curriculum.

What is needed is a shift in attitude, away from the equation between nation and language, a reform of the traditional canons of language education, leading to a better understanding of the 'changing linguistic public spheres of our societies' (Gogolin, 2002: 7) and of what it means to grow up with two or more languages for language acquisition in general, and for language learning. For speakers of immigrant languages are people with a wide and complex repertoire of languages which can also be envisaged as a learning resource, as bringing a range of literacies into the mainstream classroom, potentially benefiting all children, monolinguals and bilinguals alike, particularly in the present-day context where school systems place so much emphasis on foreign language learning. However, as Anderson, Kenner and Gregory (this volume) warn us, bilingual children's knowledge should not be exploited for the sake of monolingual pupils and give rise to tokenism, as has often been the case in so-called 'intercultural' programmes. What is at stake here is the development of new relationships between the various languages of pupils in a school.

Researchers working in the field of language awareness talk of a relationship of 'reciprocity' (Perregaux, 1998), where the main idea is one of gathering all the languages spoken in a class, and sharing them in order to go beyond a situation of competitiveness or conflict. As shown by Hélot and Young (2006), such an approach can help to build the common history of a classroom without hiding pupils' differences. On the contrary, differences are valued and do not prevent the creation of a community of interest. At the same time, the monolingual habitus of the school is slowly being eroded because pupils and teachers are exposed to a much greater variety of languages and cultures than in traditional foreign language programmes.

The language awareness approach is particularly useful in the domain of teacher education, where it does not demand as much time as foreign language learning and where it can be more important to work on language attitudes than language aptitude. It is an approach that makes it possible to go beyond the monolingual framework of foreign language teaching and bilingual education. For both foreign language teaching and bilingual education are constrained by a binary vision (mother tongue/L2) which needs to be reframed because we live in a world where the multiplicity of languages and cultures has become the norm. These remarks are not meant to imply that language awareness should replace foreign language teaching or bilingual education, but rather to point to the inclusive dimension of such an approach, which proposes a reflection on all languages irrespective of their categorisation in the curriculum, including the language of schooling. It is an approach which does away with the minority–majority dichotomy, and which supports knowledge acquired in the home context. It can also enable teachers to expand their vision of literacy teaching and understand the importance of concepts such as 'heteroglossic literacy' (Ball & Warshauer Freedman, 2004; Gogolin, 2001), even if they are not familiar with all the languages of their pupils.

Hornberger (2002: 30) reminds us that 'multilingual policies are essentially about opening up ideological and implementational space in the environment for as many languages as possible'. While we agree with this proposition, we would like to make two final points concerning immigrant languages: first about their integration in the mainstream language curriculum and secondly as to how their status can be improved. As explained below in the chapters by Hélot and Anderson *et al.*, subsuming immigrant languages within curricula designed originally for foreign languages means that all learners are considered as monolinguals, that their linguistic and cultural background is ignored and their specific learning needs forgotten. However, there is a great difference between children who start learning a second language at school and those who learn at school a second language they speak at home. The former are monolingual, the latter bi- or multilingual. The question, then, is the extent to which schools are prepared to support bilingualism developed in the home context. Research has shown that the first language of bilingual children should be supported by a rich linguistic environment and both cultures valued. We know today that providing literacy in the first language facilitates the development of literacy in the socially dominant language of schooling. Yet in France, for example, mainstream education still gives priority to the acquisition of the French language.

Anderson *et al.* (this volume) provide the example of Wales, where separate frameworks have been developed for those learning Welsh as a mother tongue and those learning it as a second language. It is precisely what O'Laoire (this volume) suggests should be done in the case of Ireland, where the needs of mother tongue speakers of Irish have not been specifically addressed because such pupils are being schooled in bilingual programmes where a majority of the pupils do not speak Irish at home. This does not mean that bilingual programmes should necessarily separate mother tongue speakers and second language learners of the same language, but that the different needs of pupils should be acknowledged and addressed pedagogically. It is rather paradoxical that the special educational needs of minority language speakers should be silenced, not only in second language learning programmes but in bilingual programmes as well; but as the two chapters on Catalonia and Ireland show, the prevailing monolingual framework of reference constrains the integration of other minority languages.

As to improving the status of immigrant languages, it is obvious that it is not enough to decree policies preaching the value of plurilingualism, as long as on the linguistic market some languages have far more value than others. Although, as argued by O'Riagain and Lüdi (2003: 15), 'linguistic practices are not to be understood as solely determined by economic considerations in the strict sense ... When an individual adopts a strategy with regard to the acquisition and use of a language, the profit that is realised may be symbolic or cultural, rather than simply or primarily economic'. This is quite clear in the case of Irish in Ireland, for example, as explained by O'Laoire (this volume). Gogolin (2002: 11) also criticises the notion of linguistic market, explaining that 'in modern European societies there probably exists more than one linguistic market' and we should acknowledge this when thinking of language education for the future. Her recommendations insist on the right for children who grow up with two or more languages to be guaranteed access to literacy in the family language when it differs from the language of schooling.

However, as Escobar Urmeneta and Unamuno remind us here, it is difficult for schools to overcome the conditions that favour the reproduction of social differences. At present, bilingual education remains, on the whole, strongly promoted as a way of improving foreign language learning, mainly benefiting monolingual learners, while pupils who speak immigrant minority languages – and who are bilingual – are offered mother tongue classes in their languages of origin on a minimal basis, as shown by the European Commission report of 2004 quoted above. Fighting for linguistic equality and the linguistic rights of immigrant children to be educated in their mother tongue means that we cannot satisfy ourselves with such inequality, or as shown in the four contributions below, we cannot accept that the languages of immigrant minority pupils be left on the margins.

Notes

1. Up to 1994, Spanish was the official language of Argentina. This status was abolished by the Constitutional Reform of that year.
2. 'Ethnoeducation' is a term coined in Colombia and used to refer to bilingual and bicultural education aimed at the ethnic minorities. This is known as 'Intercultural Bilingual Education' (IBE) in other Latin American countries.
3. For a comprehensive description of the situation in the countries of the European Union, see the Euridyce survey published in 2004: *Integrating immigrant children in schools in Europe*, http://www.eurydice.org/portal/page/portal/Eurydice/showPresentation?pubid=045FR (Euridyce is a European Commission network of information on education in Europe: www.eurydice.org).
4. The Council of Europe web page (http://www.coe.int/t/dg4/linguistic/Division_EN.asp) makes the following distinction between multilingualism and plurilingualism. We shall respect this terminological distinction here. 'Multilingualism' refers to the presence in a geographical area, large or small, of more than one 'variety of language' i.e. the mode of speaking of a social group whether it is formally recognised as a language or not; in such an area individuals may be monolingual, speaking only their own variety. 'Plurilingualism' refers to the repertoire of varieties of language which many individuals use, and is therefore the opposite of monolingualism; it includes the language variety referred to as 'mother tongue' or 'first language' and any number of other languages or varieties. Thus in some multilingual areas some individuals are monolingual and some are plurilingual.
5. For more details see the Council of Europe report by Salt (2005) entitled *Current Trends on International Migrations in Europe*, which is the 14th annual report presented to the Council of Europe on the main aspects of the evolution of cultural migrations in Europe: http://www.coe.int/T/E/Social_Cohesion/Migration/Documentation/Publications%20and%20reports.asp.
6. There are no standardised designations to refer to these languages; many different terms are used depending on sociopolitical contexts, such as for example 'immigrant', 'migrant', 'heritage', 'community', 'non-European minority', 'allochthonous minority' etc. For the sake of consistency, in this introduction we shall use the term preferred by Extra and Gorter, 'immigrant minority languages'.
7. Its first article states that 'affirmative conventions and action programmes on regional, minority and immigrant languages within the context of a multicultural Europe should be based on a non-exclusive acknowledgement of the existence of all these languages as sources of linguistic and cultural enrichment' and Article 6: 'Education in regional, minority and immigrant languages should be offered, supervised and evaluated as part of the regular curriculum in preschool, primary and secondary education.'
8. http://www.coe.int/t/dg4/linguistic/.
9. http://www.ecml.org.
10. http://www.coe.int/t/dg4/linguistic/Migrants1_EN.asp#TopOfPage.
11. http://www.coe.int/t/dg4/linguistic/Migrants1_EN.asp#P44_6142.

12. See the Common European Framework of References for Languages (2001) for a definition.
13. See note 12.
14. See: http://portal.unesco.org/culture/en/ev.php-URL_ID = 13066&URL_DO = DO_TOPIC&URL_SECTION = 201.html. In 1999, UNESCO also proclaimed the International Mother Language Day (21 February) to celebrate the world's 6000 or so languages. This year (2007) the focus was on promoting linguistic diversity and multilingual education. In 2001 the Council of Europe created the European Day of Languages (26 September) to promote an awareness of linguistic and cultural diversity.
15. It was adopted unanimously at the 31st UNESCO General Conference. It aims to have a significant impact on humanising globalisation and making it more culturally sensitive. It was an opportunity for States to reaffirm their conviction that intercultural dialogue is the best guarantee of peace and to reject the theory of the inevitable clash of cultures and civilisations.
16. The research carried out in the USA on the theoretical concept of funds of knowledge (Moll *et al.*, 1992) should be more widely known; it provides a new perspective for the study of households as dynamic settings with abundant social and intellectual resources.
17. Article 25a of the declaration of the seventh conference of ministers responsible for migration affairs held in Helsinki in September 2002 states that the positive contribution that migrants make to society should be recognised.

References

Abbate-Vaughn, J. (2004) Two-way bilingual immersion (Twi) with low income urban student populations: Dilemmas of Equity. In *Actas del Simposio Bilinglatam 2004*. Buenos Aires: ESSARP.

Akinci, M.A., De Ruiter, J.J. and Sanagustin, F. (2004) *Le Plurilinguisme à Lyon. Le Statut des Langues à la Maison et à l'École*. Paris: L'Harmattan.

Baker, C. (1995) *A Parents' and Teachers' Guide to Bilingualism*. Clevedon: Multilingual Matters.

Ball, A.F. and Warshauer Freedman, S. (eds) (2004) *Bakhtinian Perspectives on Language, Literacy, and Learning*. Cambridge: Cambridge University Press.

Barriga Villanueva, R. (2007) La cara oscura del bilingüismo en México. In *Actas del Simposio Bilinglatam II 2007*. Bogotá: Universidad de los Andes.

Beacco, J.C. and Byram, M. (2003) *The Guide for the Development of Language Policies in Europe. From Linguistic Diversity to Plurilingual Education*. Strasbourg: Language Policy Division, Council of Europe.

Bhabha, H. (1994) *The Location of Culture*. London: Routledge.

Bourne, J. (2003) Remedial or radical? Second Language Support for curriculum learning. In J. Bourne and E. Reid (eds) *Language Education, World Yearbook of Education 2003* (pp. 21–34). London: Kogan Page.

Bullock, S.A. (1975) *A Language for Life*. London: HMSO.

Byram, M. and Leman, J. (eds) (1990) *Bicultural and Trilingual Education: The Foyer Model in Brussels*. Clevedon: Multilingual Matters.

Centre for English Language Teacher Education and Applied Linguistics (CELTEAL) (2005) International Conference on Interrogating Third Spaces in Language Teaching, Learning and Use. University of Leicester, 27–28 June, 2005.

Cerquiglini, B. (2003) *Les Langues de France*. Paris: PUF.

Common European Framework of References for Languages (2001) On WWW at http://www.coe.int/t/dg4/linguistic/CADRE_EN.asp. Accessed 12.2.08.

Creese, A. and Martin, P. (eds) (2003) Multilingual classroom ecologies: Interrelationships, interactions, and ideologies. *International Journal of Bilingual Education and Bilingualism* 6 (3&4), 161–167.

Cummins, J. (1986/2001) Empowering minority students: A framework for intervention. *Harvard Educational Review* 71 (4), 649–675.

Cummins, J. (2000) *Language, Power and Pedagogy: Bilingual Children in the Crossfire*. Clevedon: Multilingual Matters.

Declaration of Oegstgeest (The Netherlands) (2001) Moving away from a monolingual habitus. In G. Extra and D. Gorter (eds) *The Other Languages of Europe*. Clevedon: Multilingual Matters.

de Mejía, A.M. (2002) *Power, Prestige and Bilingualism. International Perspectives on Elite Bilingual Education*. Clevedon: Multilingual Matters.

ESSARP (1995) *The Scholastic Association of the River Plate 1985–1995*. Buenos Aires: ESSARP.

Eurydice (2004) *Integrating Immigrant Children in Schools in Europe*. Directorate General for Education and Culture European Commission. On WWW at http://ec.europa.eu/education/policies/lang/doc/com596_en.pdf. Accessed 5.2.08.

European Charter for Regional and Minority Languages (1992) ETS n°148. On WWW at http://conventions.coe.int/Treaty/EN/Treaties/Html/148.htm. Accessed 12.2.08.

European Language Portfolio (2000) On WWW at http://www.coe.int/t/dg4/portfolio/default.asp?l=e&m=/main_pages/welcome.html. Accessed 12.2.08.

Extra, G. and Gorter, D. (eds) (2001) *The Other Languages of Europe*. Clevedon: Multilingual Matters.

Extra, G. and Yagmur, K. (2004) *Urban Multilingualism in Europe. Immigrant Minority Languages at Home and at School*. Clevedon: Multilingual Matters.

Fishman, J.A. (1976) *Bilingual Education. An International Sociological Perspective*. Rowley, MA: Newbury House.

Fishman, J.A. (1977) The social science perspective. In Centre for Applied Linguistics (ed.) *Bilingual Education: Current Perspectives*. Arlington, VA: CAL.

Fishman, J.A. (1982) Sociolinguistic foundations of bilingual education. *Bilingual Review/La Revista Bilingüe* 9, 1–35.

Flores, J. (1993) *Divided Borders*. Houston: Arte Público Press.

Fraser, N. (1994) Rethinking the public sphere. A contribution to the critique of actually existing democracy. In B. Robbins (ed.) *The Phantom Public Sphere* (pp. 1–32). Minnesota: University of Minnesota Press.

Freeman, R.D. (1998) *Bilingual Education and Social Change*. Clevedon: Multilingual Matters.

García, O. (1993) Understanding the societal role of the teacher in transitional bilingual classrooms: Lessons from the sociology of language. In K. Zontag (ed.) *Bilingual Education in Friesland. Facts and Prospects*. Leeuwarden/Ljouwert: GCO/MSU.

García, O., Skutnabb-Kangas, T. and Torres-Guzmán, M.E. (2006) *Imagining Multilingual Schools. Languages in Education and Glocalization*. Clevedon: Multilingual Matters.

Gogolin, I. (1994) *Der Monolinguale Habitus der Multilingualen Schule*. Münster: Waxmann-Verlag.

Gogolin, I. (2001) Heteroglossic Literacy. Kommunikationsgewinn im Informationszeitalter. In R. de Cillia, H-J. Krumm and R. Wodak (eds) *Kommunika-*

tionsverlust im Informationszeitalter (pp. 77–85). Wien: Verlag der Österreichischen Akademie der Wissenschaften.

Gogolin, I. (2002) *Linguistic Diversity and New Minorities in Europe, Reference Study.* Language Policy Division, DG IV, Directorate of School, Out of School and Higher Education, Strasbourg: Council of Europe.

Graddol, D. (2006) *English Next.* London: British Council.

Gutierrez, M.J. and Fairclough, M. (2006) Incorporating linguistic variation into the classroom. In R.A. Salaberry and B.A. Lafford (eds) *The Art of Teaching Spanish. Second Language Acquisition from Research to Praxis.* Washington: Georgetown University Press.

Hamel, R.E. (2003) El español como lengua de las ciencias frente a la globalización del inglés. Diagnóstico y propuestas de acción para una política iberoamericana del lenguaje en las ciencias. Manuscript, UAM, México, D.F.

Hamel, R.E. (2006) The development of language empires. In U. Ammon, N. Dittmar, K.J. Mattheier and P. Trudgill (eds) *Sociolinguistics – Soziolinguistik. An International Handbook of the Science of Language and Society. Ein internationales Handbuch zur Wissenschaft von Sprache und Gesellschaft* (2nd edn, Vol. 3). Berlin, New York: Walter de Gruyter.

Hélot, C. (2005) Bridging the gap between prestigious bilingualism and the bilingualism of minorities: Towards an integrated perspective of multilingualism in the French education context. In M. O'Laoire (ed.) *Multilingualism in Educational Settings* (pp. 49–72). Tübingen: Stauffenburg Verlag.

Hélot, C. and Young, A. (2006) La diversité linguistique et culturelle à l'école. Comment négocier l'écart entre les langues/cultures de la maison et celle(s) de l'école? In C. Hélot, E. Hoffmann, M-L. Scheidhauer and A. Young (eds) *Ecarts de Langue, Écarts de Culture. A l'École de l'Autre* (pp. 207–220). Frankfurt: Peter Lang.

Hornberger, N. (1989) Continua of biliteracy. *Review of Educational Research* 59 (3), 271–296.

Hornberger, N. (1991) Extending enrichment bilingual education. Revisiting typologies and redirecting policies. In O. Garcia (ed.) *Bilingual Education Focusschrift in Honor of Joshua A. Fishman on the Occasion of his 65th birthday* (pp. 215–234). Philadelphia: John Benjamins Publications.

Hornberger, N. (2002) Multilingual language policies and the continua of biliteracy. *Language Policy* 1, 27–51.

Hornberger, N. (ed.) (2003a) *Continua of Biliteracy: An Ecological Framework for Educational Policy, Research and Practice in Multilingual Settings.* Clevedon: Multilingual Matters.

Hornberger, N.H. (2003b) Afterword: Ecology and ideology in multilingual classrooms. *International Journal of Bilingual Education and Bilingualism* 6 (3–4), 296–302.

King, K. (2005) Enrichment bilingual education in the Andes. In A.M. de Mejia (ed.) *Bilingual Education in South America.* Clevedon: Multilingual Matters.

Lindholm-Leary, K.J. (2005) *Review of Research and Best Practices on Effective Features of Dual Language Education Programs.* San José: San José State University.

Lüdi, G. and Py, B. (1996) *Être Bilingue.* Berne, Switzerland: Peter Lang.

Martin, P., Bhatt, A., Bhojani, N. and Creese, A. (2004) *Final Report on Complementary Schools and their Communities in Leicester.* Leicester: University of Leicester.

Nussbaum, L. (2003) Immigration et dynamiques polyglossiques en Catalogne. In L. Mondada and S. Pekarek (eds) *Plurilinguisme, Mehrsprachigkeit, Plurilingualism* (pp. 15–28). Tübingen: Francke.
O'Riagain, P. and Lüdi, G. (2003). *Bilingual Education: Some Policy Issues*. Language Policy Division, DG IV, Directorate of School, Out of School and Higher Education, Strasbourg: Council of Europe.
Patiño, C. (2005) La enseñanza del español. *Vigía del Idioma*. Bogotá: Academia Colombiana de la Lengua.
Perregaux, C. (1998) Esquisse d'un nouveau monde. In J. Billiez (ed.) *De la Didactique des Langues à la Didactique duPplurilinguisme, Hommage à Louise Dabène* (pp. 291–298). Grenoble: CDL, LIDILEM.
Ricento, T. and Hornberger, N.H. (1996) Unpeeling the onion: Language planning and policy and the ELT professional. *TESOL Quarterly* 30 (3), 401–427.
Ruiz, R. (1984) Orientations in language planning. *NABE Journal* 8 (2), 15–34.
Skilton-Sylvester, E. (2003) Legal discourse and decisions, teacher policymaking and the multilingual classroom: Constraining and supporting Khmer/English biliteracy in the United States. *International Journal of Bilingual Education and Bilingualism* 6 (3–4), 168–184.
Torres-Karna, H. and de Kanter, E. (2004) Language revitalization through the implementation of a dual immersion program. In *Actas del Simposio Bilinglatam 2004*. Buenos Aires: ESSARP.
UNESCO (1953) The *Use of Vernacular Languages in Education*. Paris: UNESCO.
UNESCO (2001) *Universal Declaration on Cultural Diversity*. On WWW at http://portal.unesco.org/ci/fr/ev.phpURL_ID=15879&URL_DO=DO_PRINTPAGE&URL_SECTION=201.html. Accessed 5.2.08.
UNESCO (2003) *Education in a Multilingual World*. Education. Position Paper. Paris: UNESCO Publishing.

Part 1

The Americas

Chapter 2

Teaching Spanish and Spanish in Teaching in the USA: Integrating Bilingual Perspectives

OFELIA GARCÍA

Introduction

Spanish has been formally taught in the USA since the early part of the 19th century. Since the early 20th century, the public school has made it a subject of study. As we will discuss, however, this tradition of teaching Spanish as a foreign language has rarely admitted the ways of using the Spanish of Spanish speakers in the USA. US schools have had little interest in developing the English–Spanish bilingualism of their Anglophone students.

After the amendments to the Immigration Act of 1965, the increasing number of students from Latin America began challenging traditional programs of teaching Spanish as a foreign language. In the late 1960s, Spanish in teaching started to be used in transitional bilingual education programs for recently arrived Spanish-speaking students. Programs of teaching Spanish for Spanish speakers (also called teaching Spanish as a heritage language) started to crop up as well. Despite the use of Spanish in teaching in bilingual education programs, and the teaching of Spanish as a heritage language, US schools have not shown much interest in maintaining and developing the English–Spanish bilingualism of US Latino students.

In the 21st century, Spanish has increasingly acquired status as a global language. With this new trend, Spanish is seen less and less as the minoritized language of poor, immigrant, brown US Latinos. The 'in' sounds of Ricky Martin, Shakira, Enrique Iglesias, Reggaeton and the 'sexiness' of Penelope Cruz and Salma Hayek have affected the presence of Spanish in US schools. As we will see, a new trend that we might characterize as the teaching of Spanish as a global language can also be evidenced in the USA, this time with Spain spurring the efforts. The interaction between Spanish as a global language on the one hand, and Spanish as the minoritized language of US Latinos, has spurred the development of a more integrated way of using and teaching Spanish in US classrooms.

More than anything else, the blending of local and international interests brought about through globalization has spurred support for an integrated model of bilingual education that has the potential to bridge the gap that has always existed between the teaching of Spanish as a foreign language, the teaching of Spanish as a heritage language and the use of Spanish in bilingual teaching. And yet, despite its potential, the integrated bilingual education model known as two-way bilingual education or two-way dual language education sometimes fails to liberate itself from the monoglossic language ideologies that have always supported language in education policies in the USA.[1]

Nevertheless, two-way dual language education can offer a space where students and teachers are forced to work in the gap created by different traditions of language education. Sometimes, with an enlightened teacher, the teaching and the learning advance notions of bilingualism that go beyond the elite ones of foreign language education programs or the minority ones of transitional bilingual education programs.

This chapter reviews the different traditions of teaching Spanish and Spanish in teaching that are present in the USA today – foreign language teaching, heritage language teaching, bilingual education and global language teaching. It then focuses on the potential of two-way dual language bilingual education to bridge the gap between the different language in education policies, attitudes, practices and pedagogies. The chapter ends by examining one specific two-way bilingual education classroom that transcends the limitations of the model by working in the gap, rather than bridging the gap. This is then the story of how schools and teachers unconsciously work against dual language structures that are externally imposed, enabling plurilingual and pluriliteracy practices and the heteroglossia[2] of children's discourse in the 21st century.

The Teaching of Spanish as a Foreign Language

The territory that is today the USA has had Spanish speakers on its soil from its founding. According to Kloss (1977), Spanish in the USA can be said to have special rights because it was spoken by original settlers. Spanish is also the language of many US citizens. It is the language of Puerto Ricans, US citizens since 1917 through the Jones Act (García *et al.*, 2001). It was the language of the Mexicans who found themselves on the US side of the border after the Treaty of Guadalupe-Hidalgo (1848) that ended the Mexican–American War. Spanish is also the language of the 42 million plus US Latinos who live in the USA,[3] some recently arrived immigrants, others having been in the USA for two, three or even more generations. Despite the great presence of Spanish speakers in the USA today, Spanish has always been taught in the USA as if it were a foreign language. The teaching of Spanish profession has constructed an ideology of *foreignness* that has been present from its inception and continues to shape the profession even today.

The tradition of teaching Spanish as a foreign language in the USA did not begin formally until 1816 when George Ticknor occupied the first Harvard Professorship of French and Spanish[4] (For more on this, see Grattan Doyle, 1926; Leavitt, 1961; Nichols, 1945; Spell, 1927). This elite Spanish teaching tradition, focusing on the reading of the literature of Spain, was continued by such well known American *literati* as Henry Wadsworth Longfellow, James Russell Lowell, Washington Irving and William Prescott. The teaching of the literature of Spain was restricted to the university, and consisted of reading the literature, while using English for the discussion. Its aim was not bilingualism but merely acquiring literary understandings. The Modern Language Association, founded in 1883, claimed that the aim of modern language study was 'literary culture, philological scholarship and linguistic discipline'. Little attention was paid to Spanish then.

In 1917, the American Association of Teachers of Spanish (now the American Association of Teachers of Spanish and Portuguese, AATSP) was established, focusing on the teaching of Spanish, especially at the secondary level. But the primary intent of the American Association of Teachers of Spanish was made obvious in its early motto: 'The war will be won by the substitution of Spanish for German'. Its first president, Lawrence Wilkins, promoted the teaching of Spanish, instead of German, at the secondary level but prevented its inclusion in the elementary school curriculum and the hiring of 'foreign' teachers. Spanish was taught at the secondary level in the same ways that it had been previously taught at the university, that is, with an emphasis on reading (García, 1993, 2003).

The first editor of *Hispania*, the journal of the AATSP, Aurelio Espinosa, was of Hispanic descent, but he was also against the hiring of native speakers and the teaching of a Latin American variety of Spanish. In an article entitled, 'Where is the best Spanish spoken?', Espinosa (1923: 244) says: 'The best modern Spanish ... is that spoken by the educated people of Old and New Castile'. In another article, written in 1921, he writes: 'American teachers must do in the future 99 percent of the teaching of Spanish ... ' (Espinosa, 1921: 281), showing his aversion to hiring teachers of Latino background. Clearly the model of Spanish to be taught in US high schools and universities had little to do with the Spanish of its citizens.

In 1929 the Modern Foreign Language Study issued national recommendations regarding the teaching of languages other than English. The study recommended that reading be the primary aim of foreign language study and that it be limited to two years (Coleman, 1929). In 1949, the report 'What the High Schools ought to teach' characterized foreign language study as useless and time consuming. And around the same time, Harvard's 'General Education in a Free Society' report commented that foreign language study was only useful in strengthening students' English (Huebener, 1961).

Despite this monolingual Anglophone ideology of the 'foreignness' of languages other than English, and their usefulness only in improving English skills, Spanish started to be increasingly heard in US discourse. The Radio Age first brought the sounds of Spanish speakers of the American Southwest to all. And shortly afterwards, the Air Age gave evidence of the first airborne diaspora in US history, that of Puerto Ricans (García, 1993, 2003). Nevertheless, the Spanish language profession continued to ignore this population.

In 1958, and as a result of the launching of Sputnik, the National Defense and Education Act gave financial assistance for the teaching of foreign languages as a 'defense' strategy (Harden, 1981). New language teaching methodologies such as the Audio-Lingual approach were developed, books were printed and teachers were hired. For the first time, attention was given not to the reading of the literature of Spain, but to listening and speaking proficiency. 'Castellano' or Castilian, the Spanish variety that had been touted as prestigious for being the variety of the central part of Spain and of Madrid, became enthroned in the nation's secondary schools, taught by Anglo teachers who had spent a short time in Spain and who themselves had limited productive proficiency in Spanish.

The new emphasis on listening and speaking of the Audio-Lingual approach also created the need for teachers who were proficient in Spanish. In 1965, *Hispania* published an article entitled 'The Bilingual Mexican American as a potential teacher of Spanish' (Wonder, 1965). For the first time, it was acknowledged that US Latinos might indeed be an important resource as teachers of Spanish.

Despite the emphasis on *foreign* language programs in teaching Spanish in the USA, the growth of such programs can be directly correlated to the growth of the Spanish-speaking population in the USA. Table 2.1 presents the number of students of Spanish in public secondary

Table 2.1 Number of students of Spanish in public secondary schools in the USA, by year

1915	*1948*	*1958*	*1968*	*1978*	*1990*	*2000*
35,882	442,755	691,024	1,698,034	1,631,375	2,611,367	4,057,608

Source: Draper & Hicks (2002: 5, table 1)

Table 2.2 Region of birth of foreign-born US population: 1910–2000

	1910	*1930*	*1960*	*1970*	*1980*	*1990*	*2000*
Europe (%)	87.4	83.0	75.0	61.7	39.0	22.9	15.8
Asia (%)	1.4	1.9	5.1	8.9	19.3	26.3	26.4
Africa (%)	–	0.1	0.4	0.9	1.5	1.9	2.8
Oceania (%)	0.1	0.1	0.4	0.4	0.6	0.5	0.5
Latin America (%)	2.1	5.5	9.4	19.4	33.1	44.3	51.7

Source: US Census Bureau, Pop Division No. 29 and Summary File 3

schools in the USA and shows the tremendous increase that has taken place in the last decade. Table 2.2 then shows the region of birth of the foreign-born US population in the 20th century, again showing the rise of immigration from Latin America in the last decade. A comparison of both tables makes evident that as the number of immigrants from Latin America has grown, the number of students of Spanish in public secondary schools has also increased. The interest in studying Spanish in the USA is associated with the greater communicative need of monolingual Anglophones to interact with the growing bilingual Latino population in the USA, as well as with recently arrived monolingual Spanish speakers. It also has much to do with the desire of US Latinos to study Spanish, be educated bilinguals and be able to use Spanish in jobs where such proficiency might be necessary. The growing interest in learning Spanish both by US monolingual Anglophones and bilingual US Latinos is grounded in the growing English–Spanish bilingual reality of the USA – a reality that is often ignored.

That there is great interest in studying Spanish in the USA today is a well known fact. Draper and Hicks (2002: 2) report that in 2000, those who study Spanish represent 68.7% of students in Grades 7–12, while French represents 18.3%, German 4.8%, Latin 2.7% and Italian 1.2%.

And yet, we continue to teach Spanish in the USA as if it were a foreign language, dismissing the possibility of using the Spanish-speaking practices of the US population as a resource in enhancing capacities to understand and speak Spanish. For example, there are few native Spanish language teachers in US schools. Although figures for Spanish teachers *per se* are not available, only 31% of public school teachers, Grades 7–12, are native speakers of the language (Rhodes & Branaman, 1999: 45). US high school textbooks of Spanish most often give instructions and explanations in English, not only because of the children, but also because the teachers need it. The teaching of Spanish in the USA is always mindful of the limited bilingualism of its teachers.

One way in which native Spanish speakers are kept out of the teaching profession is through teacher certification requirements. In New York, teacher candidates must have the equivalent of a major in Spanish in college, excluding anyone who may be a native speaker of Spanish and may have studied in a Latin American or Spanish University anything but Spanish language, literature or philology. Furthermore, becoming certified as a Spanish teacher most often requires passing stringent examinations given in advanced English, whereas the Spanish language level required of the specialization examination is less than demanding. Thus, teacher candidates who are not native speakers of Spanish often have more opportunity to become certified as teachers of Spanish, even though their fluency in Spanish may be limited. As a result of these practices, and despite the growth of the Spanish-speaking population, teachers of Spanish are scarce.

This vision of Spanish acquisition from a monoglossic point of view is also reflected in the final assessments that are supposed to measure Spanish language proficiency. For example, in New York State, the English Regents exam is given after three years of high school study of a language other than English. It is supposed to be the pinnacle of Spanish language attainment. But the Regents Examination cannot be passed by a monolingual Spanish speaker, for it requires English language ability and only limited Spanish language ability. What follows is an example of the Listening Section of an English Regents:

The teacher says while students listen:

You are listening to the radio in Spain and you hear:
Subway to Sally es un grupo musical que se ha apoderado de las listas de popularidad en gran parte de Europa. Y no es para menos, pues estos siete alemanes han podido hacer una mezcla de lo más extraño, ya que combinan melodías de la Edad Media con música típica europea y sonidos de metal moderno. Así que si eres una de las personas que le gusta escuchar cosas nuevas en la escena musical, este disco es para ti.

The teacher then reads the following question and answer options, with students reading along:

What is unique about this group's music?
(a) Their music is played on all the major subways in Europe.
(b) Their music combines old melodies with modern sounds.
(c) Their music features an orchestra.
(d) Their music is only sold in Germany.

The Spanish Regents also includes a reading and a writing section. In the reading section, the questions and the options are also in English, although the reading selection is in Spanish. In the writing section, the situation presented and the points to be included are all in English, which the students must then write in Spanish. It is clear that today the teaching of Spanish tradition in the USA continues to see Spanish as a foreign language, denying the existence of the many who are bilingual in the USA. Even in high schools for immigrant newcomer Latino students in New York City, students cannot take the Spanish Regents because they have to learn English first.

The teaching of Spanish as a foreign language continues to be one more monoglossic mechanism that prevents, through its ideology, traditions and pedagogies, the full development of the bilingual potential of all US citizens.

The Teaching of Spanish as a Heritage Language

In 1978, Guadalupe Valdés organized, through the support of the National Endowment for the Humanities, a first seminar to study the teaching of Spanish to Spanish speakers. Language pedagogues began to realize even then that the foreign language education approach simply did not work to teach the many US Latinos who were studying Spanish (see, for example, Gaarder *et al.*, 1972). Valdés, Lozano and García-Moya published the first complete treatment of the subject in 1981.

In the last decade of the 20th century, much scholarly attention has been paid to the teaching of Spanish to bilingual US Latinos (see, for example, AATSP, 2000; Colombi & Alarcón, 1997; Draper & Hicks, 2000; Roca & Colombi, 2005; Valdés, 1997). And yet, as Valdés *et al.* (2006) make evident, theories concerning the teaching of Spanish to US bilinguals remain underdeveloped, while teaching programs themselves, especially at the secondary level, are almost nonexistent. For example, according to Draper and Hicks (2002) programs of Spanish for Spanish speakers only had 141,212 students in fall 2000, making up only 1.9% of secondary school students who are enrolled in Spanish courses. This is a minuscule figure compared to the number of children 5–17 years of age who claim to be Hispanic in the 2000 census – a total of 8,595,305, with 2,590,250 speaking only English at home, and 5,970,217 also speaking Spanish at home. It is clear that the US school system is in no way developing the potential for bilingualism that the sheer number of Latino students would make possible.

Table 2.3 details the number of students that were reported to be in classes of Spanish for Spanish speakers by state, as well as the number of Spanish speakers in the state. It is instructive to realize that there is little relationship between the number of Spanish speakers in a state and the number of students in Spanish for Spanish speakers classes. In fact, the number 2 and number 4 states in terms of Spanish speakers (California

Table 2.3 Number of students in Spanish 7–12, and Spanish for native speakers, and number of Spanish speakers by state[a]

State	*Spanish classes*	*SNS classes*	*Number Spanish speakers*
Alabama	27,918	0	89,729
Alaska	12,925	0	16,674
Arizona	88,151	2,609	927,395
Arkansas	40,119	0	82,465
California	547,993	58,321	8,105,505
Colorado	71,520	2,113	421,670
Connecticut	54,734	0	268,044
Delaware	12,537	0	34,690
D.C.	5,651	167	49,461
Florida	158,576	24,163	2,476,528
Georgia	135,727	4,000	426,115
Hawai'i	6,500	0	18,820
Idaho	26,802	796	80,241
Illinois	200,373	5,932	1,253,676
Indiana	86,403	0	185,576
Iowa	71,872	98	79,491
Kansas	50,498	1,497	137,247
Kentucky	66,078	1,957	70,061
Louisiana	43,819	0	105,189
Maine	20,428	0	9,611
Maryland	92,101	2,713	230,829
Massachusetts	94,653	2,794	370,011
Missouri	161,612	4,776	246,688
Minnesota	101,758	3,036	132,066
Mississippi	27,627	0	50,515
Missouri	132,084	3,981	110,752
Montana	11,789	0	12,953

Table 2.3 (*Continued*)

State	*Spanish classes*	*SNS classes*	*Number Spanish speakers*
Nebraska	54,676	0	77,655
Nevada	30,827	908	299,947
New Hampshire	21,448	632	18,647
New Jersey	112,365	3,308	967,741
New Mexico	17,284	4,579	485,681
New York	446,299	0	2,416,126
North Carolina	120,073	0	378,942
North Dakota	13,171	392	8,263
Ohio	177,838	0	213,147
Oklahoma	61,162	0	141,060
Oregon	58,427	1,732	217,614
Pennsylvania	226,184	525	356,754
Rhode Island	15,253	450	79,443
South Carolina	66,224	1,953	110,030
South Dakota	14,186	421	10,052
Tennessee	68,102	0	133,931
Texas	456,384	0	5,195,182
Utah	45,043	0	150,244
Vermont	9,068	0	5,791
Virginia	116,782	3,454	316,274
Washington	106,465	3,167	321,490
West Virginia	17,054	0	17,652
Wisconsin	142,129	104	168,778
Wyoming	10,684	317	18,606
Total	4,757,373	140,897	28,101,052

[a]The number of students in Spanish 7–12 and Spanish for native speakers is derived from Draper & Hicks (2002). The number of Spanish speakers by state is from US Census Bureau, 2000, Summary File 3

and New York) do not even report the number of students in such classes, making evident that such classes do not truly count.

Valdés *et al.* (2006) show that even in California, where the number of Latino students makes up an important part of secondary school students, there is little interest in the teaching of Spanish to US Latino students, efforts are not organized and a theory of teaching Spanish to Spanish speakers has yet to be developed.

In the last decade, and under the restrictions imposed by the No Child Left Behind Act (2001), US schools have increasingly paid attention to English literacy and Math, leaving behind other school subjects and paying little attention to Spanish (see, for example, Dillon, 2006: 1). In New York City, for instance, Latino high school students follow structured academic programs that leave no room in the student's program to take Spanish. It has been reported, for example, that in 2004 Latino students at the High School for the Humanities were taking a special academic intensive program, *Ramp Up*, that left no time in their programs to study Spanish (Prozzo, personal communication, 2004).

There has also been a recent shift in referring to this activity not as 'Spanish for Spanish speakers' or as 'Spanish for Native Speakers' but as 'Spanish for heritage language speakers'. The use of 'heritage' language has been used in Canada since 1977, the beginning of the Ontario Heritage Languages Programs (Cummins, 2005; Cummins & Danesi, 1990). The term was not embraced in the USA until the Center for Applied Linguistics and the National Foreign Language Center organized the First Heritage Languages in America conference at the University of California at Los Angeles in 1999 (Cummins, 2005). Cummins (2005: 586) suggests some reasons for the change:

> [R]ecent academic initiatives in relation to heritage languages can be seen as an attempt to establish an independent sphere of discourse where heritage language support can be debated on its own merits rather than viewed through the lens of preexisting polarized attitudes towards bilingual education and immigration. Heritage language advocates perceive, correctly I believe, that there is little likelihood of any reduction in the volatility of the bilingual education debate.

I have suggested elsewhere that this shift in naming points to an unfortunate silencing of Spanish itself (García, 2005). From a position of existence and presence, Spanish has been relegated to a position of heritage, something not relevant, something past. And in so doing, this turn of events contributes to the silencing of an approach that has used Spanish in teaching US Latinos – bilingual education, the subject of our next section.

Spanish in Teaching: Bilingual Education

Traditionally, foreign language education programs in the USA have started in the seventh grade, although full attention is not paid until the secondary level in the ninth grade. Thus, although the teaching of Spanish is primarily a secondary level phenomenon,[5] Spanish is used in teaching mostly in bilingual education programs at the elementary level where the greatest number of recently arrived immigrant children are found.

The use of languages other than English in bilingual education programs is not limited to the 20th century. Throughout the 19th century German was used to teach in many schools in cities such as St. Louis, Milwaukee and Cincinnati, as well as in the rural areas of the Mid-West (Daniels, 1991; Dicker, 1996). Likewise, in places like New Mexico, Spanish has been used to teach from the time it became a territory at the end of the Mexican–American war, and even after being granted statehood in 1912 (for more on this history, see Hernández-Chávez, 1995). But clearly the second half of the 20th century saw renewed activity in using Spanish in various ways to educate US Latinos.

In 1968, the Bilingual Education Act, also known as Title VII of the Elementary and Secondary Education Act, for the first time provided federal funds to school systems that organized and implemented bilingual education programs to teach the nation's failing Spanish-speaking students. These students were mostly Mexican–Americans in the Southwest and Puerto Ricans in the Northeast.[6] The bilingual education programs that were organized in these early years adopted a *developmental* model that had been used successfully by elites all over the world, mostly teaching half the day in English and half the day in Spanish. This was also the kind of program implemented at the Coral Way Elementary School in Dade County, established by recently arrived Cuban refugees who wanted to ensure that their children maintained and developed their Spanish language abilities, while learning English. Programs for US Latinos which used Spanish in teaching became known as maintenance bilingual education. As bilingual education programs grew, and the nation's Spanish-speaking population increased, bilingual education programs became limited to transitional bilingual education models, using Spanish only as a tool to learn English and for only a limited period of time – generally three years.

The growth of transitional bilingual education programs promoted publication of learning material in Spanish. Spanish language publishers such as Santillana expanded their operations to include the USA. Children's books and high school textbooks were translated into Spanish as well.

Despite the attention to Spanish that bilingual education promoted, the field and practice of bilingual education had little to do with that of foreign language teaching. The professionals associated with the National Association for Bilingual Education (NABE) remained distant from those in the American Association of Teachers of Spanish and Portuguese (AATSP) or even the American Council on the Teaching of Foreign Languages (ACTFL). In philosophy and orientation, the bilingual education profession never saw Spanish in isolation from English, whereas the foreign language profession focused on Spanish only. Whereas bilingual educators positioned themselves in a *heteroglossic* context, giving attention to the multiplicity of discourses that the children brought and that they were acquiring, foreign language educators adopted a *monoglossic* ideology with Spanish positioned as the focus of attention. However, in actual classroom practice, more Spanish could be heard in bilingual education classrooms where students with limited English proficiency learned English, than in foreign language classrooms where students and teachers learned Spanish.

Bilingual education in the USA started to come under attack in the 1980s, as the English-Only movement gathered force (for more on this, see Crawford, 1992). Today, political pressures have significantly restricted opportunities for bilingual education. California, Massachusetts and Arizona have declared bilingual education illegal. Changes in federal education laws also make it difficult to use Spanish in teaching. In 2001, Title VII of the Elementary and Secondary Education Act (the Bilingual Education Act) was eliminated as part of the authorization of No Child Left Behind (NCLB). E. Garcia (2005: 98) describes these changes:

> Whereas the 1994 version of the Bilingual Education Act included among its goals 'developing the English skills ... and to the extent possible, the native-language skills' of LEP students, the new law stresses skills in English only. The word *bilingual* has been completely eliminated from the law.

Table 2.4 displays the changes in naming of offices and laws that have occurred in the last five years. The silencing of the word 'bilingual' from US discourse is noticeable.

In an era of globalization, when supranational and transnational structures have started to replace the national, and when there is multidirectional flows of goods, services, money, people, information and culture across borders, and going faster and further than ever before (Held *et al.*, 1999; Mittleman, 1996), the USA is showing less interest than ever in developing the bilingualism of its citizens. Wright (2004: 163–165) referred to this by saying:

Table 2.4 Changes in naming and silencing of the word 'bilingual'

Office of Bilingual Education and Minority Languages Affairs (OBEMLA) →	Office of English Language Acquisition, Language Enhancement and Academic Achievement for LEP students (OELA)
National Clearinghouse for Bilingual Education (NCBE) →	National Clearinghouse for English Language Acquisition and Language Instruction Educational Programs (NCELA)
Title VII of Elementary and Secondary Education Act: The Bilingual Education Act →	Title III of No Child Left Behind, Public Law 107-110: Language Instruction for Limited English Proficient and Immigrant Students, 2001

> Some of the most robust resistance to globalisation comes from within the United States itself. As the remaining and only superpower, the United States dominates in a number of key areas but is not reciprocally dominated. The U.S. government is able to guard its sovereignty and autonomy in the classic manner of the nation state. The national group exerts pressure on its members to be patriotic in a way that has become increasingly more difficult in many other Western states ... [W]e appear to be witnessing asymmetric developments within globalisation: loss of economic autonomy and political sovereignty for many states; continuing economic autonomy and political sovereignty together with the survival of some elements of traditional 'one nation, one territory, one language nationalism for the United States'.

At present, only one model of bilingual education seems to have gained limited public support in some parts of the USA – two-way dual language programs.[7] The contemporary two-way dual language model integrates students with different linguistic profiles, incorporating children who are learning English, those who are bilingual, and those who are learning a language other than English (Cloud *et al.*, 2000; García, 2006; Lindholm-Leary, 2001; Torres-Guzmán, 2002; Valdés, 1997). The idea of dual language programs is that these diverse students attend classes together. Instruction is rigidly split between the two languages, mostly following a 50–50 approach, with half of the time spent in English and the other half in Spanish. Dual language programs predominate at the elementary level. The integrated nature of the two-way dual language model makes it difficult to implement at the high school level, as the more specialized, academic register of a second language required for secondary subject instruction is remarkably difficult to achieve within the short four-year period of a US high school education.[8] We will consider these two-way dual language bilingual programs as a model that holds the promise to integrate attitudes, practices and pedagogies on the teaching of Spanish and Spanish in teaching, and on elite bilingualism (seen as the acquisition of Spanish by Anglophones) and folk bilingualism (seen as the acquisition of English by recent newcomers and immigrants). First, it is important that we consider one more trend in the teaching of Spanish that may greatly affect the potential of two-way dual language education programs in the USA in the future, Spanish as a global language.

The Teaching of Spanish as a Global Language

In the last decade, US Spanish, spurred by the globalization of Spanish, has shifted position. As a matter, of fact, some say that Spanish has become 'fashionable'. For example, Álvarez Martínez (2001) says:

> Cuando afirmamos, pues, que el español está de moda, lo que estamos diciendo es que ahora nuestra lengua, lengua oficial de veintiún países, es el centro de atención de gran parte del mundo.
>
> When we say then that Spanish is fashionable, what we're saying is that now our language, an official language of 21 countries, is the center of attention of a great part of the world.

Recently, when I posed the question of whether Spanish was fashionable or not to my graduate students, most referred to the increasing global influence of Spanish. For example, one pointed to the recognition that Spanish architects such as Calatrava have achieved, as well as the success of films with Spanish-speaking actors such as *Y tu mamá también* and *Mala Educación*, both featuring Gael Garcia Bernal of Mexico (Turchinsky, personal communication, 23.3.06). Another student mentioned the role of the media in promoting not only chic, good-looking and interesting Spanish speaking actors and singers (Penelope Cruz, Salma Hayek, Pedro Almodóvar, Jimmy Smits, Alejandro González, Gael García and Cecilia Roth), but also writers such as Gabriel García-Márquez and Isabel Allende (Valdivieso, personal communication, 23.3.06). But another student warned that the status of Spanish in the USA has more to do with economic and social realities than with fashion, which generally implies a passing trend (Bucuvalas, personal communication, 23.3.06).

Spain has capitalized on the global influence of Spanish, and its economic potential, to launch a program to teach Spanish as a global language. On 11 May 1990, the Instituto Cervantes was established to 'Agrupar y potenciar los esfuerzos en la defensa y promoción del español en el extranjero.' [Group and potentialize the efforts in the defense and promotion of Spanish abroad.] (Sánchez, 1992). In a decade, the Instituto Cervantes has opened 34 centers in the world, including three in the USA – in Albuquerque, New Mexico, Chicago and New York City.

The Instituto Cervantes offers classes in Spanish. It also has its own virtual classroom – AVE (*Aula Virtual de Español*). Its activities include the teaching of Spanish to children as demonstrated by the virtual program *Mi Mundo en Palabras* [My World in Words], which offers Spanish language teaching material designed for 7–9 year olds. In addition, the Instituto Cervantes offers an Exam for an Official Diploma of Spanish as a Foreign Language (DELE) and a program to prepare teachers of Spanish (for more information, see http://www.cervantes.es).

With regards to the teaching of Spanish to Spanish speakers, however, the language-in-education policies of the Instituto Cervantes mirror those of the USA. Despite the interest in teaching Spanish, the Instituto Cervantes has shown little interest in teaching Spanish to Spanish speakers. For example, in New York City during the fall of 2005, the Instituto Cervantes offered 95 sections of Spanish. Only one section was for Spanish for Spanish speakers (García, 2007).

Attempts at Integrating Perspectives: Two-way Dual Language Classrooms

When I posed the question to my graduate students of whether Spanish was fashionable, a Mexican–American student replied:

> I believe White people perceive Spanish as fashionable when they speak it, even cute, but dirty when Latinos speak Spanish ... As a bilingual person, my Spanish has never been considered fashionable. As a matter of fact, I have often been told to stop speaking Spanish. (Armenta, personal communication 23.3.06)

It is precisely the ability to build on the 'fashionable' appeal of Spanish for all, at the same time that it may offer US Latino students the possibility of developing their bilingualism, that makes two-way dual language education programs promising. Despite the limitations of the two-way dual language education model (see, for example, García, 2006; Valdés, 1997), the programs, as instituted in practice, have the potential to integrate attitudes, practices and pedagogies concerning bilingualism that have traditionally been looked at separately.

In one sixth-grade dual language classroom in NYC in which I have spent some time,[9] there are 17 eleven-year olds, all showing the linguistic and cultural complexity that characterizes urban societies in the 21st century. Three of the children have arrived this academic year, but seven are considered English Language Learners. Two of them are not of Latino ancestry. One is a second generation Pakistani who has lived in this

Spanish-speaking neighborhood of Washington Heights her whole life. Her mother says that everyone in the neighborhood in which the school is located always speaks Spanish to her, and that she would want her daughter to be able to understand and reply. The other is African–American. Her mother is of mixed Puerto Rican ancestry, although far removed. Eleven of the children were born in the USA, although many have been back and forth to many Spanish-speaking countries. For example, R. was born in New York, but left for the Dominican Republic at the age of two. He then lived in New York from five to seven, returning to the Dominican Republic once more at seven. At the age of 11, he has now recently arrived in New York.

The children also have mixed origin parenting. For example, P. was born in the USA. Although his father is a first generation Puerto Rican, his mother was born in the USA of mixed Puerto Rican and Dominican parentage. P., however, lived in Puerto Rico for seven years.

Although most of the children in this classroom are Dominicans – the dominant group in this predominantly Spanish-speaking neighborhood – there are also first and second generation Latino children of Salvadorean, Colombian, Ecuadorian, Puerto Rican and Mexican ancestry. It is important to note that over 25% of the New York City population is Latino, and in the 2000 US census, Latinos constituted close to 2 million people. Although Puerto Ricans are still the most numerous group, the NYC Latino population has diverse national origins, as shown in Table 2.5. Many of the US born children in this classroom have parents who have been born in different Latin American countries. At least one of the US born children has an African–American mother and a father of Latino background who doesn't live with her.

The heterogeneity of the children, combined with the commitment to the importance of Spanish in this school, allows this classroom to function as a space that bridges the gap created by the different attitudes towards Spanish in the USA. At the same time, these classrooms make use of pedagogies that provide multiple entry points to the teaching of Spanish and the teaching in Spanish (as well as English), working precisely in the gap that has always existed between these two approaches (and languages). Before we look at pedagogies, it is important to study the differences in attitudes toward Spanish that this more integrated approach develops in children. As we will see, the children in this sixth grade dual language classroom feel very differently about Spanish than do many adult Latino students who have not experienced dual language bilingual education.

Integrating attitudes: Spanish to get along

All the children in this sixth grade classroom seem to hold Spanish in high regard, and despite the fact that Spanish and English are separated

Table 2.5 Latinos in New York City[a]

	2000	*%Latino2000*
Puerto Rican	789,172	36.5
Dominicans	406,806	18.8
Mexican	186,872	8.6
Ecuadorian	101,005	4.7
Colombian	77,154	3.6
Cuban	41,123	1.9
Honduran	25,600	1.2
Salvadoran	24,516	1.1
Peruvian	23,567	1.1
Panamanian	16,847	0.8
Guatemalan	15,212	0.7
Argentinean	9,578	0.4
Venezuelan	6,713	0.3
Nicaraguan	6,451	0.3
Chilean	5,014	0.2
Costa Rican	4,939	0.2
Bolivian	2,942	0.1
Paraguayan	1,658	0.1
Uruguayan	1,907	0.1

[a]These figures are derived from US Census 2000, Summary File 3. An underestimation of all Latino groups except Cubans, Mexicans and Puerto Ricans may have occurred in 2000 because the 'other Hispanic' category was open-ended. In NYC between 1990 and 2000, the Other Hispanic category jumped from100,644 to 401,108

for instruction, both languages have been integrated in ways that define who the children are. As one boy told me, 'Even though Spanish runs through my heart, English rules my veins.'

Latino children here understand the importance of Spanish, in their homes, their lives, their neighborhood. Spanish here is not simply an instrument to communicate today with their Spanish-speaking parents or in their Spanish-speaking neighborhoods. It is impressive how many of these students refer to language as an instrument to 'get along'. A boy who came to the USA when he was a kindergartner tells me:

> I was born with Spanish, and I would never leave the Spanish. I'll keep Spanish. Spanish was born into my life because anywhere I go I see somebody or a friend and that person might know Spanish, and in the future I might know Spanish, and we might be able to **get along**. (my emphasis)

For these children both English and Spanish are important to get along. A boy tells me, 'In the Heights, you see a lot of Latinos and stuff, and Latinos are everywhere, and Americans are everywhere. Everywhere you go you bump into a Latino or an American . . . .' And another girl says: 'There are a lot of Latinos out there, and Americans, and a lot of Americans that don't know Spanish and a lot of Latinos that don't know English. It would be better for both of them to know both languages.' It is evident to me that these children have learned the importance of language to get along, as they have negotiated with classmates who do not speak the language of instruction, whether English or Spanish.

To these children, Spanish is not a barrier. Rather, it is one more way of communicating with the many who speak it and are learning it. As one of them told me, 'Most of the people around here in Washington Heights speak Spanish. There are families in my block that speak Spanish. The Russians are learning Spanish. The French are learning Spanish.' The Pakistani girl remarked with incredible naturalness about the presence of Spanish in her neighborhood. Talking about her trip to Pakistan, she said with superiority: 'I went to Pakistan. What's different is they speak Urdu, and they don't know how to speak Spanish, and over here, we speak only English and Spanish.' The ubiquitousness of Spanish in this community was driven home for me when one of the children started talking about how important English was for her. She said: 'English is special for me because let's say you go to England, or Brooklyn. There people speak English. It's very special; it's like a privilege.' It turns out that in this girl's eye, one has to go to England or Brooklyn to speak English only!

These children have learned that Spanish is spoken and heard beyond the home. Sure, there are some that tell me that their parents do not speak Spanish. A girl says: 'I speak Spanish in my home because my mom doesn't know that much English. It really helps.' But there is another one who points to all the people with power that he has heard speaking Spanish:

> My friends from my neighborhood speak Spanish. And in school, the principal, the Assistant Principal, most of the teachers. Bush speaks a little bit of Spanish. In a speech of the campaign he started saying some Spanish.

Spanish not only has reality beyond the neighborhood. Students see it as an economic resource for their own futures, and for those who are presently monolingual English speakers. Speaking about the African–American girl in this classroom, a Latino boy tells me: 'We're lucky to learn Spanish when we're trying to get a job. She's even luckier because she's black.' This same boy expressed how sorry he felt for monolinguals, and with extreme confidence said to me: 'Spanish is everywhere for them. They could face Spanish in the future, so why not learn it now?'

It is in the attitude expressed towards how students learn both languages that the pedagogies and language uses of this dual language school are made evident. Students seem to enjoy learning and using both languages in this way. One Latino boy tells me: 'This is where I learned my English, and practicing my English and Spanish.' This school is not only the place where Latino students learn English, but where they rehearse using both their languages. And speaking of the African–American girl who has learned Spanish in this school, another boy tells me:

> I really like this program in this school. Like A., she came into this school, not learning Spanish, and A., she learned Spanish with people helping her. You get other students to help in Spanish and English, yes.

As we will see, the collaborative nature of the pedagogy used in this school reflects in methodology the idea that language must be used to 'get along', and so, children help each other as the other language is acquired and developed.

The use of Spanish in instruction is non-controversial in this setting. A recently arrived boy told me: 'Spanish is as good as English, and if you don't know in English, you need to learn it in Spanish, became some people can understand what you're saying.' And so, the use of Spanish in education is not questioned, it is simply natural, it is a gift, a collaborative venture of 'getting along', important for peaceful living, as well as effective learning.

Integrating pedagogies: Spanish to learn along

What two-way dual language bilingual education programs have in common is a philosophy of developing the bilingualism of children. To do so, they separate the use of language. Sometimes, this is done by having side-by-side classrooms, with two teachers who teach in only one language switching children every day, every half day or even every week. Other times, one teacher assigns a different language to either days or times or subjects or activities. For example, at a recent visit to a New York City school, M. wears a red apron for Spanish days and a blue apron for English days. These are also the colors which are used to write the two different languages throughout dual language education programs in the city. Our sixth grade teacher simply changes the 'channels' of a make-believe television that she has on the blackboard. She regularly says: 'Y ahora voy a cambiar el canal y we're going to speak in English because we're in New York 1!' [We're now going to change the channel and we're going to speak English because we're in New York 1!]

New York City has adopted a 'Balanced Literacy' model to teach reading and writing. For dual language bilingual classrooms, this has the advantage that both English and Spanish are taught as mother tongues using the Reading and Writing Workshop Model (for more on the workshop model, see Au, 2006; Au & Carroll, 1997; Calkins, 1994; O'Neill & Velasco, forthcoming). The Literacy Workshop model builds on collaborative groups or pairs working on literacy activities, individual independent reading and writing, and explicit whole-group instruction done during a mini-lesson. It is in the collaborative nature of instruction that the workshop model introduces the 'Trojan Horse' to the language separation of the model. For it turns out that even though the teacher separates languages strictly and children are expected to work in a specific language, the collaborative nature of the literacy activities, coupled with the heterogeneous levels of language proficiency that children hold in Spanish and English, makes the actual language practices of children in these two-way dual language classrooms much more fluid than expected.

Spanish in dual language classrooms is used not only to get along, but also to learn along – with Spanish native speakers, with second and third generation US Latinos for whom Spanish is a passive or non-existent 'heritage' language, with foreign language speakers – integrating perspectives, building multiple entry points for learning, and scaffolding instruction for the increasing bilingual and bidialectal US students. Children themselves constantly negotiate language to learn alongside their peers who might have different linguistic and cultural profiles.

The pedagogy of dual language bilingual education classrooms do not fit within an ESL model or a sheltered English model. Neither does it fit within a Spanish as a Foreign Language (SFL) or a Spanish as a Second Language (SSL) or even a Spanish for Spanish speakers (SSP) or a Spanish as a heritage language (SHL) model. In its own way, two-way dual language bilingual education pedagogy is all of this and much more. It builds on the children's collaborative spirit to learn, play and imagine, and in so doing, and despite the language separation which reflects a respect for the two languages, it integrates the children's bilingual practices and their attitudes toward their own bilingualism, precisely by working in the gap that US society continues to artificially maintain.

Integrating languages to learn along and get along

Despite the teacher's language separation, the children themselves provide much evidence of an integrative discourse which, despite trying to respect the space for the language being used in instruction, goes beyond what we might expect. In collaborative groups and pairs, children often use one language or the other, going back and forth as they negotiate their emotional and intellectual connections with students who might have different linguistic profiles.

For instance, during a Book Club period observed last spring in the same sixth grade class described above, five students were reading the same novel in Spanish independently. They were told to put post-it notes on a specific page to write out personal connections to a text or pose a question. I notice that one US born girl writes:

> *Yo tiene miedo en la noche. Porque un dia* in second grade my father took me to the movies to watch the Exorcist and in the night I can't sleep.
>
> I'm afraid at night. Because one day ...

One language is not just sufficient for this girl (it is written here exactly as it appears), and thus, even though she starts in Spanish, the language of the lesson, she continues in English, possibly the private language in which she expresses connections and fears.

When the dialogue for this group starts, one boy reads one of his questions in a post-it, and a second child engages him in dialogue:

Child 1: *¿Por qué el niño le tiene miedo al lobo?* [Why is the boy afraid of the wolf?]
Child 2: The what?
Child 1: The *lobo*. You know, wolf.
Child 2: No, *pero* he's still scared.
Child 1: But they're not going to get any help.

The conversation started in Spanish, the language of instruction, but Child 2 asked for clarification of the word 'lobo' in English and eventually Child 1 ends this short exchange in English. The next child, however, then asked another question in Spanish.

Children also are capable of using language to improve their possibilities of getting along. During another Spanish language period, the teacher asks students to read independently in silence.

Teacher: Ok. *Trabajo independiente por favor, en silencio.* [Work independently, please, in silence]
Child 1: Ms. X, I want the other one. It's better than my own.
Child 2: She has it! *Mira, ella lo tiene.* [Look, she has it.]

Although bilingual, this particular teacher is an Anglo, and thus Child 1 capitalizes on his fluency in English and uses English to try to get the teacher's attention to get a newer copy of the book they're reading. But Child 2, comfortable in both languages, responds first in English, and then repeats it in Spanish, making sure that the entire class pays attention to what he's saying and that everyone, no matter their proficiency, is engaged with him.

In the exchange that follows, a student is reading a Spanish essay. When the others start to laugh at him, he immediately switches to English, hoping to save face and engage with all his classmates:

> Mi hermano me tiro una bola de nieve y yo me puse bravo. Cogi y [laughter from children] But! he threw it at my face!!!!!!!! Cogi y lo tire a mi hermano
>
> My brother threw a snowball at me and I got mad. I took ... [laughter from the children] But! he threw it at my face!!!!!!! I took it and threw it at my brother.

The integrative use of language by children in this two-way dual language bilingual education program certainly fills the gap in Spanish in education that we have noticed. Rather than bridge the distance between teaching Spanish, and using Spanish to teach; or teaching Spanish to US Latinos and US Anglos, or seeing Spanish as a resource or a problem, or seeing bilingualism as an elite optional venture or a folk needed venture, this particular classroom is a good counterexample to the current silence surrounding bilingual education and even foreign language education in Spanish.[10] Children's natural voices, name and shape, perhaps, a more integrated bilingual future.

Conclusion

This examination of the various traditions of teaching Spanish and Spanish in teaching reveals the potential of two-way dual language bilingual education programs to fill the separations and inadequacies which have characterized language education programs in the USA. In working in the gap, these programs are capable of overcoming what Wright (2004) has pointed out to be the 'one nation, one territory, one language nationalism' ideology which works against the globalization processes that the USA has championed in the rest of the world. We have seen how this is successfully done in one particular sixth grade classroom where students and teachers unconsciously work against dual language structures externally imposed, enabling not only plurilingual and pluriliteracy practices, but also constructing a heteroglossic discourse that is integrative because it reflects and respects our language and cultural differences.

The reality is that the two-way dual language education movement in the USA has been slow to develop; and the community, political and professional support has been less than desirable. The accountability measures of the new NCLB Act, and the emphasis on English-only assessments, have made schools cautious to introduce educational programs that take away time from English-only instruction. Parents have also felt this pressure. Concomitantly, the different language education professions in the United States have shown very little interest in this model.

To develop and grow, this more integrated bilingual model called two-way dual language education must continue to seek the support of language majority parents.[11] Beyond the parents, this model must be supported by language professionals other than bilingual educators. In particular, the Spanish language profession could lend support to this bilingual model, yet Spanish language professionals, steeped in a monoglossic ideology, often have more in common with English language professionals, including ESL professionals, than with bilingual professionals.

The alienation of Spanish language educators, often international teachers, and the bilingual education educators, mostly US-based, is also reinforced by philosophy, as well as where these programs are found in the academy. Bilingual educators focus on language education only as an aspect of a child's holistic education, whereas Spanish language educators are only concerned with language itself. Furthermore, Spanish language programs are mostly housed in Arts and Sciences divisions alongside English, whereas bilingual education programs are in Schools of Education. At the college level, Spanish language professionals teach the language, in much the same way as ESL professionals teach English to international and immigrant college students. Bilingual professionals, however, are involved in the education, as well as the teaching of languages, only at the school level. At the college level, their only role is teacher education. Thus, there is little collaboration among professionals concerned about the future of Spanish in the USA.

To advance the position and the potential of two-way dual language bilingual education models in the future would require that professionals and adults collaborate in the same ways as the children in the sixth grade class described. That would require the ability to work in the gap, to hold a heteroglossic view of how language is negotiated – aspects that adult professionals in the education business in the USA have rarely learned to navigate. The potential for integrating bilingual perspectives through two-way dual language bilingual education is great. The reality, however, is difficult to expand beyond the few programs with enlightened and courageous principals, teachers, parents and students, willing to fill in, at least temporarily, and in a specific space, the space between policy and reality of the increasingly multilingual discourse of the USA.

Acknowledgements

I want to thank Cambria Russell for the help given me in the preparation of this paper. I'm grateful to Leah Mason for her help in putting together Table 2.3.

Notes

1. We use monoglossic in the same sense used by Del Valle (2000, 2006) and used in an earlier paper (García, 2007).
2. We use heteroglossia in the ways given to us by Bakhtin (1981), with competing discourses coexisting and languages hybridised in a certain discursive dialogic space.
3. This is the figure given in the 2005 American Community Survey. There are also many undocumented who were not counted.
4. Some of the early history provided in this paper is based on my paper, García (1993).
5. The teaching of foreign languages in the elementary school has always been much more common in private schools. Rhodes and Branaman (1999: 12) state that in 1997, 24% of public elementary schools reported teaching foreign languages.
6. For more on the history of bilingual education, see especially Crawford (2004) and Garcia (2005).
7. We will adopt here the label that is most often used to describe these programs – two-way dual language or simply dual language. The reader is warned, however, that this use of dual language in opposition to bilingual education is another manifestation of the silencing of the word bilingual. In effect, dual language programs are a kind of bilingual education program, a two-way bilingual education. Although dual language education models are favored in public discourse and many US school systems are developing such programs, in reality there are few such programs. For more on this in New York City, see Torres-Guzmán (2002).
8. This has also been noted in the case of English immersion high schools in Hong Kong by Marsh *et al.* (2000).
9. I am grateful to Dana Erickson from Amistad School and to her sixth graders for opening up their class to me. I am also grateful to the principal, Miriam Pedraja, who provided me with access. The interviews were carried out during the spring of 2005.
10. The emphasis by US government officials is on teaching the 'critical' languages – Arabic, Chinese, Russian, Hindi and Farsi – according to the National Security Language Initiative. Spanish is not considered critical.
11. In New York City, for example, except for Gifted and Talented programs where few Latino children are found because of the inadequacies of the gifted tests given in English only, most dual language education classrooms have Latino children with different linguistic profiles.

References

Álvarez Martínez, M.A. (2001) El español como lengua extranjera en las universidades españolas. Centro Virtual Cervantes. II Congreso de la Lengua Española. On WWW at http://www.congresosdelalengua.es/valladolid/ponencias/activo_del_espanol/1_la_industria_del_espanol/alvarez_m.htm. Accessed 1.08.

AATSP (American Association of Teachers of Spanish and Portuguese) (2000) *Spanish for Native Speakers: AATSP Professional Development Series Handbook for Teachers K 12. A Handbook for Teachers* (Vol. 1). Fort Worth, TX: Hartcourt College Publishers.

Au, K.H. (2006) *Multicultural Issues and Literacy Achievement.* Mahwah, NJ: Lawrence Erlbaum.

Au, K.H. and Carroll, J.H. (1997) Improving literacy achievement through a constructivist approach: The KEEP Demonstration Classroom Project. *Elementary School Journal* 97, 203–221.

Bakhtin, M.M. (1981) *The Dialogical Imagination.* Austin: University of Texas Press.

Calkins, L.M. (1994) *The Art of Teaching Writing.* Portsmouth, NH: Heinemann.

Cloud, N., Genesee, F. and Hamayan, E. (2000) *Dual Language Instruction. A Handbook for Enriched Education.* Boston, MA: Heinle and Heinle.

Coleman, A. (1929) The teaching of modern foreign languages in the United States. *Publications of the American and Canadian Committees on Modern Languages, Volume 12.* New York: Macmillan.

Colombi, M.C. and Alarcón, F.X. (eds) (1997) *La Enseñanza del Español a Hispanohablantes: Praxis y Teoría.* Boston: Houghton Mifflin.

Crawford, J. (ed.) (1992) *Language Loyalties: A Source Book on the Official English Controversy.* Chicago, IL: University of Chicago Press.

Crawford, J. (2004) *Educating English Learners: Language Diversity in the Classroom* (5th edn). (formerly Bilingual Education: History, Politics, Theory, and Practice). Los Angeles: Bilingual Educational Services.

Cummins, J. (2005) A proposal for action: Strategies for recognizing heritage language competence as a learning resource within the mainstream classroom. *The Modern Language Journal* 89, 585–592.

Cummins, J. and Danesi, M. (1990) *Heritage Languages: The Development and Denial of Canada's Linguistic Resources.* Toronto: Our Schools/Our Selves and Garamond Press.

Daniels, R. (1991) *Coming to America: A History of Immigration and Ethnicity in American Life.* New York: Harper Perennial.

Del Valle, J. (2000) Monoglossic policies for a heteroglossic culture: Misinterpreted multilingualism in modern Galicia. *Language and Communication* 20, 105–132.

Del Valle, J. (2006) U.S. Latinos, *la hispanofonía*, and the language ideologies of high modernity. In C. Mar-Molinero and M. Stewart (eds) *Globalisation and the Spanish-speaking World* (pp. 27–46). London and New York: Palgrave.

Dicker, S. (1996) *Languages in America.* Clevedon: Multilingual Matters.

Dillon, S. (2006) Schools cut back subjects to push reading and math. *The New York Times* 26 March, Sunday Late Edition – Final Section 1; Column 5; National Desk, p. 1.

Draper, J.B. and Hicks, J.H. (2000) Where we've been; What we've learned. In J.B. Webb and B.L. Miller (eds) *Teaching Heritage Language Learners: Voices from the Classroom* (pp. 15–35). Yonkers, NY: American Council on the Teaching of Foreign Languages.

Draper, J.B. and Hicks, J.H. (2002) *Foreign Language Enrollments in Public Secondary Schools, Fall 2000*. Yonkers, NY: American Council on the Teaching of Foreign Languages.
Espinosa, A. (1921) On the teaching of Spanish. *Hispania* 4, 269–284.
Espinosa, A. (1923) Where is the best Spanish spoken? *Hispania* 6, 244–246.
Gaarder, A.B., Walsh, D., Barker, M.E., Cantero, H., Guerrero, A., La Fontaine, H., Munoz, M.O., Olstad, C. and Perales, A.M. (1972) Teaching Spanish in school and college to native speakers. *Hispania* 55, 619–631.
Garcia, E. (2005) *Teaching and Learning in Two Languages*. New York: Teachers College Press.
García, O. (1993) From Goya portraits to Goya beans: Elite traditions and popular streams in U.S. Spanish language policy. *Southwest Journal of Linguistics* 12, 69–86.
García, O. (2003) La enseñanza del español a los latinos de los EEUU. Contra el viento del olvido y la marea del inglés. *Ínsula* julio–agosto, 679–680.
García, O. (2005) Positioning heritage languages in the United States. *Modern Language Journal* 89 (4), 601–605.
García, O. (2006) Lost in transculturation: The case of bilingual education in New York City. In M. Putz, J.A. Fishman and J. Neff-Van Aertselaer (eds) *Along the Routes to Power: Exploration of the Empowerment through Language* (pp. 157–178). Berlin: Mouton de Gruyter.
García, O. (2007) Lenguas e identidades en mundos hispanohablantes. Desde una posición plurilingüe y minoritaria. In M. Lacorte (ed.) *Lingüística Aplicada del Español* (pp. 377–400). Madrid: Arco.
García, O., Morín, J.L. and Rivera, K. (2001) How threatened is the Spanish of New York Puerto Ricans? Language shift with vaivén. In J.A. Fishman (ed.) *Can Threatened Languages be Saved? Reversing Language Shift Revisited* (pp. 44–73). Clevedon: Multilingual Matters.
Grattan Doyle, H. (1926) *Spanish Studies in the United States*. Washington: Government Printing Office.
Harden, T.K. (1981) The National Defense Education Act: A turning point in federal aid. Eric Document 212084.
Held, D., McGrew, A., Goldblatt, D. and Perraton, J. (1999) *Global Transformations*. Cambridge: Polity Press.
Hernández-Chávez, E. (1995) Language policy in the United States: A history of cultural genocide. In T. Skutnabb-Kangas and R. Phillipson (eds) *Linguistic Human Rights: Overcoming Linguistic Discrimination* (pp. 141–158). Berlin: Mouton.
Huebener, T. (1961) *Why Johnny Should Learn Foreign Languages*. Philadelphia: Chilton.
Instituto Cervantes. http://www.cervantes.es/. Accessed 1.4.06.
Kloss, H. (1977) *The American Bilingual Tradition*. Rowley, MA: Newbury House.
Leavitt, S.E. (1961) The teaching of Spanish in the United States. *Hispania* 44, 591–625.
Lindholm-Leary, K. (2001) *Dual Language Education*. Clevedon: Multilingual Matters.
Marsh, H.W., Hau, K.T., Kong, C-K. (2000) Late immersion and language of instruction in Hong Kong high schools: Achievement growth in language and nonlanguage subjects. *Harvard Educational Review* 70 (3), 302–347.
Mittleman, J. (1996) *Globalization: Critical Reflections*. Boulder: Lynne Reiner.
Nichols, M.W. (1945) The history of Spanish and Portuguese teaching in the United States. In H. Grattan-Doyle (ed.) *A Handbook on the Teaching of Spanish*

and Portuguese with Special Reference to Latin America (pp. 99–146). Boston: D.C. Heath.

O'Neill, J. and Velasco, P. (forthcoming) Understanding the power of scaffolds. Unpublished manuscript.

Rhodes, N. and Branaman, L.E. (1999) *Foreign Language Instruction in the United States: A National Survey of Elementary and Secondary Schools*. Washington, D.C.: Center for Applied Linguistics.

Roca, A. and Colombi, M.C. (eds) (2003) *Spanish as a Heritage Language in the United States. Research and Practice.* Washington, D.C.: Georgetown University Press.

Sánchez, A. (1992) Spanish language spread policy. *International Journal of the Sociology of Language* 95, 51–69.

Spell, J.R. (1927) Spanish teaching in the United States. *Hispania* 10, 141–159.

Torres-Guzmán, M.E. (2002) Dual language programs: Key features and results. *Directions in Language and Education* 14, 1–16.

Valdés, G. (1997) Dual-language immersion programs: A cautionary note concerning the education of language-minority students. *Harvard Educational Review* 67, 391–429.

Valdés, G., Lozano, A.G. and García-Moya, R. (eds) (1981) *Teaching Spanish to the Hispanic Bilingual. Issues, Aims, and Methods.* New York: Teachers College Press.

Valdés, G., Fishman, J.A., Chavez, R. and Perez, W. (2006) *Developing Minority Language Resources. The Case of Spanish in California.* Clevedon: Multilingual Matters.

Wonder, J.P. (1965) The bilingual Mexican–American as a potential teacher of Spanish. *Hispania* 48, 97–99.

Wright, S. (2004) *Language Policy and Language Planning. From Nationalism to Globalization.* Hampshire and New York: Palgrave Macmillan.

Chapter 3

Plurilingual Latin America: Indigenous Languages, Immigrant Languages, Foreign Languages – Towards an Integrated Policy of Language and Education

RAINER ENRIQUE HAMEL

Indigenous Bilingual Education and Elite Bilingual Schools: Setting the Stage

In Latin America[1] two different types of population have created their own specific domains of bilingual practice including that of bilingual education: domains relating to indigenous education and domains relating to elite private education which was originally organised by European immigrant communities. Over 500 indigenous languages (IL) are spoken alongside the national languages by some 30 million people, mainly within their historical territories, but also in the new urban and rural areas resulting from migration.[2] Schooling for the children of indigenous peoples[3] is provided by the state in a public subsystem of indigenous primary education known as 'intercultural bilingual education' (IBE) that functions mostly in rural indigenous areas. These schools, which are generally poorly equipped and staffed, use the two languages for a variety of functions in content-based teaching and learning. Pedagogical achievement is generally extremely low in all countries, according to national standards and programmes defined by and for the mainstream population.

On the other hand, immigrant languages other than Spanish and Portuguese, resulting from a wave of European immigration which became massive during the second half of the 19th century, have played a significant role in the development of private institutions, such as British, French, Italian or German bilingual schools that now form a sector of 'elite bilingual education' (EBE). Most of them were founded by immigrant groups to cater initially for their own communities in their heritage languages. Much later, they incorporated the countries' national language and curriculum and opened their doors to students from outside the immigrant community. In the 20th century, those schools associated with prestigious and internationally powerful language communities developed into 'global language schools' (Banfi & Day, 2004) that serve a significant segment of the countries' economic and power elites who seek prestigious and differentiated education of high standard for their offspring, alongside the needs of the shrinking immigrant communities.

The two types of communities and their schools position themselves at opposite poles of social stratification and the scales of extreme inequality that characterise all Latin American countries, and their actors hardly ever cross paths or exchange words. Nevertheless, their spaces and educational systems share psycho- and sociolinguistic challenges which lend themselves to comparison and confrontation at certain levels of abstraction. From a macrosociolinguistic perspective, both communities exist as enclaves in sociohistoric formations of nation-state-building processes oriented towards European models of linguistic and cultural homogeneity that seek to assimilate those who are different, irrespective of differences of origin, historical legitimacy and status. Thus, in most Latin American countries both the state and mainstream society traditionally considered their representative citizens to be monolingual speakers of the national language beyond the common rhetoric of support for IL, the value of immigrant communities and the necessity of foreign language learning.[4] This strong monolingual ideology often stirs up suspicion about true citizenship, national loyalty and the lack of assimilation in those who are native speakers of other languages, even if they are equally proficient in the national language, as happens in the USA[5] and, to a lesser degree, in Canada. Therefore, any stable bi- or multilingualism, and the existence of language maintenance oriented communities – be they indigenous or immigrant – face adverse sociolinguistic conditions and will have to develop specific ideological, cultural and linguistic justifications for maintaining their bilingual domains, such as schools, churches or social clubs within an otherwise monolingual context.

Enclave or heritage language schools have demonstrated how mother tongue maintenance oriented education can be successful, without jeopardising the development of high proficiency in both content areas and in the national language. When some of these institutions developed into elite bilingual schools, they profited from top level input in modern applied linguistics and foreign language teaching techniques provided by their countries of origin. Although indigenous schools obtained considerably less support from applied linguistics and modern teaching techniques, in contrast, they received a wealth of anthropological and sociolinguistic insight in identifying complex intercultural and multilingual contact situations.

I will argue that these two spaces and their respective education systems share several common problems and possible solutions, and that the complex interplay of linguistic, cognitive, cultural and socioeconomic factors in the explanation of success and failure, as well as in the design and implementation of promising strategies could greatly benefit from an exchange of experience and expertise across the systems. It is my contention that a reciprocal, unbiased process of exchange and mutual learning could foster the growth of multilingual spheres and the transition towards pluricultural nation states where cultural and linguistic diversity is seen as global enrichment (Hamel, 2008a, 2008b).

In this chapter, I will first outline some general characteristics of each educational setting with regard to the macro level of policy and the micro level of curriculum. I will then explore some basic differences as well as shared problems and solutions in order to postulate possible avenues of pedagogical cooperation. Finally, I will discuss aspects of an integrated interpretation of language and education policy in Latin America.

Indigenous Education in Latin America

From colonisation to the modern nation state

From the beginning of colonisation in 1492, conflict arose between the new colonial languages and the pre-existing multilingual systems of communication based on over 1000 native languages. The colonial powers developed two basic strategies of ethnic and language policy in Latin America in relation to the indigenous population which took shape after Independence in the early 19th century. The first and generally dominant strategy considered the assimilation (i.e. dissolution) of Indian peoples and the suppression of their languages and cultures a prerequisite for the building of a unified colonial empire and later of homogeneous nation states. A second strategy favoured the preservation of Indian languages and cultures in this process, without sacrificing the ultimate goal of uniting nation and state.

As a result, a gradual process of language shift took place, which accelerated during the 19th and 20th centuries. The two strategies materialised in education and Spanish teaching – the main pillars of cultural policies for the Indians – through two basic approaches which differed considerably in their cultural and educational philosophy and methods, their view of sociocultural integration and, above all, in their manner of using and teaching Spanish or Portuguese. The first strategy was aimed at linguistic and cultural assimilation through direct imposition of the national language, leading to submersion or fast transitional programmes, to use modern terminology. It was seen as important that education in the colonial language should actively contribute to language shift and cultural change. The national language was to be the sole target and medium of instruction, and teaching materials, content and methods were the exclusive preserve of the dominant society. The second strategy involved transitional and some rare maintenance programmes. In most cases, diverse bilingual methods were introduced where the Indian languages played a subordinate, instrumental role as languages of instruction and for initial alphabetisation (for overviews see Hamel, 1994, 2000).

Today, the debates about indigenous education centre around two fundamental issues. The first relates to a macropolitical and anthropological dimension. Given the difficulties of building homogenous nation states fashioned on the European model and the strengthening of indigenous movements during the last decades of the 20th century, the question arises whether the dominant societies and the state apparatus will insist in pursuing their historical strategy of forced assimilation. In most Latin American countries a powerful alternative emerges that strives for the transformation of the existing nation states into plurilingual and pluricultural polities which approach their existing diversity from an enrichment perspective. Autochthonous First Nations, African descent and the differentiated European heritage should converge as three distinct roots in the forging of a new type of nation and Latin American integration that reconciles unity with the preservation of cultural and linguistic diversity. As in the past, education plays a central role in the development of pluricultural societies. If this process is to succeed, the earlier ideological orientation to use education as a central tool of assimilation and homogenisation will have to give way to new policy approaches that come to terms with and foster diversity.

In view of previous failures with submersion and fast transitional programmes for the indigenous population, a number of new modalities have emerged since the 1970s. Colombia has developed its own model of ethnoeducation based on indigenous worldviews and teaching methods. However, this is sometimes identified with top-down state education by autonomous indigenous movements (CRIC, 2005). In most other countries, bilingual and bicultural programmes were designed to help to preserve and foster ILs. The bicultural component was replaced by a new concept of 'intercultural' education in the late 1980s, which implied a new approach: a cultural relationship of mutual understanding and respect which should not be limited to the indigenous population but should involve the whole[6] school population of the countries concerned. In the case of Indian students, the idea is to develop indigenous culture through the native language and to foster ethnic identity as a basis for the learning and appropriation of national culture and values. Conversely, mainstream students should learn about indigenous cultures right from the start and be expected to develop positive values towards diversity and intercultural knowledge and practices. In areas of high indigenous population density, these students should learn one of the ILs of the region (Albó, 2002).

The second fundamental issue refers to the micropolitical domain of the cultural, pedagogical and linguistic organisation of the school itself. The debate focuses on the appropriate modalities of intercultural and bilingual education to fulfil the global objectives discussed above. More precisely, we may ask which cultural model, which pedagogical approach and what functional language distribution will be able to integrate overall cultural and linguistic aims with academic achievement in the context of an asymmetric power relation between the dominant Spanish- or Portuguese-speaking mainstream society and the indigenous peoples organised around their subordinate languages (Hamel, 1988, 2000, 2006b; Hornberger, 2000).

The pedagogical and psycholinguistic dimension relates to the question of how global sociopolitical goals may best be achieved through education. How might a given school population of indigenous children with little or no command of the national language best acquire the content areas they are supposed to learn, starting with their own cultural heritage? What understandings, orientations and ideologies do those in power generate about the role of native languages and cultures in education that would make such a programme politically viable? Would indigenous children have to abandon their native language in order to learn the national language properly and become useful citizens? Or, on the contrary, could their first languages function as efficient instruments to acquire literacy, other academic skills, second order discourses and content matters? Should monolingualism in the state language or should enrichment bilingualism be the aim of indigenous education?

The gulf between curriculum theory and educational practice in the classroom is probably even deeper in indigenous education than in other subsystems. Implementation remains the fundamental problem. At present, a range of pedagogical modalities are in use in indigenous education. In most countries, an intercultural bilingual model was officially adopted that establishes mother tongue literacy and content teaching plus Spanish or Portuguese as a second language for pupils who have an IL as their L1. However, historical discrimination and a pervasive diglossic ideology which is deeply rooted even in indigenous teachers' attitudes, raise high barriers against the implementation of a curriculum that would be more appropriate, both from a pedagogical and psycholinguistic perspective, and from the standpoint of the official declared goals of language maintenance and cultural development.

Even in the Andean (Bolivia, Ecuador, Peru) and the Mesoamerican regions (Mexico, Guatemala), which are home to over 80% of the continent's indigenous population, and where educational reforms have established IBE since the 1990s, cultural and language maintenance education still does not constitute a solid, well organised and accepted educational practice. In Mexico and elsewhere, the most widespread modality is to teach literacy and content areas in Spanish, to use the official Spanish primers for elementary education as the basic textbooks, and to make use of the IL as the initial medium of instruction where necessary (Hamel, 2008b). An increasing number of teaching materials in ILs are being used alongside Spanish primers. On the whole, due to extended poverty in indigenous regions and poor conditions of education, together with the prevalence of transitional and submersion programmes, the indigenous educational systems show the poorest results in general proficiency among the different subsystems in most Latin American nations.

Grassroots initiatives of alternative indigenous education

On the local and regional level an increasing number of experimental school projects and other local initiatives have experimented with new ways of improving indigenous education and novel relations between academic achievement and bilingual language use since the 1980s. Most new experimental projects are based on a pluricultural conception of the state and full respect for Indian peoples and their ethnic rights. They claim as their goal the maintenance or revitalisation of Indian cultures and languages. Paradoxically, they comply much more appropriately with the new laws of educational and linguistic rights, as well as with the official IBE programmes, than does *de facto* mainstream indigenous education. Notwithstanding, they are regarded as marginal or experimental both inside and outside the system.

As one example, I will report on a local initiative that I have been involved with over a number of years. In 1995 in San Isidro and Uringuitiro, two bilingual elementary schools (Grades 1–6) in Michoacán, in the west central Highlands of Mexico, the local P'urhepecha teachers introduced radical changes to the previous curriculum which had been based on fast transition to Spanish and submersion L2 Spanish instruction. Academic results had been extremely poor as most children entered primary school as IL monolinguals. Since 1995 all content areas including literacy and mathematics have been taught in P'urhepecha, the children's first language. As a first step, the indigenous teachers, especially those who were local citizens, had to convince the community and the parents to accept the new approach. Once the teachers explained that the new curriculum would not only foster their own language but also lead to higher levels of achievement in literacy, Spanish and other subject areas, the community agreed. The teachers had to create their own materials and decide on an appropriate alphabet. The most difficult part was to develop their own writing skills and the necessary academic discourse in their language to teach the content areas (Hamel, 2006b; Hamel & Ibáñez, 2000; Hamel *et al.*, 2004).

A few years later, in 1998, the teachers and communities invited our research team to study their school project and to help to improve it. As a first step, we set up an interdisciplinary research group which included indigenous teachers and researchers and designed a comparative study in five schools in two indigenous regions with highly divergent sociolinguistic characteristics: the P'urhepecha area with a high degree of IL monolingualism and linguistic vitality, and the Hñähñú (Otomí) region in the Mezquital Valley, in the state of Hidalgo north-east of Mexico City, where language shift had reached an advanced stage and children entered elementary school as almost monolingual speakers of Spanish at that time. Consequently, the IL played a very subordinate role in the Hñähñú indigenous schools. In the P'urhepecha area we included the two schools mentioned above, and another community which exhibited the same sociolinguistic characteristics, but where the school applied traditional 'Castellanización' (fast transition to Spanish). The study was based on a sociolinguistic survey, extensive classroom observation over a full school year and the administration of a specially designed battery of language proficiency tests. It revealed that much more intensive classroom interaction and meaningful learning of content matter occurred in the P'urhepecha schools based on IL teaching than in the other school in the same area. In contrast to most indigenous schools in Mexico and elsewhere in Latin America, P'urhepecha had become the legitimate, unmarked language of all bilingual interaction at school, a sociolinguistic achievement still quite exceptional in indigenous education.

The findings from the proficiency tests[7] illustrated very clearly that students who had acquired literacy in their L1 achieved significantly higher scores in both languages than those who were taught reading and writing in Spanish as L2. The battery included tests in the four skills for the three languages. The same tests in each language pair (P'urhepecha–Spanish and Hñähñú–Spanish) were applied to all students in the five elementary schools (Grades 1–6) to assess linguistic and communicative growth. Let me single out the results in one of the writing tests where students were asked to rewrite a tale that was read to them. Figure 3.1 shows the results from Grades 2 to 5 in San Isidro where students entered school almost as monolinguals in IL and developed literacy in their L1; Spanish was taught as L2, although in a rather unsystematic way at that time.

The lower part of each column represents the development of writing skills in P'urhepecha as L1, whereas the upper part stands for writing skills in Spanish as L2. Clearly, the parallel growth suggests the development of a common underlying proficiency in writing skills[8] mainly through L1, which is then transferred to or accessed from L2,

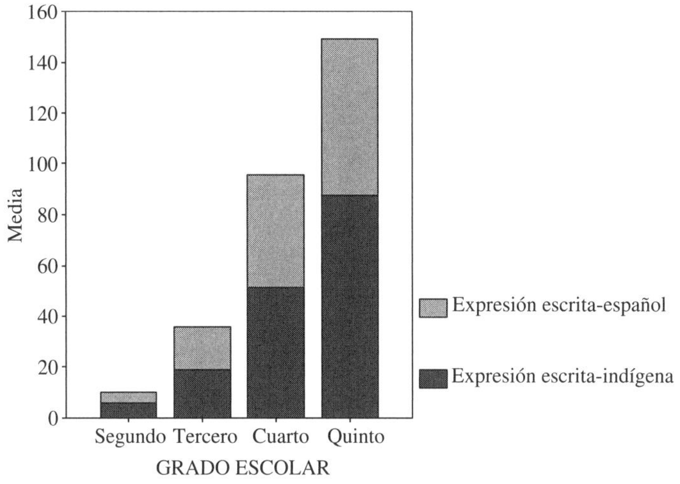

Figure 3.1 Spanish writing skill (narrative). San Isidro scores in L1 and L2. Cronbach's α is 0.93 for the Spanish and 0.87 for the P'urhepecha

especially if we take into account that students had virtually no access to literacy and to Spanish outside school.[9]

The interdependence between the two languages in the development of a cognitively demanding, decontextualised academic proficiency becomes even clearer when we compare the results of the same tests in the five schools (Tables 3.1 and 3.2).

San Bartolomé obtained by far the lowest scores in the Spanish writing test (Table 3.1). Students there entered first grade as almost monolinguals in P'urhepecha and a hybrid between submersion and a fast transitional curriculum was applied. Students in San Isidro and Uringuitiro, in contrast, achieved scores twice as high, probably because they acquired literacy in their first and stronger language, a skill they transferred to Spanish as their L2. In Decá and Defay, the Hñähñú communities where students entered school as monolingual or dominant speakers of Spanish, literacy and content matters were taught almost exclusively in Spanish. No wonder students scored the highest in this test. In these schools, Hñähñú was supposed to be taught for two hours per week, but many of the teachers who were themselves indigenous bilinguals did not systematically apply this part of the programme.

In the IL writing test (Table 3.2) the San Bartolomé students again obtained the lowest scores of all. Although they had fully developed P'urhepecha as their mother tongue and their command of Spanish was fairly poor, most of them were not able to produce acceptable written texts in their language, most likely because there was no relevant space

Table 3.1 Spanish writing skill (narrative)

Community	*L*	*N*	*Students: Types of bilingualism*		
			IL monolinguals or incipient bilinguals IL-S	*IL monolinguals or incipient bilinguals IL-S*	*S monolinguals or incipient bilinguals S-IL*
			Curriculum type & language functions		
			Submersion/ fast transition to S (SB)	*IL based maintenance with additive bilingualism (SI & UR)*	*All S curriculum with 2 weekly hours IL teaching (DC & DY)*
SB	P	158	6.523		
SI	P	82		12.617	
UR	P	79		13.631	
DY	H	137			22.415
DC	H	114			26.994

2001 application
L, language; S, Spanish; P, P'urhepecha; H, Hñäñú
SB, San Bartolomé; SI, San Isidro; UR, Uringuitiro; DY, Defay; DC, Decá
Reliability coefficients: 13 items, $\alpha = 0.8429$; standardised item $\alpha = 0.8504$

for that skill in the curriculum, and the indigenous teachers had contributed to stigmatising the IL. Their peers in the neighbouring communities of San Isidro and Uringuitiro, who acquired literacy and other academic skills through P'urhepecha in a sociolinguistic school environment where their language was highly valued, scored between three and five times higher. The big surprise for both Hñähñú teachers and researchers was the fact that the Spanish dominant or supposedly monolingual students in the Hñähñú area scored roughly three times higher than the P'urhepechas in San Bartolomé in this test. They developed literacy and other components of their academic proficiency systematically through Spanish, which was their 'stronger' language. Many of their teachers insisted that their students really did not speak Hñähñú and they did not teach the language; therefore, they said that we would do better not to apply the IL writing tests. However, the pupils did a marvellous job when writing in their ancestors' language. Especially in Grades 5 and 6, many of them managed to produce

Table 3.2 Indigenous language writing skill (narrative)

Community	*L*	*N*	*Students: Types of bilingualism*		
			IL monolinguals or incipient bilinguals IL-S	*IL monolinguals or incipient bilinguals IL-S*	*S monolinguals or incipient bilinguals S-IL*
			Curriculum type & language functions		
			Submersion/ fast transition to S (SB)	*IL based maintenance with additive bilingualism (SI & UR)*	*All S curriculum with 2 weekly hours IL teaching (DC & DY)*
SB	P	158	5.3846		
SI	P	82		18.0769	
UR	P	79		29.4872	
DY	H	137			15.5682
DC	H	114			16.3352

perfectly comprehensible and well structured texts. Our entire test results, as well as classroom observation, show consistent growth in IL from 1st to 6th grade. These results open up the prospect of helping to reverse language shift through the school, based on a programme of IL revitalisation and the development of additive bilingualism at virtually no additional educational cost.

The results seem to indicate a principle that should be taken into account in IL and education planning. In the context of asymmetric relations of conflict between a dominant national language and subordinate ILs, additive bilingualism and optimal academic achievement in content matters could probably be best accomplished if students develop literacy and other academic skills through their 'stronger' language, be that an IL or the national language. Once a sufficient threshold level[10] in the other language is attained, transfer of academic skills can develop powerfully and operate in both directions at an advanced level. These results strongly support Cummins' interdependence hypothesis and provide evidence in favour of differentiated bilingual programmes in indigenous education aimed at enrichment bilingualism and enhanced academic achievement.

In their microplanning of language in education, the P'urhepecha schools in San Isidro and Uringuitiro combined two good reasons for using their own language as fundamental instruments of communication and content teaching. From a political and anthropological perspective, the fact that P'urhepecha 'conquered' the schools that have traditionally been an instrument of state domination in indigenous areas implied a significant step towards its appropriation by the indigenous community. It fostered the P'urhepecha language, culture and ethnic identity in a significant way. From a pedagogical and psycholinguistic perspective, these schools put into practice the old but frequently contested principle (see UNESCO, 1953) that everyone, particularly children from a subordinate ethnolinguistic minority, best acquire academically demanding skills such as reading and writing in their own language if an appropriate learning environment is provided. The better they develop these skills in their L1, the better they will learn content matter and achieve proficiency in reading and writing in the national language.

In several years of cooperation with the research team, the schools developed their own validated curriculum based on L1 literacy, content teaching of most subject matters in L1 and a specially designed syllabus for Spanish as L2 (Hamel & Francis, 2006). This enrichment curriculum now serves as a model for IBE in other communities and schools. The collaborative work shows very clearly that such a curriculum is feasible and more successful than traditional submersion or transitional education. It demonstrates, furthermore, the validity of the 'common underlying proficiency' hypothesis, as success in Spanish L2 literacy is best explained through the previous development of core proficiencies and academic discourse abilities in L1, which can then be more easily accessed from L2.

In conclusion, throughout history the field of indigenous education in Latin America has represented a site of struggle between divergent orientations and programmes – assimilation versus integration with linguistic and cultural maintenance, the role and integration of indigenous and national languages – and a gulf between general programmes and their implementation. One central question that will have to be pursued further is whether the proposed function of indigenous education as a basic tool for the development of cognitive and academic language proficiency and significant academic achievement in content matters, as exemplified in the case described above, will have a chance to flourish under globally adverse economic and sociocultural conditions. We also need to ask in a more generalised sense which modalities of curriculum might be appropriate and feasible in differentiated sociolinguistic and cultural contexts.

Immigrant and Elite Bilingual Education

From immigrant to global language schools

The question as to who counts as an immigrant, in the sense of someone who represents a foreign country or culture and is not fully integrated into the national culture, is not easy to answer in Latin America. Certainly first generation newcomers qualify as such. Although the New World rule of 'jus solis'[11] is applied without exception in legal terms, descendants of immigrants may still be considered immigrants, i.e. not fully mainstreamed citizens in cultural and linguistic terms, even if their rights as citizens are respected most of the time. Such a cultural construction of ethnic distinction even applies to descendants of Spaniards in Argentina or Mexico or to Portuguese in Brazil. The blond sixth generation offspring of German immigrants, who does not speak a word of his ancestors' language, may still be affectionately referred to as 'o alemão' (the German) among friends and neighbours in southern Brazil. As the recent process of rediscovering immigrant identity in the Southern Cone shows, those who claim their ancestry without at the same time casting the slightest doubt on their Brazilian or Paraguayan citizenship, may still be regarded as a potential security risk by some mainstream civil servants.[12] All these apparently anecdotal cases are tokens of a complex and sometimes divided ethnic and national identity that provides the historical background for the analysis of immigrant communities and their institutions.

For the purpose of this chapter, I will limit my discussion of immigrant education to those cases where immigrant groups speaking languages other than the countries' national languages organised themselves as distinct ethnolinguistic communities.[13] The history of European and, to a lesser extent, Asian immigration to Latin America is well documented and needs no detailed discussion here. Let me just recall a few highlights relevant to immigrant schools. The countries of the Southern Cone (Argentina, Chile, Paraguay and Uruguay) and Brazil absorbed about 90% of the European immigration to Latin America (Rosenberg, 2001). During the period of massive immigration (1875–1930), Spaniards and Italians represented the largest immigrant groups in most countries, followed by the British, Germans, Polish, Yugoslavians (mainly Croatians) and French. Throughout that time, about 1.5 million Italians migrated to Argentina and also 1.5 million to Brazil, more than 100,000 British (mainly Welsh and Irish) and about 120,000 Germans settled in Argentina, 250,000 Germans in Brazil and 200,000 in Chile.[14] Today, between 1.3 and 1.5 million Brazilians are of Japanese and 2 million of German descent.

Around 1900, in Buenos Aires alone, Italians made up 32% of the city's population, and the number of foreigners in the overall population of

Argentina reached 42.7% (Bein, 1999). In spite of their numerical clout, the linguistic assimilation of Italian immigrants advanced even quicker than in the USA during the same period (Fontanella de Weinberg, 1979), while in terms of numbers, they could well have formed a solid linguistic enclave preserving their language.[15] Rapid and pacific assimilation was fostered by Argentina's impressive socioeconomic development, which allowed immigrant peasants and workers to attain a much higher standard of living than they had enjoyed before in most European countries. Various Argentine analysts and educators (Arnoux & Bein, 1997; Axelrud, 1999; Bein & Varela, 1998) argue that the success behind the assimilationist policy of huge numbers of immigrants and the rapid construction of a national identity based on Argentine Spanish monolingualism was largely due to the integrative force of Argentina's developmental superiority and to the high academic level of public education characterised by a republican view of state responsibilities and models of European positivism.

Although immigrants from countries and regions of low socioeconomic status, such as Italians and Poles, maintained networks and founded social organisations within their communities, they rarely set up specific educational institutions of their own. In contrast, the British, French and German settlers adopted a different pattern of immigration. Rural immigrants from the UK, especially the Welsh and the Irish,[16] settled in distant and isolated rural areas specifically because they wanted to set up their colonies and their own educational and religious institutions, as they had suffered from oppression back in Britain. Urban middle-class English immigrants, in turn, established themselves as soldiers, businessmen or set up large-scale modern agricultural projects. Given their perceived superiority and their close links to the British government, they formed enclaves in big cities such as Buenos Aires, Santiago, Montevideo or Rio de Janeiro, very similar to the Germans and French.

German colonisation consisted initially of a professional middle class who migrated mainly to Brazil, Argentina and Chile in the mid-19th century. Later, rural colonisers created large estates in closed network communities and founded German villages in Brazil, Argentina and Chile. Finally, immigrants from working and professional middle class backgrounds arrived in the first half of the 20th century (Bernecker & Fischer, 1992; Rosenberg, 2001).

For 1990, estimates establish some 500,000 speakers and almost 2 million citizens of German descent for Brazil, 300,000 speakers and 1 million descendants for Argentina, and 20,000 speakers out of 200,000 descendants for Chile (Born & Dickgießer, 1989).[17] In all Latin American countries, the German-speaking settlers founded their own schools, churches, hospitals and other social institutions. Initially, they maintained strong links with their home governments, commerce, churches and cultural institutions. Southern Brazil hosted the largest German colonies in Latin America, which preserved their communities mostly segregated from the Brazilian society, maintaining their language, endogamic kinship, their institutions and traditions. World War II, however, meant a dramatic threat to the German, Italian and Japanese colonies, which suffered repression in most Latin American countries and experienced a rapid process of language loss and cultural dissolution. Today a vast majority of descendants under 60 are either national language monolinguals or limited speakers of the heritage language (Bärnert-Fürst, 1994; Ziebur, 2000).

In sum, a complex array of factors explain the divergent patterns of cultural behaviour and ethnolinguistic vitality exhibited by different immigrant groups: numbers and density of immigration; profession and socioeconomic as well as perceived social status in relation to the host society; rural versus urban settlement implying relative isolation versus integration; religion; the type of relationship with their fatherland; and the international status of the home countries and their languages. These multiple factors explain why, for example, sheer numbers of immigrants alone do not explain organisational patterns and the creation of educational and other institutions by each immigrant group.[18]

Ethnolinguistic vitality developed out of specific combinations of these factors. Immigrant communities that achieved successful cohesion typically shared a common cultural, linguistic and geographical background. They built up dense 'colonies' with multiple and close-knit internal network relations. Their members often belonged to a professional middle class, or they achieved rapid economic success which moved them to a social status equivalent to the upper middle or upper class of the host country. Segregation including endogamic marriages and distinct religious practices maintained over several generations played a key role in community building, either because the groups settled in isolated rural areas or because they practised deliberate segregation in the cities, a conduct often based on attitudes of superiority and racism towards the host society. Such customs were reinforced through the preservation of intensive relations of kinship, commerce and politics with their fatherland, especially in the case of immigrants from powerful countries who spoke prestige international languages. Mostly enclave colonies decided to create their own schools right from the beginning. Preserving their language and traditions were central motives to construct their own institutions. Not surprisingly, the British, French and German settlers created the most important and powerful immigrant schools in Latin America.

Most of these schools went through three historical phases (Banfi & Day, 2004). They were founded as community or heritage language schools in the 19th or early 20th century to provide the children of the settlers with appropriate education, especially in rural areas where very often no other schooling was available. Teaching was conducted entirely in the immigrant language in most cases, and no students from outside the community were admitted.[19] In contrast to heritage language experiences in developed countries studied in more recent times (see Cummins, 1995 for Canada and Hornberger, 2005 for the USA and Australia), the Latin American bilingual schools did not function as complementary or after-school institutions, but provided full and exclusive education for their students. In most cases they enjoyed high status because they represented the educational system of the most developed European countries at the time. As we have seen when discussing indigenous educational policy, after their independence from Spain at the beginning of the 19th century, the new bourgeoisies in the newly independent Hispano American republics turned away from 'decadent' Spain and focused their search for models of nation building, modernisation and education on France, Great Britain and Germany. Immigration from those countries was encouraged, and the immigrant communities and their institutions were considered ambassadors and models for the development of the host countries' own system of public education.[20]

This explains why the leading immigrant schools were seen as attractive by the local 'high society'. In their second phase, they gradually weakened their character of being enclave and ethnic community schools and joined the group of national elite schools, together with Catholic and other private institutions, opening their doors to the children of the countries' economic and power elites. Although many leading personalities in public life became alumni over time, those schools with formal support from their countries of origin never lost their ambiguous status of being both national *and* foreign. Therefore they often found themselves the target of nationalist attacks and sanctions.[21] Due to shrinking numbers of immigrants and ongoing language shift, in spite of efforts of maintenance, education in these schools gradually became bilingual, and a wide variety of dual language programmes were implemented.

The era of globalisation based on neoliberal economy which began in the 1980s has had a worldwide impact on education. In Latin America, the imposed drastic reduction of state expenditure and the welfare state severely affected public education. Military dictatorships in Argentina, Chile and Uruguay brutally damaged a long history of outstanding quality and a democratic, humanistic tradition in public education. In Mexico and elsewhere a similar process of educational impoverishment came about without military action. The decline of public education at the primary and secondary levels led to an increase in private education which has risen from 15% to over 25% in the last 20 years in Mexico.

In most Latin American countries, virtually no families from the middle and upper classes send their children to public primary and secondary schools any more. Thus, the traditional class character of private bilingual schools is now being reinforced by the increasing class division in Latin America; the growing gulf between rich and poor.

The imposed impoverishment of public education, no doubt a significant trademark of worldwide neoliberal globalisation under the influence of the World Bank and the International Monetary Fund, has increased the importance of these schools as part of the small group of elite institutes that offer modern, international technology and curriculum together with class segregation and the promise of moulding the future leaders of business and politics at national and international level. Only those former heritage schools that were able to modernise and keep pace with the dynamics of swift globalisation could compete with other top private schools for the offspring of the economic and political elite. High-quality education has become an expensive commodity, and private schools have to offer their services and develop marketing strategies like any other enterprise in this increasingly competitive and capitalised market.

Bilingual enrichment curriculum and teaching practices

In Latin America, curriculum and teaching practices have undergone significant transformations in response to changes in policy and school population resulting from the transformation from immigrant to global bilingual schools.

At the beginning, fragile schools were created by the urgent need of immigrants to educate their children, especially in rural areas. Those who had any subject knowledge or who had finished secondary school would help with teaching the best they could. The curriculum was what they remembered from their own schooling, or was taken from the schoolbooks that had survived the long journey from Europe. Better organised parties brought their teachers with them, and wealthy families could afford their own private 'institutrice'.[22] Later on, Spanish was introduced almost as a foreign language in the enclave communities to provide the necessary language skills in dealing with the external society. Content matter was usually taught entirely in the immigrant language.

This second phase of dual language education was marked by two convergent processes that triggered significant changes in curriculum and language policy. As the immigrant schools became attractive for the national elites and opened their doors to their offspring, they had to offer a curriculum that could satisfy the educational needs of their new customers. At the same time, general laws of public education promulgated during the last quarter of the 19th century established requirements not only for public, but also for private institutions that sought state recognition and certification.[23] Except for very conservative governments, there was little controversy about general educational orientations and basic content, as the educational credo of most Latin American liberal elites was based on the same European principles of modernisation, positivist instruction, and the role of science, technology and foreign languages. The question was rather that of a new power relationship which the increasingly nationalist governments wanted to establish to extend their control over the schools, to cultivate patriotism among their students and thus contribute to the assimilation of the immigrant communities.

A wide array of curricula, most of them hybrid in nature, came into being as an outcome of permanent negotiations and the attempt to conciliate sometimes divergent orientations.[24] Some schools taught the national syllabus as the core curriculum, and the foreign language area as an extracurricular programme. In most cases, a dual system of parallel curricula, staff and management developed. The schools had to hire teachers with quite different qualifications for each track (Banfi & Day, 2004). Very often, the requirements of each system increased the work and study load and unnecessarily doubled certain content matters such as Maths, Natural Sciences and Humanities, which were taught in both languages. Some schools maintained segregated tracks, separating the descendants of immigrants, as supposedly native speakers, from nationals who were learning the immigrant language as a foreign language.

The German Humboldt School in Mexico City may serve as an example. It is the largest German school in the system of *Auslandsschulen* (schools abroad) supported by the German government. The director is always a senior teacher and civil servant sent by the German government to constantly renew the relationship with the home country and to ensure that German guidelines and levels of achievements are observed. The vice-director is a civil servant from the Mexican Federal Ministry of Education, often with experience in the foreign language school sector.

Today, over 80% of the student population does not speak any German at entrance level, and their families cultivate no specific links with German culture or history. Students are divided into three sections: the mother tongue track caters for native speakers or bilinguals with a significant proficiency in German who use at least some German at home. From kindergarten to the 12th grade most content matters are taught in German, although the Mexican curriculum requirements are also met, which implies a heavier course load than in most other Mexican schools. Students use German schoolbooks and programmes, even for their English classes taught by German teachers, to the same level as their peers in German public schools. They may present the *Abitur*, the German leaving certificate that grants access to university studies in

Germany. At the same time they sit in for the Mexican equivalent as the implementation of the high school degree follows the guidelines of the Universidad Nacional Autónoma de México, Mexico's and Latin America's largest university.

The bilingual track caters for students who are dominant in Spanish but have some German background in their families, although German is not systematically spoken. They follow a similar programme to that of the mother tongue track but with lower requirements in German, and share courses in Spanish with the other tracks. Finally, the German as a foreign language track starts with partial immersion in kindergarten and primary school including reading and writing. Later on, most subjects are taught in Spanish, although content teaching in German continues for some subjects, as also happens in the bilingual track.

The transition from dual language schools still rooted in their immigrant community to modern elite schools with strong links to global educational development is still under way in Latin America. The impact of globalisation on education in the region as outlined above has had significant consequences on the reorganisation of bilingual schools, their student population and on curriculum and language policy decisions. Those schools that compete for the top social stratum of society have adjusted their curriculum to international requirements, including the introduction of IT and other modern technologies, both in organisation and as subject matters. They have improved their teaching methods and materials to meet top international standards, and are committed to surpassing official standards established for public schools in quality and quantity including additional competencies and activities.

Advanced additive bilingualism in highly valued languages, first and foremost in English, has gained significant weight in Latin America and elsewhere in the era of globalisation (de Mejía, 2002; Phillipson, 1992).[25] The Colombian 'National Programme of Bilingualism 2004–2019', a government initiative to transform Colombia into a massively bilingual country in Spanish and English within 15 years (Valencia, 2007; see de Mejía & Montes Rodríguez, this volume), represents a prospect launched to catch up with globalisation via the language highway of the world's most globalised language and the international society it represents. At the same time, it promises significant profit and empowerment for private corporations that teach the foreign language and train teachers for that purpose. Public institutions are often seen as incompetent to lead this process, even to teach or train teachers to the required advanced bilingual level.[26]

As the profile of the student population from the national or local economic and power elite with few links to an immigrant background is largely the same for the whole field of expensive private schools, the bilingual schools compete with the attraction of strong bilingual programmes right from the start, with exchange and study-abroad prospects in industrialised countries and with improved study and job opportunities for their graduates. As an extra value, international degrees like the renowned International Baccalaureate (IB), a French *baccalauréat* or a German *Abitur* add a cutting edge to the value of these institutions.

Banfi and Day (2004) call these schools 'global language schools'. The concept is certainly applicable to the institutions that teach English. The rise of English as the world's only fully global language (Crystal, 1997; Hamel, 2006a), the hyper central language in De Swaan's (2001) and Calvet's (1999) gravitational model of the world language system, has induced a process of decline for super central languages, such as French, Spanish, German or Italian, that once competed with English on the global scene. As a result, a process of differentiation between bilingual schools emerged. Prestigious institutions, such as the French, German, Italian or Japanese schools, are experiencing a crisis of identity and orientation. Their traditional trademark, a prestige language and culture they represent and teach, has suffered from this decline and does not help them as much as in the past to compete on the market under new conditions. The 80% of parents with no link to German culture who send their children to the 'Humboldt Schule' in Mexico do so because they expect German discipline and excellence in education, and because the school is considered to be one of the best and most expensive in the country. For many, the fact that their children will have to learn German is taken as a necessary price to pay, rather than an asset. Therefore, the other bilingual schools have to offer English as a strong third language and promise that their students will attain a high level of English language proficiency. Accordingly, some advertise themselves as trilingual schools in an attempt to take a lead over schools that are 'only' bilingual.[27]

In elite bilingual schools, students are expected to achieve high levels of academic proficiency in content matter and bi- or multiliteracy; they acquire competence in both cultures, and advanced IT related skills. Even more important, they have to develop the appropriate values and leadership competences that will qualify them to occupy executive positions in the economy and politics that either their parents already hold or that they hope their offspring will aspire to. To achieve these goals and to justify costly fees, these schools have to mark a clear social and educational distance with the available public school system and with cheaper private schools. This includes the pressure to attain significantly higher levels of achievement in all existing instruments of comparison and evaluation.[28]

In general, elite bilingual schools accomplish their mission to achieve high academic levels and to give their graduates excellent perspectives for further education and professional success. A series of problems remain, however, that need to be taken into consideration in the light of a discussion of appropriate language and educational policies.[29]

Elite bilingual schools share a model of enrichment plurilingualism as a societal perspective and additive bi- or multilingualism as an individual goal.[30] None of the languages involved is under threat or clearly stigmatised as inadequate for advanced content teaching or communication. Students usually come from literate backgrounds where bi- and multilingualism is appreciated and, most importantly, children are systematically encouraged, rewarded and recognised for the bilingualism they develop in the world's 'good' languages. The schools' history is part of each country's history of immigration and nation building. Initially, these institutions fulfilled the dual role of providing education where the state was not in a position to supply it, and of organising the immigrant communities as a central institution of immigrant identity building and the preservation of languages and culture.

In the process of gradual integration of their communities into the host country's society, they opened their doors to non-immigrant students belonging to the middle and upper classes and thus became a significant force for national development, in some cases providing models for the design of the public school system. At the same time, their development led to conflict and constant negotiation with national educational authorities. Both aspects: diverse educational cultures and programmes as well as integration and reciprocal transfer, have shaped their identities and roles. The fact that bilingualism has been established as a visible and positive trademark in a domain of social prestige has helped to add an enrichment perspective and to soften the Latin American policy of building homogeneous and monolingual nation states.

Two Systems of Bilingual Education: Differences and Similarities

Bilingual education at societal poles: Inequality and educational success in Latin America

At first sight, the two types of bilingual schooling seem to have little in common. Luxurious buildings identify private elite schools that attract the rich and the powerful. Skewed adobe hutches or plain cement block buildings in the middle of an isolated Indian village embody the other type of bilingual schools. These institutions represent two extremes in Latin America, one of the world's most unequal regions. According to the Gini coefficient, hardly any country in Africa or Asia exhibits such an abysmal distance between the rich and the poor as do Brazil or Mexico, who are among the world's champions of inequality (CIA World Factbook, 2006; United Nations, 2006) (see Tables 3.3 and 3.4).[31]

Table 3.3 Proportions of inequality

Country	*10% poorest (share of country's GNP)*	*10% richest (share of country's GNP)*
Brazil	0.7%	64.1%
Mexico	1.2%	57.6%

Table 3.4 Monthly income and school fees in Mexico's elite bilingual schools (in US$ 2006)

Professions & fees	*US$*
Director of National Health Care Institution	20,000
Lowest salary in the same institution	101
Minimum wage in Mexico	101
Associate Professor B, public university	850
American School in Mexico City, monthly fee at Senior High School	1,055
German School in Mexico City, monthly fee at Senior High School	740

The figures chosen represent this extreme inequality. Students who attend the leading and most expensive bilingual schools in Mexico, Brazil, Colombia or Bolivia belong to the top 10% of the population where more than half of the countries' wealth is concentrated.[32] Indigenous school children, obviously, fall within the lowest income group in countries where 40–60% of the population lives below the extreme poverty mark.

The significance of the correlations between social class and academic achievement has been revealed in many studies over the past 50 years and needs no further discussion.[33] The policy debate in the neoliberal era of globalisation focuses on how to improve educational achievement among the lower and lowest classes of society without changing the economic model or increasing their income first and improving other components in the quality of their lives. This debate encompasses all countries, from the USA[34] to the Third World.

The World Bank, which has largely displaced UNESCO in education policy debates and has been imposing guidelines for education for the Third World over the past 20 years, has emphasised the need to improve the quality of public education as a means of overcoming underdevelopment. At the same time it forced poor countries to reduce state expenditure and to open up state controlled sectors including education for privatisation. The progress of education, as the new discourse goes, will help countries to leave poverty behind and enter the knowledge society of the future. Enhancement in education is sought and promised if the countries follow the rules of the World Bank, alongside growing impoverishment, the reduction of stable and well paid jobs and the deindustrialisation of Third World countries.[35] The history of European industrialisation reveals, however, that the extension and improvement of public education came about as an *outcome* of industrial development and the creation of more and more sophisticated and demanding jobs in the factories and not vice versa. Once economic development required differentiated higher skills and technological, abstract thinking, the educational system not only learned how to provide these competencies successfully, but also how to make sense of them for the actors involved.

Similarly, autonomous indigenous education rooted in the cultural models and modes of production of a non-capitalist society will succeed in providing quality instruction and making sense of its ways of producing knowledge, in as much as it succeeds in mobilising and activating the cultural capital and funds of knowledge of its society while, at the same time, managing to find a way of appropriating the knowledge of the dominant society. That is what *inter*cultural education is all about, as we shall see later.

The general debate on education in Latin America, and more specifically the discussion about indigenous bilingual education, reflects the problems of an educational model that is created from outside which runs counter to economic development. Ecuador has lost 50,000 of its 150,000 primary school teachers via emigration since the 1990s due to its disastrous economic development. In Mexico in recent years, the neoliberal government has supported IBE and distributed teaching materials, and infrastructure including Encyclomedia, a new computer- and Internet-supported technology for primary education, on the one hand. At the same time, the government has demolished the basis of survival of the indigenous peoples by destroying subsistence agriculture through the import of corn and beans at highly subsidised prices from the USA based on the NAFTA agreement. It eroded the ecology of the indigenous habitat via the ruthless development of agrobusinesses and monocultural plantations. In recent decades, several million poor peasants, many of them Indians, were forced to leave their villages and work as migrants in the northern plantations. Between 2000 and 2006, 3.4 million poor Mexicans crossed the border to seek work and survival in the USA, more than at any time before in Mexican history. Thousands of indigenous villages resemble ghost towns today. In the P'urhepecha communities I have been working with, schools lose up to 80% of their students for several months of the year.

Acute inequality imposes severe restrictions on education as an instrument of national integration, able to create opportunities for social mobility and reduce existing achievement gaps within common objectives of quality, knowledge and competencies. Thus, indigenous educational systems are typically found at the lowest levels on national evaluations testing general standards in most Latin American countries. Extreme poverty, malnutrition, and deficient teacher formation and payment all limit the possibilities of harnessing the enormous intellectual, cultural and linguistic potential of indigenous school children and their communities. Nevertheless, in spite of overall adverse conditions, exciting learning dynamics occur once we leave the level of macro-evaluations and focus on the micro level of the classroom and individual learning processes.

From a sociological perspective of educational policy, elite bilingual schools, as part of a system of socioeconomic stratification and power relations, have, by and large, contributed to the increase in class divergence and to the deepening of the socially grounded achievement gap between private and public education. This may not be the fault of the institutions and their staff. On the whole, however, these schools and the fee-paying communities that sustain them participate in the reproduction of an ideology of elitism that is not based on merit but on socioeconomic segregation and, very often, on a sense of superiority of the developed countries they represent and from which the schools draw in part their prestige. However, their privileged position does not exempt them from structural and pedagogical problems, some of which are similar to those found in indigenous education.

The integration of psycholinguistic and sociolinguistic factors

In terms of bilingual education typology and language acquisition related to academic learning, IBE and EBE share interesting points in common relating to academic achievement, language use and ethnolinguistic identity. The question arises as to how psycholinguistic, sociolinguistic and pedagogical factors interact with each other and with their socioeconomic contexts.

Since Chomsky's (1959) paradigmatic critique of Skinner's behaviourism and the nature of language acquisition processes, an important strand of thinking and research assumes that all children are born with a similar language acquisition device that allows them to acquire two or more languages simultaneously or consecutively, to develop cognitively demanding academic skills and to transfer or enhance access to these competencies from any of their languages. If, controlling for differences in aptitude, striking differences appear in achievement, these dissimilarities will have to be interpreted in terms of contextual differences where socioeconomic and ethnolinguistic factors play a significant role. Thus, the fundamental psycholinguistic postulates about the equal, innate equipment of children for the acquisition of various languages and the development of academic proficiency poses a severe critique of the socioeconomic conditions that give rise to such a dramatic achievement gap among the student populations in industrialised and developing countries alike.

The specific functions and weight of different factors that determine educational success and the role of schooling for the development of ethnolinguistic identity are central to a critical, comparative analysis of elite and indigenous bilingual education and the exploration of potential bridges. In both cases the interdependence between the languages involved turns out to be crucial for academic achievement and the development of enrichment bilingualism. I will here narrow the discussion to the relationship between psycholinguistic and sociolinguistic factors, embedded in the more general pedagogical and socioeconomic context of the two types of bilingual education.

As we have seen, many of the private bilingual schools basically combine two types of approaches. The bilingual immigrant students are exposed to a strong component of L1 literacy development and content teaching, whereas the monolingual national language group is often schooled in immersion programmes in the foreign language at entrance level. These syllabuses integrate the advantages of L1 development in one case and immersion in the immigrant/foreign language in the other, as a means of developing highly proficient bilingualism within an enrichment perspective. Once an advanced threshold level of proficiency in both languages is achieved, the two cohorts can be integrated in a number of content areas that may be taught in either language.

In contrast, *submersion* or fast *transitional* programmes in indigenous education show extremely poor results, comparable to the low achievement of Hispanic immigrant students of low socioeconomic status in the US who are schooled in similar programmes. Achievement and proficiency rates in literacy and other academic skills fall significantly behind compared to L1-based enrichment programmes and the general school system in most national evaluations.

If we compare then *immersion* and *submersion* education, at first sight, the programmes look similar in terms of curriculum structure, as in both cases monolingual or incipient bilingual children are taught entirely or predominantly in the 'other' language.[36] How, then, can the strikingly divergent results in academic achievement and in the development of proficient bilingualism be explained? Certainly, a narrow psycholinguistic explanation will not suffice. In the case of immersion, students typically belong to the upper middle class with a rich educational family background. They voluntarily enter course programmes that enjoy strong parental and school support. More important, they are immersed in a prestige language, and their mother tongue is another prestigious language that is never in danger – nor is their identity – throughout their studies.

Conversely, students in submersion and fast transitional programmes typically belong to a stigmatised ethnolinguistic minority of low socioeconomic status. The two languages involved usually maintain an asymmetric relationship of diglossia and of language conflict. Their mother tongue is considered of low prestige and little functional value, an obstacle for the acquisition of the national language and for academic achievement. Thus, submersion programmes constitute an attack on students' identity. These psycho- and sociolinguistic factors explain to a large extent the striking differences in school success and the development of language skills in the two contexts. The divergent values attached to the languages involved reflect sociocultural and economic differences between dominant majority and subordinate minority groups which are then internalised by the students and the education community at large.

This general framework is well supported by research and general educational evidence (see Skutnabb-Kangas, 2000 for references). It may offer an explanatory basis to account for educational success and failure, but only on a very general level. Much inquiry is still needed to explain in detail exactly how psycholinguistic, sociolinguistic, curriculum design, socioeconomic factors and power relations interact in each case. The political and pedagogical challenge will be to significantly improve indigenous education and transform it into a system that empowers indigenous communities and peoples, that fosters their ethnic identity, that upgrades and strengthens their languages to improve their curriculum and teaching as a basis for enhanced academic achievement.

Integration and conflicting orientations in bilingual education

Both systems of bilingual education exhibit problems of integration on various levels: (1) the internal integration of curriculum and school communities; (2) the external integration or indeed segregation from the sociocultural context of their host countries; and (3) the integration into a global community of education and other international networks. Let me examine these ideas in more detail.

Elite bilingual schools

The internal integration of curriculum and school communities. One of the most significant challenges that affect most of these schools is how to integrate curriculum, teaching methods, the academic development of their students and their educational community. From the beginning, students have to struggle with the implementation of two national curricula that may conflict on various levels. Frequently bureaucratic regulations and their inflexible implementation lead to unnecessary replication of content matter that run counter to any pedagogically based teaching strategy of integration and transfer of competencies and knowledge. Often two separate curricula and their teaching staff exist side by side with little communication and acquaintance with the other language and curriculum. Furthermore, staff are not always fluently bilingual, and teachers tend to adopt role models and align with one or other of the language groups that compete with each other and jealously defend their territories. Differentiated salaries for local and 'imported' staff may also be a source of resentment and conflict.

In my own experience working with elite bilingual schools, I realised that, paradoxically, very little is known about bilingualism and the way bilingual children acquire and use their languages as part of an integrated communicative repertoire.[37] Dichotomising folk theories about separate language domains and the 'terrible danger' of interference and mixing abound, and little is known about modern theories of bilingual education, such as the common underlying proficiency hypothesis, the transfer of cognitively demanding academic skills from one language to the other, or the development of languages through content teaching. Therefore, coordination between teachers of the two language groups in important matters of content and learning strategies often remains weak and subject to divergent cultural orientations. This seems particularly worrying because the integrated development of fundamental cognitive academic skills and the coordination of the languages involved turns out to be a central concern for any successful bilingual syllabus.

Conversely, a bilingual programme that raises barriers between languages, which fails to organise its syllabus in an integrative way and to build multiple transfer routes of knowledge and competencies between them, is destined to failure in the long run, no matter what other advantages it may offer on a daily basis. Integrated multilingual repertoires of communication and academic development, rather than separate language domains, should be the object and the target of any bilingual programme. Common practices evolving out of the orientations described above cast doubt on the depth of conviction about additive bilingualism and enrichment biculturalism in these educational communities. A significant number of schools are aware of these problems and are in the process of working on them with their staff, students and parents. Further research, which is surprisingly rare in the field of EBE compared to other bilingual systems, will have to clarify these questions that seem central for successful future developments.

External or national integration. As we have seen, the integration of EB schools has caused problems as they were founded as segregated immigrant institutions. Today some of these problems, which are related to divergent, sometimes conflicting orientations, are clearly evident. Many students from immigrant and non-immigrant backgrounds feel alienated after they leave because the French, English or German schools taught them more about the history or present politics of the European countries than about their own. Such teaching is certainly not limited to factual knowledge; more importantly, it conveys a value system that may conflict with that of the host country, especially when marked socio-economic differences are shaped into stereotypes that, in turn, reinforce ideologies of superiority.

In addition, many EB schools maintain little communication with the public school sector and rarely share their professional resources and know-how with less privileged institutions, the ministries of education and the universities, although there are notable exceptions. Over the years, many Latin American universities have developed a significant body of knowledge in applied linguistics. However, although academics in these countries participate in international networks, these are seldom connected with the private bilingual school sector.

Integration into a global community of education. Conversely, in-service teacher training is often provided by specialised institutions from the countries of reference, such as the ministries of education or overseas affairs, and cultural institutions like the British Council, the Alliance Française, the Goethe Institut or the ZfA.[38] These organisations are eager to transmit their particular and culturally biased strand of teaching methods and cultural values; yet at the same time, they often show little knowledge and interest in the broader cultural context and pedagogical traditions of the Latin American countries these schools work in. Their experts operate worldwide and covertly strive to reproduce not only close professional links but also dependency on the metropolitan countries they represent.[39] Moreover, their courses are often limited to the foreign language teachers and exclude the local staff who teach the national curriculum in Spanish or Portuguese.

The present-day dynamics of globalisation have caught many national EB schools in a process of transition that gives rise to a number of contradictions. On the one hand, traditional networks between specific schools and their European countries of reference are strictly segregated and compete with each other. They seem to be reminiscent of the traditional relationships of dependency between the old European empires and their overseas colonies and counterparts. Although today the old empires are integrated into the European Union, they still operate as individual nation states in their international relations. Therefore, contemporary practices cannot easily be labelled as a process of integration into global society; they may indeed increasingly conflict with globalisation itself.

On the other hand, global integration emerges as a decisive force in an era of national disintegration and international incorporation into what Hardt and Negri (2000) have called the 'Empire', the new invisible world government formed by international corporations that rule the world without democratic legitimacy and dissolve nation states and their governments. At the same time, a growing number of autonomous and regional organisations and movements have entered the global scene. These call for an alternative model of globalisation to that imposed by international corporations. In fact, EBE in Latin America, together with private universities, increasingly incorporates their members into the emerging global arena, which creates new, deterritorialised 'third cultures' and international networks that encompass international management customs, the international community of science and technology, fashion, music and other fields of culture with their own discourses and language use, as well as their own counter movements (Calhoun, 1992; García Canclini, 1999; Hamel, 2006a).[40]

For those who distinguish between globalisation and US-Americanisation and sustain that the position of English as the only global language may decline in the future – Graddol (2006) from the English Company upholds that never again will the dominance of English be the same as during the 20th century – a new perspective of international plurilingualism comes into sight that calls for further elaboration. New assessments of future language needs and opportunities assign a high value not only to any kind of bilingual skills as such, but especially to those that include less widely spoken languages. English monolinguals will soon find themselves at a disadvantage, while English and Spanish bilinguals, though potentially extremely important as they can communicate with a quarter of the world's population as first or foreign language speakers, will find fewer opportunities than trilinguals in English, Spanish and Vietnamese. And, surprisingly, the role of some lesser used languages, even those with no official status, such as most ILs, will probably rise when combined with international languages. The genetic knowledge potential of ILs, i.e. the biological and other non-mainstream knowledge enshrined in them, may well lead to a significant rise in their value in a future society of knowledge, according to Skutnabb-Kangas (2003).[41]

In sum, integration in its multiple dimensions – integration of parallel curricula, integration of the languages taught and used for content teaching, integration of a school population with diverse cultural and linguistic background, integration into the educational system of the host countries and into the global society – emerges as a formidable challenge for EBE whose schools range among the best and most highly prestigious in Latin America.

The perspectives outlined above, uncertain and speculative as they may sound at present, suggest that EB schools will be well advised to attend to problems of integration in several domains. Although at first sight national and international integration may appear as mutually exclusive targets, a pluralistic orientation of cultural and linguistic enrichment and intercultural learning could point to ways in which both objectives reinforce each other. In terms of language choice, they could open up a truly global arena where English plays a significant role but where plurilingualism is the main goal. Several languages could be included in their programmes in flexible combinations. Most important is the development of basic cognitive and academic skills that have been identified as predictors for both successful multiple language learning and other highly valued academic skills. Non-integrated curricula and ideological barriers between languages, their syllabuses and staff are certainly not the best basis for such developments.

Indigenous education

Problems and challenges of integration emerge for indigenous education and language planning in Latin America too, though in different ways. Nevertheless, these can also be traced to similar levels of internal, external and international integration.

Internal integration. A truly intercultural curriculum requires that content matters and competencies from indigenous funds of knowledge and world views, as well as from national programmes, be integrated in a culturally and pedagogically appropriate fashion. In order to counteract historical imbalance and relations of dominations that subordinated and fragmented indigenous cultures, many syllabuses have given priority to the indigenous content at the beginning of the programme. First, children should know and appropriate their own culture in order to build a solid base of competencies and values. Starting from this fund of knowledge, the idea is that they will learn about national and global societies and cultures later on, in order to integrate knowledge and competencies from several sources without diluting them.

In similar fashion, where the IL is the children's stronger or exclusive language, it is seen as important that education including literacy acquisition should develop predominantly in the IL, with the national language taught as L2. In many areas, including urban settlements, advanced IL shift moved the national language into the role of the stronger language of primary socialisation. There, education should develop predominantly in that language with the IL as L2. IL immersion could also provide a successful strategy where sociolinguistic conditions and attitudes permit such an approach.

The IBE approach, which exists more as a model than as an established practice today, is facing a series of difficulties that cannot be discussed here at length. Indigenous funds of knowledge need to be identified, recovered and reconstructed from oblivion and fragmentation, and systematised to serve as input for the indigenous part of the curriculum. The appropriate integration of such an intercultural curriculum that avoids imbalance, unsuitable misrepresentation of indigenous knowledge funds via 'Western' systematisation, and dichotomised juxtaposition presents a significant challenge for curriculum design. As we have seen, the role and the functional integration of the two languages and strategies for their teaching as L1 and L2 or two first languages posit similar yet unsolved problems. Last but not least, such programmes will probably only work where indigenous students, teachers and communities are empowered and gain a significant degree of autonomy over their government and education.

External or national integration. Here again, the appropriate degree of integration and distinctiveness of the indigenous educational systems poses problems that need to be taken into account. Experiences range from imposed national programmes that care little or nothing for diversity, to programmes that practice *de facto* segregation. Indigenous education as a subsystem of elementary education needs to develop strategies that will lead to both a sheltered territory and the necessary transfer of knowledge in a process aimed at an appropriate integration without assimilation.

Integration into a global community of education. Although at first sight indigenous education in isolated villages seems to have little relation with global issues, a closer look reveals that today indigenous communities and their members participate actively in the process of globalisation in various ways. First, international migration has become the hope of survival of millions of Indians throughout Latin America. Many migrants 'discover' and reinforce their ethnic identity and language use in the USA or Europe, where they build up lively local as well as transnational communities (Besserer & Kearney, 2006) and develop their cultural (Rosaldo, 1994) or ethnic citizenship (de la Peña, 1999, 2002) without a traditional territorial base, although the existence of their home communities as points of reference plays a significant role. As their migration differs sharply from historical one-way immigration, they frequently return to their home villages and maintain close network links with their communities, including significant financial support for their kin and villages.[42] Their homecoming introduces many facets of globalisation into their towns: new consumer goods and habits of consumption, US and pocho – Mexican transnational – culture, music, Spanglish, English, computers and the Internet.

All such dynamics constitute in themselves powerful processes of education, learning and reorientation for adults and children. The systems of formal education both in Latin America and in the target countries of migration (USA, Canada, European Union) have shown considerable difficulties and resistance to new circumstances and needs of migrants, even more so to indigenous migration that has so far remained largely invisible. The Mexican government has set up special programmes for indigenous migrant children in the north of the country where many work in modern plantations, in the main cities, and programmes back home in the communities for returning children. In addition, although cooperation exists with education departments in a number of US states to cater for migrants, indigenous school children find little specific attention paid to their needs.

The main challenge involves the transformation of existing curricula to include competencies and content that might be helpful for survival and empowerment in migration. Increasingly, indigenous communities in Mexico demand bilingual education, but including English, as they know that their destiny will take them northwards. Such claims have so far been considered disruptive and counterproductive for the implementation of traditional IBE programmes by educational authorities. However, traditional curricular and educational ideologies do not hold anymore. The migrants themselves, who creatively integrate their own languages, Spanish and English, into a powerful communicative repertoire, show the pathways for innovation.

A second strand of powerful globalisation stems from a process of increasing homogenisation, rather than integration, of IBE in Latin America. The World Bank, the Inter-American Development Bank, UNESCO and the influential aid agencies from industrialised countries (USAID, GTZ, DANIDA, etc.) have cooperated with local governments to develop models for indigenous education. In most countries, except Mexico and Brazil, First World cooperation agencies, their money and their experts have played a decisive role.[43] Significant pilot projects and educational reform programmes have been negotiated between governments, foreign aid agencies and their experts, and the growing indigenous movements in some countries. In particular, collaboration has developed across state borders, especially in the Andean region that shares the macroethnic groupings of Quechuas and Aimaras.[44] However, this integration has mainly operated from the top down. Based on a common agenda established by powerful donors, a handful of international experts intervened as consultants in educational reforms. Therefore, paradoxically, most reform programmes that should reflect the acclaimed diversity of indigenous cultures and peoples look very much alike and reflect variants of the same basic model that uses, except in Colombia, the common label of 'intercultural bilingual education'. In addition, international cooperation, a euphemism for Third World aid for development that has been present in Latin America for some 50 years, has on the whole rather deepened dependency than helped to overcome it and foster independence and sustainability, as has always been its declared goal.

In sum, the IBE system also exhibits problems and needs of internal integration and modernisation, as well as international integration, that bear certain similarities to those of EBE, but it also differs from the latter in significant ways.

Towards an Integrative Perspective of Language and Education Policy

Differences and similarities between IBE and EBE have been a substantive part of my personal and professional life. An immigrant family history that started in Chile and spans over a century today has placed me in the privileged position of experiencing the acquisition of native bilingualism in German and Spanish from birth and the learning of several other languages as an immensely enriching process. It includes the transmission of native bilingual proficiency in the same languages to my fourth-generation immigrant Mexican children that have all been actively involved in bilingual maintenance education. For almost 30 years now, I have also been able to develop a deeply inspiring professional experience working with indigenous communities, in Mexico and elsewhere, with their cultures, languages and educational endeavours.

While I observed with satisfaction my children's multilingual growth that included periods of immersion in Portuguese and the almost effortless acquisition of English as a third language, when living with them in the USA at a young age, I experienced, studied and supported the intensive struggles of indigenous children of the same age who acquired their bilingual skills in a context of stigmatisation, inappropriate schooling and economic hardship, but also support from their parents. Every step that seemed so easy for my children usually involved enormous efforts and drawbacks for their indigenous peers. Although the abysmal socioeconomic differences and their educational effects sometimes caused frustration, they also constituted a challenge for me to help the indigenous children to gain access to positive and encouraging experiences with bilingualism the same way as my own children did. It also meant engaging in political and professional action to support the indigenous communities' endeavour to maintain and invigorate their cultures and languages, and to obtain the most appropriate form of bilingual education for their children.

No doubt the parallel experience of bilingual development helped me to improve my own understanding of bilingualism and to transfer insights from one context to the other. It is within this autobiographical context that I now undertake the challenge of considering possible bridges between the two systems that are so far apart, in order to contribute to the development of an integrative perspective on bilingual education and language policy in Latin America.

Mutual learning and cooperation

To find bridges over troubled water will not be easy, both in conceptual and policy-driven terms and, even more so, in terms of concrete cooperation. When I stated at the beginning of this chapter that the two bilingual systems are located at the extreme poles of society whose actors hardly ever cross paths or exchange words, this was not meant to be a metaphor but a description of real practice. Little cooperation exists between these areas inside and outside institutions. Although from a comparative academic perspective many common topics come to mind, concrete implementation will probably depend on local initiatives that manage to overcome existing barriers. Additionally, contrastive analysis is only able to lay the ground for a more theoretical and conceptual integration of perspectives in language and education policies for bilingual education.

Complementary knowledge and experience

In the previous section I outlined a number of structural problems in each system. Although many of them will have to be attended to separately, others could serve as a basis for possible cooperation. A starting point might be to explore the different funds of knowledge, capacities and experiences in each field that could be mobilised as complementary knowledge to converge creatively in the development of proposals for change and better practice.

In many Latin American countries, indigenous education was for a long time strongly influenced and even administrated by anthropologists, as it was anthropological insight that developed an understanding of how indigenous societies existed and survived as distinct but subordinate ethnolinguistic social aggregates in the context of nation states. Anthropological theory developed frameworks to interpret the dynamics of these contacts as either assimilation and acculturation, or independent endoculturation and integration without the loss of a distinct identity. Sociolinguistics provided complementary knowledge about the relations between languages and their speakers, postulating concepts such as diglossia, language conflict, shift and maintenance.

Together they shaped our understanding about the central role of language and other cultural components in the construction of ethnic identity. The conditions of communication, or its impossibility, across cultures constituted the argument to create a distinct system of education, either pursuing the states' goal of transition and assimilation, or, on the contrary, the maintenance of cultures and languages within the system. The new intercultural bilingual approach focuses on the idea that indigenous worldviews and funds of knowledge including the IL should be placed at the centre of indigenous education and should constitute a stimulus for educational development. Such a course of action would empower indigenous societies to gain control over an educational system, which in the past has been an instrument of domination. It should at the same time create a better platform than immersion or fast transitional programmes to gain access to the national language and content areas belonging to the national curriculum.

As we can see, anthropological thought and, to a lesser extent, sociolinguistics were present in the planning and the implementation of indigenous education. Conversely, the system has always been weak in terms of psycholinguistic and pedagogical input to create appropriate teaching methods that would help to enhance the indigenous students' learning under given sociolinguistic, psychosocial and cultural conditions.

On the other side, EBE has not been a topic of significant research until recently (see de Mejía, 2002). Even less did it attract the attention of academic disciplines as bilingual education has done both in industrialised countries and the Third World. On the other hand, EBE enjoys significant international capital in the fields of applied linguistics and foreign/second language teaching, L1 development in a context of diasporas, language through content teaching and the use of modern teaching technologies. There seems to be an acute lack, however, of anthropological and sociolinguistic insight to apply to the understanding of intercultural relations and possible conflict between languages, both inside the schools themselves and in relation to their integration into local and national host societies. Banfi and Day (2004) also mention a lack of self-evaluation.

Areas of cooperation and mutual learning

Both systems share a number of central tasks and problems, despite other differences. The basic question of how children develop competence in two or more languages for everyday communication and academic learning needs further attention in relation to curriculum design and teaching methodology. Both systems have to improve a curriculum that develops content matter from two different sources, assigns functions and spaces to each language and achieves high academic proficiency in the languages and content matter. Furthermore, the curriculum should be integrated so as to foster optimal transfer between languages and content areas in the development of competencies and skills. Last but not least, the curriculum should comply with sometimes divergent regulations and will have to be politically and culturally acceptable for students, staff, the communities at large and government authorities.

Let me single out just two common problems. The pursuit of the objectives enumerated above requires, among other things, appropriate teacher training for bilingual education. Certification for teaching-specific subjects including mother tongue and foreign or second languages will not suffice, nor will certification as primary school teachers. Both systems struggle with the development of high proficiency in L2, especially when there is little external support for that language. German or French schools encounter difficulties in their students achieving high levels of proficiency in these foreign languages even when they start at an early age with intensive language programmes. Similarly, indigenous schools in densely monolingual IL areas experience difficulties in teaching Spanish as L2. In both cases, teaching methodologies and student motivation need to be revised.

Over the past 20 years, indigenous education in Latin America has attempted to compensate for its deficit in pedagogy, psycho- and applied linguistics by drawing on bilingual education experiences in the USA, Canada and certain European countries,[45] as well as within Latin America itself, as I mentioned earlier. Although EBE is certainly farther away to serve as a model, there are aspects of EBE experiences that could well contribute to indigenous education. One of the most important refers to the invaluable experience of creating contexts of learning where children develop self-reliance in their own languages and cultures, where they can be confident in their capability of learning and where the whole environment stimulates enrichment education. Successful experiences, their examples and their narratives play a significant role in any educational context.

In addition, and in a more technical sense, indigenous IB schools could greatly profit from L1 development and L2 teaching methodology based on a communicative approach. Content teaching, i.e. the development of linguistic and communicative proficiency in a second language through the teaching of significant content matters, both at beginner and at advanced level, constitutes another area where EBE tends to be successful, whereas in most cases, indigenous schools are just beginning to develop such an approach. Transfer of cognitively demanding academic skills or higher-order discourses from one language to the other might be improved in both areas of bilingual education through exchange and mutual learning. In-service teacher training which includes immediate collaborative application of new techniques is another potential area of fruitful exchange. Academic bodies could help by identifying other important areas of comparative, collaborative research.

For elite bilingual schools it would certainly be an enriching experience to introduce an anthropological perspective into their work, both on the micro level of their internal integration of languages, cultures and learning communities, and on the macro level of societal integration. In the USA, Canada, Asia and Europe there have been a wealth of studies carried out recently on intercultural education, cultural diversity in schools and on related topics. De Mejía (2002: 67) explains why ethnocentrism and taboos about discussing culture have obstructed the development of an (inter)cultural perspective in foreign language teaching in the past, although there is an increasing awareness of its relevance for the development of communicative and cultural competence (Alred *et al.*, 2003). Certainly, the avoidance of potentially conflictive topics may play a role in EBE too. These schools, however, exist right in the contact zone where different cultures and languages interact and create new hybrid worlds of their own. To review their often dichotomised curriculum and their teaching practices from an intercultural learning perspective could help them to reach a higher level of integration. Given the drive towards intercultural national curricula for mainstream education in many Latin American countries, EBE could take a leading role in that process based on their own experience of enrichment education.

Furthermore, cultural diversity in other fields, such as indigenous education, could become an interesting topic for discussion in EBE, which might help these schools review their own situation in the light of an apparently distant example.[46] Such teaching units could create general language and intercultural awareness, including cases of diglossia and language conflict, and the way subtractive language teaching stigmatises subordinate languages and creates or reinforces ideologies of superiority.

Language and Education Policies in Latin America: From Monolingualism and Multilingualism to Plurilingualism

To interpret the language and education policy behind the two types of bilingual education from an integrated perspective is not an easy task. It requires a broad conceptual framework that goes beyond traditional models of language policy and language planning. Within such a framework, language policies should be understood as historical processes of language change (i.e. the change of whole systems of communication) where state institutions and other social forces intervene. Such a process not only implies a transformation of discursive and linguistic structures and uses (e.g. standardisation, diffusion, shift, revitalisation, etc.), but also and fundamentally a change in the relationship that the actors involved establish with their own language(s) and others in the field as part of overall power relations (see Hamel, 1993, for a discussion of this approach in language policy theory).

The previous analysis of bilingual education has revealed the existence of multiple links between language and education policies connecting all language types involved: the national language(s) of each state, as well as indigenous, immigrant and foreign languages. In addition, choices on the macro level of state decision and the micro level of institution, classroom interaction, and individual orientations and skills are related. The analysis of decisions and activities should not be limited to overt governmental intervention, as other social forces and sometimes hidden actors also play a significant role. Experienced language planners (e.g. Baldauf & Kaplan, 2003) maintain that language policy decisions are generally taken by politicians, to the exclusion of language specialists and their expertise. Furthermore, the case of Latin America clearly shows how bilingual programmes and their institutions are largely determined by policy decisions that go far beyond language and education policy as such, and represent the intervention of sometimes conflicting social forces and actors from inside and outside each country.

When we analyse the language policies concerning the two types of bilingual education and their communities in Latin America, we realise that the common factor which allows for an integrated interpretation is their relationship with the state and the dominant society as they developed over time. Within such a historical perspective, we can identify three broad ideological orientations[47] in language and cultural policy that correspond to historical phases, but survive at the same time as competing positions today (see Figure 3.2).

Colonialism developed *monolingualism* and *monoculturalism* as the dominant position that was reinforced by the nascent republics after Independence. This orientation denied the indigenous populations the right to exist as distinct ethnic peoples, e.g. in 19th-century Argentina, or it erased its presence and visibility, as happened in Brazil during the early colonial period (Orlandi, 1993). During the 19th century, when the new republics promoted massive immigration from Europe, this orientation was apparently questioned. At that time the distinction between positive and negative minorities and between positive and negative bilingualism was born.[48] Racist and social considerations prevailed over the aim of building homogeneous nation states and admitted, at least for a time, the presence of European immigrants and their languages, as long as they did not challenge the status of Spanish or Portuguese as the national languages. In any case, as we have seen, many of the republics

MONOCULTURALISM - MONOLINGUALISM
Diversity denied
Ideological Orientation: Cultural Exclusion

↓

MULTICULTURALISM - MULTILINGUALISM
Diversity recognised as a 'problem'
Ideological Orientation: Cultural Inclusión

↓

PLURICULTURALISM - PLURILINGUALISM
Diversity assumed as a resource of enrichment
Ideological Orientation: Cultural and Intercultural Base

Figure 3.2 Ideological orientations in language and cultural policy

developed assimilationist policies. A late expression of a monocultural and monolingual orientation can be found in President Getulio Vargas' nationalist policy towards immigrant communities in Brazil in the 1930s, analysed above.

This monolingual ideology was challenged at the end of the 19th century by a competing orientation that I want to frame as *multiculturalism* and *multilingualism*. Multiculturalism acknowledges the existences of ethnolinguistic minorities but defines diversity negatively as a problem ('the Indian problem') that needs attention. It accepts a certain tolerance for minority rights as an inevitable, but uncomfortable necessity. The cultural theory behind this position promotes cultural inclusion (Bullivant, 1984). It distinguishes between global, universal cultures such as the European cultures which can express any knowledge including science, and local cultures which can only articulate their own idiosyncratic wisdom. Such an orientation developed mainly, but not exclusively, in Latin American countries with a high proportion of indigenous population (Bolivia, Peru, Ecuador, Guatemala or Mexico) during the 20th century. Today, this concept of multiculturalism still constitutes the dominant mainstream orientation, not only in Latin America, but also in the USA, and in many European countries as well. The cultural and linguistic expressions of indigenous and other minorities are recognised both as a problem *and* as a right, and their existence is seen as a barrier to national unity.

Pluriculturalism and *plurilingualism* represent a third orientation based on an enrichment perspective. This vision shares with multiculturalism a similar recognition of factual diversity, but differs in its interpretation of this diversity as an asset and potential cultural capital for the nation as a whole.[49] It is grounded in a cultural base theory as developed by the Colombian 'etnoeducación' or the foundations of intercultural education which emerged in Venezuela in the 1970s (Monsonyi & Rengifo, 1983). It assumes that, provided appropriate *Ausbau*, all languages and cultures can express and convey universal knowledge based on their own worldview, interactional styles and languages (see also Stairs, 1988). This orientation was already present as a minority current in early colonial days (e.g. De las Casas, 1542), but only gained momentum as a challenge to previous orientations since the 1970s and 1980s when indigenous movements developed all over Latin America and claimed their right to be recognised as peoples with their own cultures and educational needs. This position, which argues for intercultural and bilingual education and promotes additive bilingualism, has made inroads into sectors of the mainstream society and has aligned itself with other groups that share an enrichment view and the acceptance of different kinds of diversity.

Although the three orientations each represent a certain historical period when they were hegemonic, they still survive and embody competing positions in contemporary society. The fundamental question today is how to move from a multilingual and multicultural orientation that recognises diversity but sees it as a problem, to a plurilingual and pluricultural perspective within the broader context of a general transformation of Latin American societies. Internal pressure, mainly from indigenous movements and civil society at large, and external conditioning from globalising trends, are forcing nation states to open up and enter a process of change.

Several actors come into play in this language and education policy debate. For the conservative forces in each state that represent large segments of the dominant society, assimilation is still an overall goal. Therefore, enclaves where distinct ethnolinguistic groups, communities and peoples reproduce their separate identities, preserving their languages and cultures, constitute a challenge, even a threat to the dominant conception of the state. They are still under suspicion for not being loyal citizens, as they speak a different language, whether they are fluent in the national language or not. Many members of minority groups and subordinate peoples have internalised this traditional hegemonic view and develop defensive attitudes about their languages and language use. Here, a new language policy is called for to transform the relationship that the actors involved maintain with their own languages and the prevailing language constellation.

Bilingual communities and their educational systems at the two poles of societal stratification can also contribute significantly to this transformation in their own ways. They can join their voices with growing sectors in most Latin American societies who increasingly understand and appreciate diversity as an asset for societal enrichment and the broadening of democracy. In particular, they can demonstrate how the specific funds of knowledge stemming from their heritage cultures – indigenous and immigrant – make significant contributions and enrich the dominant societies. The unquestionable educational leadership of elite bilingual schools based on successful enrichment bilingualism can help to further erode the unsustainable ideology of monolingualism as the natural and convenient state of existence of a nation. And the unquestionable legitimacy of indigenous group claims to be recognised as peoples and to have their linguistic and educational rights respected may work towards the same goal from a different societal pole.[50]

There can be little doubt that IBE for indigenous peoples will only succeed if assimilationist pressure is removed as a result of significant changes in the dominant sectors of Latin American society and if these embrace a pluricultural enrichment orientation. Such a transition to a pluricultural and plurilingual viewpoint could open new ways of looking at immigrant and global bilingual schools, in which heritage language knowledge could be seen as a valuable resource for the nation as a whole. Furthermore, new light could be shed on the prospect of massive foreign language learning in public education, not only in the private sector as happens today. Recently, it has become clear that language and education policies for majorities and minorities can no longer be dismissed as marginal components of state policy that may be dealt with outside the domains of mainstream power relations. They have become a touchstone to evaluate the quality of democracy, pluricultural commitment and the construction of modern states in most parts of the world.

Acknowledgements

Research on indigenous education in Mexico was funded by research grants from the Mexican National Council for Science and Technology (CONACYT) and the Ford Foundation. I am grateful to Anne-Marie de Mejía and Nancy H. Hornberger for insightful comments on an earlier version and for helping to put my English into shape.

Notes

1. It may be surprising that the question of which countries belong to 'Latin America' is not as clear as it should be. I will use the term 'Latin America' but limit my discussion to those countries that evolved out of Spanish or

Portuguese colonisation, a unit which in Spanish or Portuguese is usually called 'Ibero America'.

2. Figures for languages and numbers of speakers are matters of debate. Diverging typologies (e.g. Ruhlen, 1987 for Amerindia; Suárez, 1983 for Mesoamerica; and Rodrígues, 1986 for Brazil) count between 300 and over 1000 languages, and national censuses typically underrate native language speakers.
3. In the past, indigenous populations have often be labelled as 'ethnic minorities' as part of a discursive process to subordinate them. One of the central claims of the indigenous movements over the past decades has been to be recognised as peoples, even as nations (e.g. União das Nações Indígenas in Brazil or First Nations in the USA), i.e. as societies with their own organisation and identity that existed prior to the arrival of the conquerors and distinct from the dominant society, independently of the numbers of their members, which may range from a few dozen to several million. Therefore, the term 'minority' is hardly used any more for them in the specialised literature.
4. A caveat against overgeneralisation should be made at this point. Certainly, there are significant differences between countries like Argentina, Brazil, Chile and Uruguay, which experienced massive European immigration and had a small percentages of indigenous populations (none in Uruguay since at least the 19th century), and countries based on a symbiosis – albeit unsettled – between indigenous high cultures and Spanish immigration such as Peru, Bolivia, Ecuador, Guatemala and Mexico. The general trend towards the construction of homogenous nation states and a Mestizo or white population of native speakers of the national languages is shared to differing degrees by all Latin American countries.
5. During the US presidential campaign in 2004, John Kerry, the democratic candidate, was accused by the republicans of being able to speak fluent French, insinuating that he was not a true American. See many similar cases in the USA in Hamel (1999), Macías (1997), Valdés (1997) and Zentella (1997).
6. A new Law of Education passed in Bolivia in 1994 established that education had to be intercultural in the whole country and bilingual in areas of high percentages of indigenous population (Albó & Anaya, 2004; López, 2005). Mexico introduced the concept of IBE in the early 1990s and passed a General Law of Linguistic Rights for the Indigenous Peoples in 2003 which established the right to mother tongue education (Hamel, 2008a; Pellicer *et al.*, 2006). Brazil had its own development after the new Constitution of 1988 which established general rights for the indigenous population. Specific educational laws followed in 1995 and after 2000 (Ministério da Educação, 2002).
7. Between 2000 and 2007, some 7000 individual tests were applied in annual series. Their results, which have not yet been analysed in detail, seem to point in the same direction as the few samples analysed here.
8. See Cummins (2000) for an updated version of his theoretical framework that includes the interdependence and the common underlying proficiency hypotheses.
9. For our Spanish L2 programme and its rationales, see Hamel *et al.* (2004); for the debate about access in this process, consult Hamel and Francis (2006).
10. The nature and degree of such a threshold level is a matter of debate as it depends on how L2 proficiency is defined. In the case of our P'urhepecha study, students developed fairly poor conversational skills in Spanish L2

throughout their elementary schooling, given the reduced outside contact with Spanish. Limited productive oral skills seem, however, not to impede the development of comparatively more advance reading and writing skills in L2. Although further analysis of our material is needed, our findings point to L1 literacy skills as a stronger predictor of the same skills in L2 than any other factor.

11. 'Jus solis', the right of the soil, means that those who are born in the country are citizens. It contrasts with 'jus sanguinis', the right of the blood that only concedes citizenship to those who are descendants of established citizens, a principle that is still applied in a number of European countries.
12. Colleagues from Brazil reported that the new Brazilian policy of recognition, which allows immigrant minorities to be officially registered, still causes anxiety among the mainstream population and particularly among civil servants, who fear possible terrorist action against the state if the immigrant communities' claims were not satisfied (personal communication by Gilvan Müller de Oliveira in 2006). This happened long before the US and the British governments started to sow xenophobic paranoia, especially against Muslim minorities, among their population, under the smokescreen of terrorism to justify the war in Iraq.
13. This leaves out important schools such as the Mexican 'Colegio Madrid', founded by republican immigrants from Spain after the Civil War (1936–39), which played a significant role in Mexican progressive intellectual education between the 1940s and the 1980s.
14. Various authors on migration warn not to trust given figures as they vary substantially. Furthermore, statistics in themselves are not the most relevant indicators for social behaviour such as assimilation or ethnolinguistic vitality (see Baily & Miguez, 2003; Lütge *et al.*, 1981; Nugent, 1992).
15. The rapid language shift to Spanish is further explained by the fact that most Italian immigrants were peasants from the poorer southern areas of Italy who spoke very diverse dialects that were hardly intercomprehensible. Thus, communication rapidly switched to the use of Spanish or some kind of interlanguage among Italians. For general information see Baily (2003); for German immigrants to Argentina consult Micolis (1973) and Saint Sauveur-Henn (1995).
16. The Welsh migrants to Argentina fled from economic and linguistic repression in Britain; they settled in the southernmost Patagonia region in order to be able to set up their own Welsh schools and internal government (Nugent, 1992).
17. Figures, again, are difficult to trust. The numbers of speakers for 1990 here seem to be extremely exaggerated and probably include many who may still speak some isolated words.
18. Thus, Banfi and Day (2004) observe that the present-day numbers and weight of international bilingual schools in Argentina bear no relationship with the number of immigrants of each linguistic group. The Italians, by far the largest immigrant group, have only six schools compared to 100 English bilingual schools. And there is no Polish school in Argentina or elsewhere in Latin America that I know of.
19. Language use differed according to each country's regulations and the local context. Most typical immigrant schools provided the curriculum of their home countries, which meant content teaching through the immigrant language. Some included courses of the host country's national language (Spanish or Portuguese) as a 'foreign' language. The relevant point is that

these schools were controlled and administrated by the immigrant communities who often exercised significant power in their host countries.

20. My maternal grandfather arrived in southern Chile around 1900 to set up a branch of a German bank in the newly developed, prosperous town of Temuco. His position as vice-consul of the German Empire implied a close relationship not only with the German community, but also with the local authorities, including the Armed Forces, which cultivated a high esteem for the Prussian military tradition at that time. He was actively involved in the development of the local German school. On the national level, the Chilean government invited Swiss and German pedagogues in 1895 to implement a profound educational reform whose positive effects lasted until the 1960s.
21. Except for Chile, all German schools in Latin America were closed during WWII. Even before its outbreak, the Brazilian populist dictator Getulio Vargas implemented a draconian policy of forced assimilation and the prohibition of foreign language use. In 1938 he dictated a decree called the 'nationalisation of education'. It was directed against Brazil's largest immigrant communities that were later identified as enemies when Brazil entered WWII in 1942: the Italians, Germans and Japanese. The immigrant colonies were accused of maintaining a foreign nationality and of preserving and disseminating foreign values, of plotting against Brazil and of not learning Portuguese. During that time more than 1600 German schools were closed and confiscated, along with other property of the immigrant groups (Kreutz, 1994; Rambo, 2003; Renk, 2005; Seyferth, 1999).
22. This is how my grandmother arrived shortly after 1900, at the age of 17, from Northern Germany to Southern Chile. She accompanied a prosperous German landowner family already established in Chile to teach their children on their long journey round the southern cone of America and afterwards on their farm.
23. Requirements for the curriculum varied according to a number of factors: the developmental stage of each country, the location (urban versus rural) of the community schools and their orientation to be integrated into the national curriculum or not. Between 1870 and 1895 Argentina, Chile and Uruguay, among other countries, promulgated general laws for education which specified curricular requirements to be carried out in Spanish. Other countries would not interfere significantly with immigrant schools until the middle of the 20th century.
24. When my father was sent by the German government to Uruguay in 1957 to be the first headmaster in the post-Fascist era in the German school in Montevideo, I entered the first grade where literacy teaching was divided between the German and the Spanish classes. My German teacher taught me print letters, whereas script letters were simultaneously taught in Spanish. And we were warned not to mix up the two systems and never ever transfer any knowledge acquired in one language to the other.
25. For the state of the art in the teaching of Romance languages in several South American countries, see Bertolotti (2003).
26. See Banfi and Day's (2004) observation that the renowned 'Lenguas Vivas', a one-hundred-year-old public institute for foreign language teacher training in Buenos Aires, is considered not to be capable of producing highly competent bilingual teachers.
27. Thus, some German schools and Goethe Institutes launched a campaign for learning German under the slogan: 'Englisch ist ein muss, Deutsch ist ein plus'.

28. Since rankings have become popular and while the testing obsession swept over from the USA and Europe to Latin America, private schools make intensive use of their success ratings ('third position in maths in the country') as part of their marketing strategies. Under the heading 'Bicultural and trilingual education', the German Humboldt school in Mexico advertised the success of their students in the 2003 international Programme for International Student Assessment (PISA) evaluation where their students rated significantly above the national average.
29. Limited space will not allow me to approach the more technical problems of language teaching and learning in these schools. Most of them are analysed in detail in de Mejía's (2002) seminal book on elite bilingual education.
30. From an analytical perspective, societal global language orientations and individual bilingual skills and uses should be distinguished, as they do not necessarily coincide (see Fishman's 1967 classical distinction between societal diglossia and individual bilingualism). Both on the societal and the individual level, positive or negative attitudes regarding diversity in terms of a given culture and a related language may be obtained. They may however diverge between language and culture and foster an instrumental attitude, as is reflected in the slogan common in Asia: 'Yes to English, no to US–American culture' (see Hamel, 2000, 2003, 2006a for a detailed discussion).
31. Thus, the Mexican businessman Carlos Slim, the owner of Telmex, the leading Mexican telephone company, and of a large group of corporations, is the richest person in the world according to the *Fortune* review in 2007. Only in 2006 Mr. Slim increased his personal fortune by US$23 billion, from 30 to 53 billion. This increase almost triples the gross national product (GNP) of Bolivia for the same year.
32. Income on the bottom edge is much lower in other Latin American countries than in Mexico. Teachers and university professors in public institutions in Bolivia, Peru or Ecuador earn a monthly salary between US$50 and 200.
33. The PISA evaluation mentioned above identified socioeconomic differences as a strong predictor of school achievement, especially in the case of Germany, where the three-track school system channels students into lower, middle or higher (grammar school) education as early as the age of 10 (Baumert, 2006).
34. See the debate on the achievement gap and President Bush's 'No Child Left Behind' programme.
35. Chile, the Latin American champion of a supposedly successful model of neoliberal economy and high quality education, returned to its status as primary commodities exporter (copper, fruit, wine) and gave up any effort of industrialisation it shared with its neighbours of the region several decades ago. Apart from having entered the circle of the world's most unequal countries (UN Gini index of 57.1, better than Haiti with 59.2, but almost doubling India's inequality rate with 32.5, see United Nations 2006), the success of its public education has increasingly come under attack from students and staff.
36. The success of immersion education in Quebec, where these programmes first developed for middle class Anglophone students to be taught in French (see Baker, 2006; Swain & Lapkin, 1991), has motivated politicians and educators to suggest the application of the same type of programmes to subordinate immigrant and indigenous students, without taking into account sociocultural differences (see however Tucker, 1986).

37. See the special issue, Volume 7 (2–3), of the *International Journal of Bilingual Education and Bilingualism* edited by Brutt-Griffler and Varghese (2004), which contains a series of interesting papers on the bilingual educator's knowledge base on bilingualism and other related topics.
38. ZfA stands for 'Zentralstelle für das Auslandsschulwesen', the institution of the German federal government that organises the German schools abroad including the provision of German teachers and teacher training.
39. Certainly, the work of the British Council and the Alliance Française reveal a much more straightforward language policy in their former colonies in Africa and Asia, where they rarely have to contend with any competitors, than in Latin America. One of the most insightful critical reports from inside the 'Company' was written about the British Council by one of its former civil servants and language teachers, Robert Phillipson (1992), in his renowned book entitled *Linguistic Imperialism*.
40. Whether Empire really exists as an entity that is totally independent of any nation state and whether all nation states including the USA disintegrate is a matter of fierce debate. The resurgence of nationalism around the question of increasingly scarce resources such as oil, a process that includes the Middle East, India, China and several Latin American countries, casts reasonable doubt on Hardt and Negri's hypothesis. Furthermore, critics like Boron (2002) and Chomsky (2003) sustain that, on the contrary, imperialism is invigorated based on the US nation state among a few others and that the vast majority of international corporations are harboured in only seven industrialised countries (see my critique of 'Empire' related to language policy in Hamel, 2006a).
41. Perhaps for these, among other reasons, when Quechua, the most widely spoken indigenous language of the Andean region, was offered as a second language in an elite school in La Paz (Bolivia), there was a rush for the language courses that surprised most observers, not least the school administrators (personal communication by Luis Enrique López in 2007).
42. Estimates calculate the money transfers ('remesas') of Mexican migrants to Mexico at over $26 billion for 2006, out of which probably $9 billion come from indigenous migrants. Again, the latter amount equals the GNP of Bolivia. Migrant money transfers have become a prime source of national income in foreign currency for many Latin American countries that help stabilise their balance of payment and prevent local communities from starvation.
43. No doubt much of their work has been extremely beneficial and essential progress would probably not have come about in the same way without their intervention, given the lack of state resources and also political deadlocks in many countries.
44. One project that stands out among others is PROEIB-Andes, a postgraduate and research programme proposed by the German government agency GTZ and signed by five Andean states (Bolivia, Chile, Colombia, Ecuador and Peru). During its time of significant foreign financing between 1995 and 2006, it formed an indigenous leadership from many indigenous peoples in the field of IBE and educational policy and management (López, 2005). It operated under privileged conditions (high-level budget, scholarships for all students paid by the participating countries, full-time professors with high salaries, dozens of invited researchers from all over the world, generous research funding) as an enclave in the public University of San Simón in Cochabamba, Bolivia. The programme greatly influenced the orientation and

implementation of IEB in the participating countries. BilingLatAm, a Latin American network on bilingual education, started organising international symposia (2004 in Buenos Aires, 2006 in Bogotá) that explicitly seek to combine EBE and IBE perspectives.

45. This is not the topic of this text. References to this process can be found in many of the studies on indigenous education, although this kind of transfer and cooperation is rarely made a central theme.
46. Interesting examples abound. A French teacher who is at the same time an expert in indigenous languages developed an extensive unit on P'urhepecha for her 9th graders at the French School in Mexico City. This project was extremely interesting, as it allowed her students to open a window into an indigenous culture via its language structure and the way a totally different community organises its worldview and grammaticalises significant concepts. Given the grammatical complexity of most IL, working with them contributed to create language awareness and to overcome 'folk' perceptions of simple indigenous cultures. In my own experience working with EBE, I have often integrated units on indigenous education into my workshops that were usually well received.
47. I have elsewhere developed these distinctions in more detail (Hamel, 2000). My conceptualisation has certainly profited from Ruiz' (1984) seminal paper on orientations in language planning, which differentiates between language-as-problem, language-as-right and language-as-resource. In his framework, the same case could appear both as a problem *and* as a right. The distinctions presented here are slightly different. They refer to the broader context of ideological orientations of large sectors of societies in their overall view of other ethnic groups, orientations that in Latin America range from the denial of the existence of ethnic minorities to an enrichment perspective which in fact coincides with Ruiz' resource category.
48. This distinction established a clear borderline between the immigrants who could all become good Argentine citizens, and the Indians who could not.
49. In the Anglo Saxon literature the only concept used is 'multiculturalism', especially in anthropology and liberal political science (Kymlicka, 1995; Parekh, 2000; Taylor, 1994). The best critique I know of the English debate from a Latin American perspective that traces the concept back to its origins in Kant and Rawles is Díaz-Polanco (2006). A distinction becomes necessary because different orientations vis-à-vis the same material existence of diversity play a significant role both theoretically and in applied matters of language and education policy. The distinction (Hamel, 1997, 2000, 2003) is gaining relevance in the Latin American debate. The term 'pluriculturalism', less used in English, is common in French and Spanish. It recovers UN and UNESCO terminology and retrieves positive connotations vis-à-vis the more neutral 'multi'.
50. It would certainly be naïve to imagine a concrete alliance between the two sectors, given insurmountable differences of class, culture and political positioning. However, both sectors could objectively converge in their move to erode monolingual and monocultural ideological orientations.

References

Albó, X. (2002) *Educando en la Diferencia. Hacia unas Políticas Interculturales y Lingüísticas para el Sistema Educativo*. La Paz: Ministerio de Educación, UNICEF, CIPCA.

Albó, X. and Anaya, A. (2004) *Niños Alegres, Libres, Expresivos. La Audacia de la Educación Intercultural Bilingüe en Bolivia.* La Paz: CIPCA and UNICEF.
Alred, G., Byram, M. and Fleming, M. (eds) (2003) *Intercultural Experience and Education.* Clevedon: Multilingual Matters.
Arnoux, E. and Bein, R. (1997) Problemas político-lingüísticos en la Argentina contemporánea, Quo Vadis Romania? *Zeitschrift für ein aktuelle Romanistik* 3, 50–65.
Axelrud, B.C. (1999) Alcances y proyecciones de la integración regional en Argentina. In *Políticas Lingüísticas para América Latina.* Actas del Congreso Internacional 1997 (pp. 59–72). Buenos Aires: UBA.
Baily, S. (2003) Italian immigrants in Buenos Aires and New York City, 1870–1914: A comparative analysis of adjustment. In S. Baily and E.J. Míguez (eds) *Mass Migration to Modern Latin America.* Wilmington, DE: Scholarly Resources.
Baily, S. and Míguez, E.J. (eds) (2003) *Mass Migration to Modern Latin America.* Wilmington, DE: Scholarly Resources.
Baker, C. (2006) *Foundations of Bilingual Education and Bilingualism* (4th edn). Clevedon: Multilingual Matters.
Baldauf, Jr., R.B. and Kaplan, R.B. (2003) Language policy decisions and power: Who are the actors? In P.M. Ryan and R. Terborg (eds) *Language: Issues of Inequality.* México: UNAM.
Banfi, C. and Day, R. (2004) The evolution of bilingual schools in Argentina. *International Journal of Bilingual Education and Bilingualism* 7 (5), 398–411.
Bärnert-Fürst, U. (1994) Conservation and displacement processes of the German language in the speech community of Panambí, Rio Grande do Sul, Brazil. In N. Berend and K.J. Mattheier (eds) *Sprachinselforschung. Eine Gedenkschrift für Hugo Jedig.* Frankfurt: Lang.
Baumert, J. (ed.) (2006) *Herkunftsbedingte Disparitäten im Bildungswesen. Differenzielle Bildungsprozesse und Probleme der Verteilungsgerechtigkeit. Vertiefende Analysen im Rahmen von PISA 2000.* Wiesbaden: VS Verlag für Sozialwissenschaften.
Bein, R. (1999) El plurilingüismo como realidad lingüística, como representación sociolingüística y como estrategia glotopolítica. In E. Arnoux and R. Bein (eds) *Prácticas y Representaciones del Lenguaje.* Buenos Aires: Eudeba.
Bein, R. and Varela, L. (1998) Bases para la determinación de una política lingüística de la ciudad de Buenos Aires. Buenos Aires: ms.
Bernecker, W.L. and Fischer, T. (1992) Deutsche in Lateinamerika. In K.J. Bade (ed.) *Deutsche im Ausland-Fremde in Deutschland. Migration in Geschichte und Gegenwart.* Manchen: Gegenwart.
Bertolotti, V. (ed.) (2003) *Relevamiento de la Enseñanza de Lenguas Romances en el Cono Sur.* Montevideo: Unión Latina.
Besserer, F. and Kearney, M. (eds) (2006) *San Juan Mixtepec. Una Comunidad Transnacional ante el Poder Clasificador y Filtrador de las Fronteras.* México: UAM, Casa Juan Pablos.
Born, J. and Dickgießer, S. (1989) *Deutschsprachige Minderheiten. Ein Überblick über den Stand der Forschung für 27 Länder.* Mannheim: Institut für deutsche Sprache.
Boron, A.A. (2002) *Império & Imperialismo. Uma Leitura Crítica de Michael Hardt e Antonio Negri.* Buenos Aires: CLACSO.
Brutt-Griffler, J. and Varghese, M. (2004) *Introduction. International Journal of Bilingual Education and Bilingualism,* 7 (2–3), 93–101.
Bullivant, B.M. (1984) *Pluralism: Cultural Maintenance and Evolution.* Clevedon: Multilingual Matters.

Calhoun, C. (1992) The infrastructure of modernity: Indirect social relationship, information technology, and social integration. In H. Haferkamp and N.J. Smelser (eds) *Social Change in Modernity*. Berkeley: University of California Press.
Calvet, L-J. (1999) *Pour une Écologie des Langues du Monde*. Paris: Plon.
Chomsky, N. (1959) A review of B.F. Skinner's Verbal Behavior. *Language* 35 (1), 26–58.
Chomsky, N. (2003) *Hegemony or Survival. America's Quest for Global Dominance*. New York: Metropolitan Books, Henry Holt & Co.
CIA World Fact Book (2006) Field Listing – Distribution of family income – Gini index. 19 December. Retrieved on 3.1.07.
CRIC (Consejo Regional Indígena del Cauca) (2005) *¿Qué Pasaría si la Educación...? 30 años de Construcción de una Educación Propia*. Bogotá: PEBI.
Crystal, D. (1997) *English as a Global Language*. Cambridge: Cambridge University Press.
Cummins, J. (1995) Heritage language teaching in Canadian schools. In O. García and C. Baker (eds) *Policy and Practices in Bilingual Education: A Reader*. Clevedon: Multilingual Matters.
Cummins, J. (2000) *Language, Power and Pedagogy. Bilingual Children in the Crossfire*. Clevedon: Multilingual Matters.
De las Casas, B. (1542) *Brevísima Relación de la Destrucción de las Indias*. Valladolid.
de la Peña, G. (1999) Territorio y ciudadanía étnica en la nación globalizada. Desacatos: *Revista de Antropología Social* 1, 13–27.
de la Peña, G. (2002) Social citizenship, ethnic minority demands, human rights and neoliberal paradoxes: A case study in Western Mexico. In R. Sieder (ed.) *Multiculturalism in Latin America. Indigenous Rights, Diversity and Democracy*. London: Palgrave Macmillan.
de Mejía, A-M. (2002) *Power, Prestige and Bilingualism. International Perspectives on Elite Bilingual Education*. Clevedon: Multilingual Matters.
De Swaan, A. (2001) *Words of the World: The Global Language System*. Cambridge: Polity Press.
Díaz-Polanco, H. (2006) *Elogio de la Diversidad. Globalización, Multiculturalismo y Etnofagia*. México: Siglo XXI.
Fishman, J.A. (1967) Bilingualism with and without diglossia; diglossia with and without bilingualism. *Journal of Social Issues* 23 (2), 29–38.
Fontanella de Weinberg, M.B. (1979) *La Asimilación Lingüística de los Inmigrantes*. Bahía Blanca: Universidad Nacional del Sur.
García Canclini, N. (1999) *La Globalización Imaginada*. Buenos Aires, Barcelona, México: Paidós.
Graddol, D. (2006) *English Next. Why Global English May Mean the End of 'English as a Foreign Language'*. London: The British Council.
Hamel, R.E. (1988) *Sprachenkonflikt und Sprachverdrängung. Die zweisprachige Kommunikationspraxis der Otomi-Indianer in Mexico*. Bern, Frankfurt: Peter Lang.
Hamel, R.E. (1993) Políticas y planificación del lenguaje: una introducción. In R.E. Hamel (ed.) Políticas del Lenguaje en América Latina. *Iztapalapa* 29, 5–39.
Hamel, R.E. (1994) Indigenous education in Latin America: Policies and legal frameworks. In T. Skutnabb-Kangas and R. Phillipson (eds) *Linguistic Human Rights. Overcoming Linguistic Discrimination*. Berlin and New York: Mouton de Gruyter.

Hamel, R.E. (1997) Language conflict and language shift: A sociolinguistic framework for linguistic human rights. In R.E. Hamel (ed.) *International Journal of the Sociology of Language* 127, Special Issue: Linguistic Human Rights from a Sociolinguistic Perspective, 107–134.

Hamel, R.E. (1999) Los derechos lingüísticos de los hispanohablantes en California. In J. Wimer (ed.) *La Lengua Española en los Estados Unidos de América*. México: FCE, CONACULTA, Union Latine.

Hamel, R.E. (2000) Políticas del lenguaje y estrategias culturales en la educación indígena. In IEEPO (ed.) *La Educación Indígena Hoy. Inclusión y Diversidad*. Oaxaca: Colección Voces del Fondo.

Hamel, R.E. (2003) Regional blocs as a barrier against English hegemony? The language policy of Mercosur in South America. In J. Maurais and M.A. Morris (eds) *Languages in a Globalising World*. Cambridge: Cambridge University Press.

Hamel, R.E. (2006a) The development of language empires. In U. Ammon, N. Dittmar, K.J. Mattheier and P. Trudgill (eds) *Sociolinguistics – Soziolinguistik. An International Handbook of the Science of Language and Society* (Vol. 3). Berlin and New York: Walther de Gruyter.

Hamel, R.E. (2006b) Indigenous literacy teaching in public primary schools: A case of bilingual maintenance education in Mexico. In T.L. McCarty and O. Zepeda (eds) *One Voice, Many Voices: Recreating Indigenous Language Communities*. Tempe & Tucson: Arizona State University Center for Indian Education, University of Arizona American Indian Language Development Institute.

Hamel, R.E. (2008a) Indigenous language policy and education in Mexico. In S. May and N.H. Hornberger (eds) *Encyclopedia of Language and Education*. Vol. 1: Language Policy and Political Issues in Education (2nd edn). New York: Springer.

Hamel, R.E. (2008b) Bilingual education for indigenous communities in Mexico. In J. Cummins and N.H. Hornberger (eds) *Encyclopedia of Language and Education*. Vol. 5: Bilingual Education (2nd edn). New York: Springer.

Hamel, R.E. and Francis, N. (2006) The teaching of Spanish as a second language in an indigenous bilingual intercultural curriculum. *Language, Culture and Curriculum* 19 (2), 171–188.

Hamel, R.E. and Ibáñez, M.A. (2000) La lecto-escritura en la lengua propia: Educación intercultural bilingüe en la región p'urhepecha de México. *Actas de las III Jornadas de Etnolingüística* 44–58.

Hamel, R.E., Brumm, M., Carrillo Avelar, A., Loncon, E., Nieto, R. and Silva Castellón, E. (2004) ¿Qué hacemos con la castilla? La enseñanza del español como segunda lengua en un currículo intercultural bilingüe de educación indígena. *Revista Mexicana de Investigación Educativa* 20, 83–107. On WWW at http://www.comie.org.mx/documentos/rmie/v09/n020/pdf/rmiev09n20scB02n04es.pdf. Accessed 10.2.08.

Hardt, M. and Negri, A. (2000) *Empire*. Cambridge, MA: Harvard University Press.

Hornberger, N.H. (2000) Bilingual education policy and practice: Ideological paradox and intercultural possibility. *Anthropology and Education Quarterly* 31 (2), 173–201.

Hornberger, N.H. (ed.) (2005) Heritage/community language education: US and Australian perspectives. Special Issue: *International Journal of Bilingual Education and Bilingualism* 8, 2–3.

Kreutz, L. (1994) Escolas da imigração alemã no Rio Grande do Sul: Perspectivas históricas. In C. Mauch and N. Vasconcellos (eds) *Os Alemães no Sul do Brasil: Cultura, Etnicidade e História*. Canoas: Editorial ULBRA.

Kymlicka, W. (1995) *Multicultural Citizenship*. Oxford: Oxford University Press.

López, L.E. (2005) *De Resquicios y Boquerones. La Educación Intercultural Bilingüe en Bolivia*. La Paz: PROEIB-Andes & Plural.

Lütge, W., Hoffmann, W., Körner, K.W. and Klingenfuss, K. (1981) *Deutsche in Argentinien: 1520–1980*. Buenos Aires: Verlag Alemann.

Macías, R.F. (1997) Bilingual workers and language-use rules in the workplace: A case study of a nondiscriminatory language policy. R.E. Hamel (ed.) Special Issue: Linguistic Human Rights from a Sociolinguistic Perspective. *International Journal of the Sociology of Language* 127, 53–70.

Micolis, M. (1973) *Une Communauté Allemande en Argentine: Eldorado: Problèmes d'Intégration Socio-Culturelle*. Québec: Centre International de Recherches sur le Bilinguisme.

Ministério da Educação (2002) *Referenciais para a formação de professores indígenas*. Brasília: SEF/MEC.

Monsonyi, E.E. and Rengifo, F. (1983) Fundamentos teóricos y programáticos de la educación intercultural bilingüe. In N.J. Rodríguez, E.K. Masferrer and R. Vargas Vega (eds) *Educación, Etnias y Descolonización en América Latina*. México: UNESCO-III.

Nugent, W. (1992) Crossings: *The Great Transatlantic Migrations, 1870–1914*. Bloomington, IN: Indiana University Press.

Orlandi, E.P. (1993) La danza de las gramáticas. La relación entre el tupí y el portugués en Brasil. In R.E. Hamel (ed.) *Políticas del Lenguaje en América Latina. Iztapalapa* 29, 54–74.

Parekh, B. (2000) *Rethinking Multiculturalism. Cultural Diversity and Political Theory*. London: Macmillan.

Pellicer, D. Cifuentes, B. and Herrera, C. (2006) Legislating diversity in twenty-first century Mexico. In M. Hidalgo (ed.) *Mexican Indigenous Languages and the Dawn of the Twenty-First Century*. Berlin & New York: Mouton de Gruyter.

Phillipson, R. (1992) *Linguistic Imperialism*. Oxford: Oxford University Press.

Rambo, A.B. (2003) O teuto-brasileiro e sua identidade. In N.A. Fiori (eds) *Etnia e Educação: A Escola Alemã do Brasil e Estudos Congêneres*. Florianópolis: UFSC, Tubarão: Editora Unisul.

Renk, V.E. (2005) Educação de imigrantes alemães em Curitiba. *Diálogo Educacional* 5 (14), 101–111.

Rodrígues, A. (1986) *Línguas Brasileiras*. São Paulo: Edições Loyola.

Rosaldo, R. (1994) Cultural citizenship and educational democracy. *Cultural Anthropology* 9 (3), 402–411.

Rosenberg, P. (2001) Deutsche Minderheiten in Lateinamerika. Frankfurt (Oder): Europa-Universität Viadrina. On WWW at http://www.kuwi.euv-frankfurt-o.de/~ sw1www/publikation/lateinam.htm.

Ruhlen, M. (1987) *A Guide to the World's Languages*. Vol. 1: Classification. Stanford: Stanford University Press.

Ruiz, R. (1984) Orientations in language planning. *NABE Journal* 8 (2), 15–34.

Saint Sauveur-Henn, A. (1995) *Un Siècle d'Émigration Allemande vers l'Argentine*. Cologne: Boehlau.

Seyferth, G. (1999) Os imigrantes e a campanha de nacionalização do Estado Novo. In D. Pandolfi (ed.) *Repensando o Estado Novo*. Rio de Janeiro: FGV.

Skutnabb-Kangas, T. (2000) *Linguistic Genocide in Education – or Worldwide Diversity and Human Rights?* Mahwah, NJ, London: Lawrence Erlbaum.

Skutnabb-Kangas, T. (2003) Linguistic diversity and biodiversity: The threat from killer languages. In C. Mair (ed.) *The Politics of English as a World Language. New Horizons in Postcolonial Cultural Studies.* Amsterdam & New York: Rodopi.

Stairs, A. (1988) Beyond cultural inclusion: An Inuit example of indigenous educational development. In T. Skutnabb-Kangas and J. Cummins (eds) *Minority Education: From Shame to Struggle.* Clevedon: Multilingual Matters.

Suárez, J.A. (1983) The Mesoamerican Indian Languages. Cambridge: Cambridge University Press.

Swain, M. and Lapkin, S. (1991) Additive bilingualism and French immersion education: The role of language proficiency and literacy. In A.G. Reynolds (ed.) *Bilingualism, Multiculturalism and Second Language Learning.* Hillsdale, NJ: Lawrence Erlbaum.

Taylor, C. (1994) The politics of recognition. In A. Gutmann (ed.) *Multiculturalism. Examining the Politics of Recognition.* Princeton, NJ: Princeton University Press.

Tucker, G.R. (1986) Implications of Canadian research for promoting a language competent American society. In J.A. Fishman (ed.) *The Fergusonian Impact* (Volume 2: Sociolinguistics and the Sociology of Language). Berlin: Mouton de Gruyter.

UNESCO (1953) *The Use of Vernacular Languages in Education,* Monographs on Fundamental Education VIII. Paris: United Nations.

United Nations (2006) Table 15: Inequality in income or expenditure (PDF). Human Development Report 2006 335. United Nations Development Programme. Retrieved on 9.1.07.

Valdés, G.M. (1997) Bilinguals and bilingualism: Language policy in an anti-immigrant age. In R.E. Hamel (ed.) *Special Issue: Linguistic Human Rights from a Sociolinguistic Perspective. International Journal of the Sociology of Language* 127, 25–52.

Valencia, S. (2007) El bilingüismo y los cambios en políticas y prácticas en la educación pública en Colombia: un estudio de caso. Memorias del II Simposio Internacional en Bilingüismo y Educación Bilingüe en América Latina. Bogotá: Ediciones Uniandes.

Zentella, A.C. (1997) The Hispanophobia of the official English movement in the US. In R.E. Hamel (ed.) *Special Issue: Linguistic Human Rights from a Sociolinguistic Perspective. International Journal of the Sociology of Language* 127, 71–86.

Ziebur, U. (2000) Die soziolinguistische Situation von Chilenen deutscher Abstammung. *Linguistic Online* 7, 3.

Chapter 4

Points of Contact or Separate Paths: A Vision of Bilingual Education in Colombia

ANNE-MARIE DE MEJÍA and MARÍA EMILIA MONTES RODRÍGUEZ

Is Colombia a Bilingual Country Today?

According to Hamel (this volume), it is possible to distinguish two different spaces with their respective educational systems which, in different ways, aim at bilingualism or multilingualism in Latin America: areas where Amerindian languages are spoken, and areas where prestigious foreign languages (many of them originally immigrant languages) are used.

This is the case in Colombia where the terms 'bilingualism' and 'bilingual education' appear in two different contexts which have little interconnection between them: bilingual programmes in international languages offered to majority language speakers, and ethnoeducation programmes designed for members of ethnic minority communities, both Amerindian and Afro-Colombian.[1] This separation can be explained by the radically different historical and economic conditions in which these two types of educational provision have developed. However, in some aspects, related both to pedagogical matters and language policies and planning, certain points of convergence can be seen. It is our contention in this chapter that attempting to overcome this separation may help to widen the view of bilingualism and bilingual education within the country as a whole, and ensure that linguistic and pedagogical insights from each tradition are available to inform future general developments in the field.

The visions of the communities that support bilingualism in these two spaces are very different. Bilingual education in majority language contexts is associated with foreign language teaching and, as such, is connected with input from foreign-based organisations, such as the British Council, *Goethe Institut* and *Alliance Française*. The families who send their children to bilingual schools come from the Colombian middle and upper-middle classes, the international community and those working for multinational organisations, particularly in the capital, Bogotá. In contrast, the families whose children study in ethnoeducation programmes are generally of peasant (Indian and Afro-Colombian) origin, who come from isolated rural communities, and who suffer the consequences of exclusion, marginalisation and armed conflict. Ethnoeducation programmes are implemented mainly in state (public) schools which depend on the Ministry of Education at national level and the local Education Secretariats at regional level. In some cases, these programmes are partially supported by community organisations which have educational programmes (such as the Indian Regional Council established in the Cauca Department in the south-west of the country) and various NGOs, which promote the notion of 'indigenous' education with the support of international resources. The academic support comes from Colombian anthropologists, ethnographers and, more recently, ethnolinguists. Thus, as Hamel (this volume) aptly observes, 'The two types of communities and their schools position themselves at opposite poles of social stratification and the scales of extreme inequality that characterize all Latin American countries, and their actors hardly ever cross paths or exchange words.'[2]

Furthermore, in Colombia it may be noted that while bilingualism in internationally prestigious languages, such as Spanish–English, Spanish–French and Spanish–German, is considered worth investing considerable sums of money in, as it provides access to a highly 'visible', socially accepted form of bilingualism, leading to the possibility of employment in the global marketplace, bilingualism in minority Amerindian or Creole languages leads, in most cases, to an 'invisible' form of bilingualism in which the native language is undervalued and associated with underdevelopment, poverty and backwardness (de Mejía, 1998).

According to Crystal (2000), monolingualism in minority languages is steadily decreasing; a development which indicates that the vitality of these threatened languages is on the decline. Bilingualism in Spanish and an Indian language is becoming ever more generalised. This tends to result in unequal development; on the one hand, there is often a progressive development of Spanish, while at the same time there is a continuous loss of competence in the native language, characteristic of situations involving unequal states of bilingualism (Pappenheim, 2002).

The discussion about the situation of bilingualism in the country seems far from being resolved. Patiño (2005: 1) strongly questions the application of the term 'bilingual' as applied to the learning of English at primary and secondary school level in Colombia, basing his position on Appel and Muysken's (1987) definition of bilingualism in 'natural' contexts which relates to situations of language contact:

> In Colombia, the concept of 'bilingual education' refers to two different situations. In the first place, bilingual and bicultural education – also known as ethnoeducation – aimed at the ethnic minorities (...) focuses on the teaching of the majority national

> language – Spanish – to children who speak minority ethnic languages, parallel to the school use of these vernacular languages. This means that there is a fairly wide social basis both for the majority and for the minority languages.[3] (Patiño, 2005: 1)

To a certain extent, Patiño considers bilingual programmes for majority language speakers as less 'authentic', and the strong emphasis on the teaching of foreign languages is seen as a fashion, which cannot truly be considered 'bilingual' education, as evidenced by the following quotation:

> This situation (...) is that of children and young people who speak the majority language and who are being intensively taught a foreign language (...) which is also the total or partial vehicle for general teaching. However, this foreign language does not have a social basis in the country: in other words, it is not the language of any section of Colombian society.[4]

This position is in direct contrast to pronouncements in relation to the 'National Bilingual Programme' (2004–2010), promoted by the Ministry of National Education (MEN) which aims at ensuring that

> Colombian citizens will be able to communicate through English with internationally comparable standards. This will contribute to the insertion of the country in the processes of universal communication, the global economy and cultural openness. (MEN presentation, 2006)

If this does, in fact, come about, it may well be that a situation of language contact with English in 'natural' contexts will develop in the not too distant future, not only as a consequence of these changes in the educational system, but also as a result of the progressive integration of Colombia within the political ambit of the USA, a development reminiscent of the Spanish conquest and colonisation of Central and South America. This may well be seen as a danger to a national identity constructed historically within a dominant, deeply rooted Hispanic tradition.

There are differing opinions about the extent and importance of bilingualism in this part of the world. Some researchers, such as Hamel (1994), see these bilingual spaces existing as 'enclaves' within a dominant sociohistorical configuration which pays homage to the model of the homogeneous and monolingual nation state. Others, such as Iriarte (1997), consider that the two traditions of bilingualism in majority and minority languages have one thing in common: both of them may be seen as minority phenomena, if considered within mainstream Colombian education. As she observes,

> Except for a few exceptions – pilot experiences of bilingual intercultural education in Indian regions and some foreign school in the main cities in the country – primary and secondary education in Colombia has developed based on Spanish ... as the first language of 93% of the Colombian population. Therefore, it is not possible to talk about bilingualism in Colombia as a generalised issue. (Iriarte, 1997: 73)[5]

This would be true in a vision which privileges demographic factors and regional population density. In other words, if the focus is on an urban, Andean, centralist nation, it may be true that bilingualism is a very restricted issue. However, from a historical point of view, we see, in the words of Triana and Antorveza (1997: 19), that:

> There are few Colombians who have stopped to think about how our social reality has been characterised by a focus on plurilingualism and cultural pluralism, both in the past and in the present. This can no longer be confined to one or two researchers, (...) but must transcend official circles (...) so that there may be an ever increasing clear and effective recognition and so that it will constitute a defining element of cultural identity.[6]

Concepts Relating to Language and Education: Bilingualism, Multilingualism, Interculturalism, Ethnoeducation, Language Recovery

Although in the country there is no consensus as to what is precisely meant by the term 'bilingualism', in educational institutions where foreign languages are taught, most people take it to mean 'proficiency in the use of the (foreign) language' (Rey de Castro & Garcia, 1997: 5). A similar lack of precision can be seen in the designation of what is meant by the term 'bilingual schools'. While most of the long-established bilingual schools use both Spanish and a foreign language as media of teaching and learning in their programmes, there are many more recent bilingual educational institutions which, in fact, provide an intensive foreign language programme (usually ranging from 8 to 20 hours per week), rather than offering bilingual content-based teaching and learning.

According to a recent survey (de Mejía & Tejada, 2001) present-day bilingual schools can be divided roughly into two groups. The first group consists of those schools which have a strong foreign connection, such as *The German School*, with branches in Bogotá, Medellin, Cali and Barranquilla, and the *Colombo Británico School* in Cali. This type of school has close contacts with foreign governments and often receives direct financial support, or the appointment of foreign teachers to work in the schools. The headteachers are usually foreign nationals and many of the materials and books used are imported from abroad. Students often have the opportunity for direct contact with the foreign country through exchanges or supervised visits organised by the schools, and international exams, like the German *Sprachdiplom* or the *International Baccalaureate,* are offered as well as the Colombian High School Diploma.

The second group of bilingual schools are national institutions which aim at a high level of student proficiency in at least one foreign language, usually English, in addition to the first language, Spanish. Most of these establishments were founded by individuals or small groups of people, generally Colombians (Araújo & Corominas, 1996). Some examples of these schools are *The Montessori School* in Medellin and *Los Nogales School* in Bogotá. Some of these schools may be classified as bilingual institutions, in the sense that they have a high degree of contact with the foreign language, foreign teachers and use two languages as media of instruction, yet sometimes they do not class themselves openly as such, because they wish to emphasise their role as educators of Colombian citizens. The headteachers are generally Colombian.

In bilingual education programmes in majority language contexts there is generally a progression in the amount of use of the foreign language in classroom interaction during pre-primary and primary levels, with some decrease in its use at secondary or high school level, as noted by de Mejía and Tejada (2001). In 11th or 12th Grade the students are often encouraged to present international examinations, such as the TOEFL or the International Baccalaureate. This type of programme is generally considered an enrichment modality (Hornberger, 1991) in which the student's first language is valued and supported at the same time as the foreign language is developed. As there is great variety in the programmes and practices of the different private bilingual schools in the country, generalisation is difficult.

We may now ask to what extent the programme characteristics outlined above are appropriate for minority bilingual education. There are some interesting points of departure which could help towards the linguistic redesign of indigenous education, yet it must be remembered that it is not a mere case of pedagogical transference; a careful sociolinguistic examination of contextual factors is of the utmost importance.

In a similar fashion to the imprecision noted in the understanding and use of the notions of 'bilingualism' and 'bilingual education' in majority language contexts, there has been a long-standing debate going on in the field of ethnoeducation (a term coined in Colombia) and in intercultural bilingual education (IBE) (as ethnoeducation is known in other Latin American countries) in relation to the real meaning of the use of different languages in bilingual school programmes.[7] Those who believe in defending the development and the spread of language and culture in minority bilingual education disagree with the use of the term 'bilingual education' to apply to communities with their own traditions, because they consider that bilingualism may be seen as a sufficient condition, when it is really only a necessary condition.[8]

They argue that there is not only the question of two (or more) languages, but also two cultures, which are not easily integrated or harmoniously compatible. Furthermore, as the situation involves conditions of linguistic inequality, discussions about interculturalism cannot ignore questions of conflict and historical inequality existing between the societies and the languages in contact, as noted in the following quotation.

> In an intercultural, educational programme which brings together indigenous and non-indigenous people, where, in practice, there is an asymmetrical relationship – domination/submission – in the relationships between the two sides to which the term 'inter' makes reference, Indian societies and the dominant society, a revaluation of the cultural heritage of the indigenous peoples in all their 'ethnic' diversity demands coming to terms with the affective and cognitive conditions in which both types of actors, indigenous and non-indigenous, act and express themselves.[9] (Gasché, 2001)

In addition, they reject the use of the native language as a transition towards the use of Spanish, something which has happened repeatedly and which has resulted in the small number of proposals advanced for the development of indigenous languages at secondary school and at university level.

The Summer Institute of Linguistics (SIL)[10] advocates a bilingual language policy directed at evangelisation through the use of indigenous languages. This runs directly counter to policies of Indian organisations which see the permanent development of bilingualism to advanced levels of proficiency as part of a political campaign for the reclaiming of social and territorial rights. The Indian languages are thus seen as linked with the defence and recovery of cultural traditions. In contrast, the SIL aims only to work on 'bilingual education' and is not concerned with 'bilingual and intercultural education', 'ethnoeducation', 'endogenous education' or 'indigenous education'; all labels which have been used at different times during the debate.

Moreover, the question of multilingualism associated with group loyalties makes designing bilingual programmes even more complex. Many well intentioned and politically correct ethnoeducational initiatives have come to grief in this respect. The north-eastern area of the Amazon region has been the scenario for a situation which can be generalised to almost any area in Colombia.[11] Vaupés is a zone where the Tukano languages are spoken. Nowadays, while some of these

15 languages are spoken by around 2000 individuals, others have only a few dozen speakers, according to Gómez-Imbert (2000). They include the Arawak and Makú languages within a social system of exogamic alliances and differential power relations. Consequently, in the same settlement or in the same maloka[12] several different languages can be heard simultaneously, some belonging to the same family and others from different affiliations by groups which practise exogamy, so that the extended family who live under the same roof are already multilingual.[13]

Migration to towns and cities, such as Mitú, Leticia and Puerto Inírida in the southern Departments of *Amazonia* and *Orinoquia*, has led to the gradual abandonment of the indigenous territories and the subsequent increase in interethnic contact. It is impossible for the education system to implement strategies to cope, as the available teachers cannot speak all the local languages. This leads to internal disputes and complaints to the educational authorities. The minorities within the minority groups feel discriminated against, both because of the imposition of Spanish, as well as the imposition of an indigenous language which is not their own. In fact, there are many primary schools which are officially referred to as bilingual, intercultural schools, but which teach the official pensum almost completely in Spanish, without designing alternative curricular proposals (Jamioy, 1998). In such complex situations, Spanish will win out. As we have seen in the case of majority language bilingualism, generalisations are supremely difficult in these contexts, too.

Sociolinguistic and Historical Context of Language Use in Colombia

From a sociolinguistic point of view, in the case of majority language contexts English is the foreign language which enjoys the highest status in the country, particularly in the domains of education, business and tourism (Zuluaga, 1996). North American English is generally the most favoured variety due to the 'overwhelming attraction of the USA by dint of historical connections, family and teacher connection, proximity and of sheer glamour image' (British Council, 1989: 10). Except for its use as a means of communication in small expatriate communities, mainly found in the capital, Bogotá, and in the Archipelago of San Andrés, Providencia and Santa Catalina, neither English, nor any other foreign language, is generally used as a means of communication within the country. Majority language speakers of Spanish as a first language are usually interested in becoming bilingual in an international language, such as English, French, German, Italian and Hebrew (see de Mejía, 2002).

For their part, minority language groups in Colombia have generally spoken Spanish as a second language and have a minority community language as mother tongue, either a native Amerindian language, an

English or Spanish-based Creole, or Colombian Sign Language.[14] However, current diagnostic studies evidence a rise in the presence of Spanish as a first language among the new generation of minority language speakers; consequently, the learning and 'recovery' of Indian languages are increasingly being seen as school concerns (Alarcón, 2001; Fagua, 2004; Montes *et al.*, 2005; Rey, 2001; Rodríguez, 2004).

Ethnolinguistic minorities

The status and use of the minority Amerindian and Afro-Colombian (Creole) languages was greatly strengthened by the Colombian Political Constitution of 1991, where it was officially recognised, for the first time, that Colombia is a multiethnic and pluricultural nation (Article 7) and that the languages of the minority communities would be co-official with Spanish in the areas where these were spoken. Furthermore, the new constitution recognised bilingual education as the form of education to be implemented in these communities. These constitutional changes arose in reply to the demands of the organised Indian communities who, from the middle of the 20th century, began to make visible their claims for unity, land and culture. These claims coincided with international trends towards the recognition of minority rights, which resulted in constitutional reform in different Latin American countries (Pineda, 1997).

Although official recognition was hailed by the communities as a great step forward, this did not immediately change ingrained attitudes towards these minority languages, particularly the Creole languages, which are often considered examples of badly spoken or 'broken' English or Spanish.

The use of Spanish as the language of education for the indigenous ethnic groups in Colombia dates from the time of the Spanish conquest of the country in the 16th century. The Education Law of 1994 continued the groundbreaking change in language policy, initiated in the Colombian Constitution of 1991, by strengthening a policy of ethnoeducation for the minority communities in Colombia, a policy which had begun in 1978 through the publication of ministerial decrees. This has been characterised as 'a permanent social process of reflection and collective construction, by means of which the Indian communities would strengthen their autonomy within an intercultural framework' (Trillos, 1998: 73). Pineda (1997) maintains, in fact, that the only concrete evidence of constitutional principles on linguistic and cultural diversity can be seen in the policy of ethnoeducation.

The education of the Afro-Caribbean inhabitants of Palenque de San Basilio in the northern state of Bolívar, descendants of runaway African slaves, who in the 17th century constructed fortified settlements or *palenques* from which they resisted attempts by the Spanish authorities to recapture them, has traditionally been carried out in Spanish. This ignores the fact that community members speak *Palenquero* as their first language, which has the distinction of being 'the only Spanish-based Creole language which has survived in the Caribbean' (Dieck, 1998: 324). However, the fact that the language was only recognised as such in 1970 is one reason for its long exclusion from the educational domain. Another powerful reason is its traditional low status, both within the community and in the surrounding neighbourhood which led to teachers repressing the use of what they considered 'badly-spoken Spanish' (Dieck, 1998: 329).

Friedemann and Patiño (1983) show that diglossic Creole–Spanish bilingualism is no longer the main sociolinguistic characteristic of this community. Spanish is in the ascendant and there is a visible decline in the use of Palenquero among the new generation. This is due to the effect of social change and to the opening up of the community, as increasing numbers of the population are now looking for work in the nearby city of Cartagena and in other parts of the Caribbean coast, even as far away as Venezuela. However, since 1986, there has been a move by the regional authorities to develop bilingual educational provision based on the needs and cultural characteristics of the community, through initiatives such as the Black Communities Ethnoeducation Programme 'Education for identity' which has produced the first reader in Palenquero for initial literacy purposes (Pérez Tejedor, 2007).

The Caribbean island of San Andrés has a long history of multilingualism, since its original colonisation by a group of English Puritan settlers in 1631, whose tobacco and sugar plantations were worked by African slaves. After the Spanish conquered the island in 1786, the English-speaking native inhabitants were allowed to remain, provided they swore allegiance to the Spanish Crown, converted to Catholicism and communicated in Spanish. While there was nominal acquiescence to these demands, in reality language and religion became means of resistance to Spanish domination (O'Flynn de Chaves, 1998).

The multilingual reality of language use is reflected to a certain extent in the education system. The majority of schools cater for Spanish-speaking 'Continentals' and use Spanish as the medium for teaching and learning. However, several primary and secondary schools have been officially recognised as bilingual institutions, where teaching and leaning is carried out in Standard Caribbean English, and in Spanish. The English-based Creole used by the majority of the native Islander population has not been considered until recently, a language appropriate to be used in Education, and has been relegated to informal, family domains, or subsidiary school contexts, such as recreation, disciplinary talk, fights etc. (Abouchaar, 2006, personal communication; Abouchaar & Moya, 2005).

In 1998 the Christian University of San Andrés, under the auspices of the Baptist churches of the Southern United States, together with representatives of the SIL, designed a pilot project for the production of pedagogical material in 'Islander English' (Creole) to be used in three Baptist primary schools on the Island. In spite of this, however, the majority language of education in the Island continues to be Spanish.

The Afro-Colombian communities in Providencia and Santa Catalina, the most traditional of the three Colombian islands, use Standard Caribbean English (strongly associated with their regional historical patrimony), though it seems that, as this is not used as frequently as might be expected, fluency levels are declining. As Abouchaar *et al.* (2002) maintain,

> In contrast to many places in the Caribbean (Jamaica, Trinidad, Grenada and Guyana) where English, in the form of Standard Caribbean English, used in education and for State formalities, coexists with the Creole language, used for everyday communication, in Providencia the space for English has gradually been taken over by Spanish. It is probable that the lack of contact between Creole and the lexifying language leads to greater interaction between Creole and Spanish.[15] (Abouchaar *et al.*, 2002: 77)

This is also reflected in the teachers' language use. Most speak Creole as a first language and have an appropriate level of oral Spanish, but have difficulties with English (Abouchaar *et al.*, 2002).

Some of the problems noted in the development of ethnoeducation programmes with the 66 different Indian language groups and with the Afro-Colombian Creole-speaking communities derive from linguistic sources; others are a result of educational difficulties, associated with situations of marginality and lack of economic and political power of the indigenous sectors, as well as the financial state of the public education system in Colombia.

Bilingual education provision in majority language contexts

In similar fashion to the situation in the Indian communities, educational provision for the descendants of the Spanish settlers in Colombia was in the hands of the Catholic missionaries, who followed in the wake of the *conquistadores* (conquerors). At this time the languages taught in these schools were mainly Greek, Latin and Spanish. Later, after independence from Spain in 1810, the ruling class, based mainly in Bogotá, Popayán and Cartagena de Indias, sent their children to study in France and England. They, in turn, brought back books which they had translated into Spanish, thus paving the way for the teaching and learning of these languages in Colombia (Zuluaga, 1996).

In more recent times, after the Second World War in 1945, as in many other South American countries, English became the most important foreign language in Colombia, due to economic expansion, social, political and economic influence and the technological development of the USA (Zuluaga, 1996). It was taught at secondary school level, alternating with the use of French.

Bilingual education in Colombia is associated principally with private bilingual schools set up to cater for the middle and upper-middle classes (de Mejía, 2002). These are found mainly in urban areas, particularly in the cities of Bogotá, Medellin, Cali, Cartagena and Barranquilla, and have increased greatly in demand over the last decade. There are around 100 bilingual schools currently in existence in the country, most of them providing English–Spanish bilingualism. The longest established institutions were founded in the 1910s and 1920s in order to provide the sons and daughters of the representatives of multinational companies stationed in Colombia and members of the expatriate communities with access to suitable bilingual and bicultural programmes.

Since then, this type of educational provision has been extended to cater for Colombian nationals and today most of the students in bilingual schools come from monolingual Colombian families who wish to do postgraduate study abroad (de Mejía, 1996). According to results from a study carried out in two well established English–Spanish bilingual schools in Cali (de Mejía, 1994), the majority of parents surveyed wanted a bilingual education for their children to enable them to study abroad at university level and to have better job opportunities when they returned. In similar fashion, Indian parents want their children to learn Spanish and to acquire other Western knowledge in order to be able to defend themselves better against discrimination.

Most English–Spanish bilingual schools characteristically separate the two languages used as media of instruction in the curriculum across the different subject areas. Thus, Maths, Natural Science and Economics are typically taught in English (the foreign language) while Social Studies, Religious Education and Physical Education are conducted in Spanish (the first language). There are very few bilingual schools who contemplate the teaching and learning of subject areas through the medium of both languages.

All this implies a change, in that Spanish language and culture is gradually losing the importance it had during the first part of the 20th century. This is not only due to the recognition of multilingualism and the co-official character of minority languages, but also to the spread of English among the upper and middle classes in Colombia. Institutions, such as the Colombian Language Academy, have publicly expressed their worries about these tendencies in primary, secondary and higher education.

With regards to bilingual education in majority contexts, some Academy members and specialists in the Spanish language are concerned about the reduction in the number of hours and in the level of complexity of the literary and scientific topics studied in Spanish. In particular, the emphasis on the teaching of subjects, such as Science and Maths, in English at primary school level has given rise to fears that Spanish (and other foreign languages) will be seen as unsuitable for the development of scientific discourse. Frequently, this privileging of English continues into undergraduate and postgraduate programmes at university level. Patiño (2005: 1) considers that there is a danger of 'forgetting or blurring the essential difference between our native language and the foreign language taught at school'.

The Linguistics Section of the Colombian Language Academy has noted the lack of coordination and communication in these areas and has proposed that,

> Spanish programmes should be designed and implemented to achieve the basic objectives of linguistic correctness and social appropriacy, and at the same time they should be in harmony with the times in which we live: 'the information society', cyberspace and globalisation.[16] (Patiño, 2005: 1)

We cannot ignore the fact that Spanish plays an important role in the Internet and in Brazil, where it has become the second preferred language in educational institutions, thanks to the *Mercosur* trade agreement. There have also been some attempts to teach Spanish as a second language to ethnic minority groups and to increase its use. However, as ever, there is little consciousness of how this can be achieved in 'natural' community contexts, where a considerable improvement in language learning methodology is needed.

Cultural Identity and Schooling

In many well established bilingual schools, there has been a noticeable tendency towards the adoption of an instrumental perspective, with a corresponding emphasis on the material and economic benefits ensuing from being bilingual in two internationally prestigious languages. Implications of cultural contact have traditionally been ignored, on the assumption that as students generally come from the dominant elite, there is no problem in this respect. Thus, the topic of culture and cultural relations, while not totally unknown, is of relatively recent interest (de Mejía, 2005).

However, clear references to interculturalism and multiculturalism can be found in the Curricular Guidelines for Foreign Languages, which were published in 1999. Interculturalism is portrayed here as 'a vision . . . which accepts and promotes all cultural manifestations, requiring a receptivity towards the contributions of the language under study and the guarantee of the knowledge and ownership of our language and culture' (Curricular Guidelines in Foreign Languages, 1999: 23).[17] Thus, an inclusive perspective is advocated, although an understanding of differences and similarities between different cultural manifestations and ways of seeing the world is not foregrounded.

In reality, however, the situation is somewhat different. In bilingual and binational schools, the treatment of cultural issues in the curriculum can often be problematic and can lead to debate and even to conflict. De Mejía and Tejada (2001) noted in a recent study carried out in Cali that many English–Spanish bilingual schools saw the idea of biculturalism as a threat to school philosophy and national identity. Certain binational institutions are seen as the only possible cultural model, and these are rejected by many as leading to acculturation at best, and anomie and identity crises at worst. There is, thus, a need for more knowledge about alternative linguistic and cultural models which could be adapted to the specific needs of bilingual schools in Colombia.

Tomasevski (2004)[18] highlights an example of the problems related to diversity and flexibility in ethnoeducation programmes in the Afro-Colombian region of Chocó. In general, the flexibility and openness to experimentation (in some cases resulting in improvisation), characteristic of the first phase of the ethnoeducation proposal, has given way to the need to define standards and to carry out standardised testing, as well as the need to 'universalise' and extend provision. This author acknowledges that,

> Education as a cultural right demands the affirmation of collective, as well as individual rights (. . .) Imposed compulsory schooling may violate human rights for not complying with criteria of acceptability and adaptability (. . .) Being Colombian involves combining attention to diversity with a contribution to the construction of a national identity.[19] (Tomasevski, 2004: 17)

This observation reminds us that for some indigenous cultures the school is still not a native institution. Not long ago, boarding schools[20] set up for Indian children prohibited and punished the use of the native language and attacked indigenous customs and traditions, distancing students from their home culture.

An early landmark in the demand for cultural rights was the expulsion of the Roman Catholic Capuchin missionaries by the Arhuaco Indians of the Sierra Nevada de Santa Marta in 1977 (Pineda, 1997), from their territory. These missionaries, who under the auspices of the Concordat established between the Colombian State and the Catholic Church were responsible for all indigenous education, were refused entry to Arhuaco territory, as a result of their punishing native children for the use of the indigenous language and the wearing of their traditional costume. Other Andean communities, especially the Paeces, who live in the south-western Department of Cauca, now consider the school as part of the process of the reclaiming of rights which guarantee the defence of territory and the reproduction and revival of language and culture.

One radical proposal with regards to language and educational policy is to think of 'ways of living' which do not involve the school[21] but which lead to the recovery of languages and cultural institutions through ways in which members of the indigenous communities have traditionally socialised, such as family and community work, specialised knowledge, and the complex processes of masculine and feminine learning in initiations in puberty and in adolescence. In this sense, pedagogical reflections on processes of socialisation and entry into the adult world are not only valid for the 'ghetto' education which seems to characterise Indian education at the moment, but also for all members of society. It seems that this knowledge has been mainly confined to the field of anthropology, which has been largely bypassed by mainstream pedagogy, apart from certain exceptions, such as the work of Aristizábal (2000).[22]

Political–religious values, closely associated with identity, and the historical traumas related in complex fashion with language use (or with restrictions on language use in certain contexts) are other problems for language planning in processes of language 'revival' of indigenous languages in school contexts of Western origin. A particularly interesting example of this is the case of the Nonuya of the Putumayo Department, a small community in the Amazon region, which was one of the ethnic groups who survived the extermination produced by the rubber trade at the end of the 19th and the beginning of the 20th centuries. In spite of the great willingness of the new generation to learn a dying language spoken only by a few older inhabitants, the serious studies carried out by linguists and anthropologists, and the recent experience of linguistic and cultural revival of the neighbouring Andokees, this project has not been successful. As Landaburu and Echeverri (1995: 54–55) note,

> ... the linguistic search is also a ritual restoration; at the collective level (...) the project of language revival is a political ritualistic project. The search for links to the past is dangerous and complex (...). 'Revival' can not just be (...) a simple faithfulness to the past, a reconstruction of the linguistic code, a replica of rituals. Revival means fundamentally symbolic re-creation ... It is not a question of

language norms or of cultural forms but the transformation of these norms so that they can re-create cultural objects – dances, the language itself – and unite in terms of new creations.[23]

Up to now, discussion in majority language contexts has concentrated particularly on pedagogical and administrative aspects involved in the implementation of bilingual programmes, leaving aside important discussions about cultural identity and the sense of belonging to a social group. On the other hand, in minority language contexts, there has been an emphasis on the non-neutrality of languages and an overemphasis on political and anthropological issues, at the expense of discussion of how linguistic skills in the different languages may be acquired.

Conscious of these differences between the two bilingual traditions in Colombia, we may therefore ask: is it possible to have a dialogue related to the challenges posed by the maintenance and the strengthening of cultural identity outside the school? Is there a possibility that the majority school population (the elite as well as the rest of the public and private sectors) may recognise the importance of the linguistic, cultural and contextual issues that have been successfully developed in ethnoeducation programmes?[24]

Challenges and Difficulties of an Equitable Language and Education Policy

There is a great difference between the type of bilingual education available to ethnic and linguistic minority groups and that offered to students from elite groups, who constitute a tiny part of the population. Factors such as social and educational exclusion are serious problems and these are compounded by internal displacement due to the effects of the undeclared civil war.[25]

Public versus private

Recent developments have added to the weakening of ethnoeducation. The fusion of some schools and the elimination of others, due to reduced numbers of students, have seriously affected the small Indian schools scattered in areas where access is difficult.

Decentralisation has implied the transference of educational responsibilities to regions in which there is no tradition of political and administrative experience, as well as a strong resistance to the application of constitutional principles to Indians and Afro-Colombians. Tomasevski (2004: 9) also refers to the ambiguity in relation to the public and the private which affects the whole educational system, but which has particularly serious consequences for the development of ethnoeducation.

> there are two parallel educational systems in Colombia: poor education for the poor, and expensive private education for the rich. Around 30% of students are in private schools in primary, 45% in secondary and 75% in higher education (...)[26]

The indigenous schools are mostly public schools, even though in some areas there are still some contracts with the Roman Catholic Church. In some cases there are community schools financed by government transferences[27] and managed by indigenous organisations and councils.As Tomasevski (2004: 8) observes,

> the educational policies of the government weakened the right to education for the lack of guarantees for free public education for children in obligatory school age, at least. The Special Commission considers that it is important to emphasize (...) the difference between education as a product and education as a human right.[28]

We would argue, based on Tomasevski's (2004) report, that a full implementation of ethnoeducation, in which bilingualism and interculturalism are developed to advanced levels (secondary, higher education), is only possible if there are adequate financial resources. The stratification and the fragmentation of educational provision are even more dramatic at university level.

Some universities, both public and private, have special entrance requirements for indigenous students with low registration fees. However, this is still not very widespread and does not guarantee that specific cultural and language issues will continue to develop. In general, those who come from regions or from schools with a high Indian population are at a disadvantage when competing in university entrance examinations.

The bilingual teacher

The training and certification of indigenous teachers, the requirements for employment, and the conflicts generated in schools due to the presence of both indigenous and non-indigenous staff are evidence of the problematic nature of teacher training and development in these contexts. There are some interesting parallels which may be drawn with what happens in majority language contexts with respect to legal norms which regulate the employing of 'natives'. In both cases, it seems that this constitutes an exemption to the general rule and, in both cases, native-speaking teachers are seen as guaranteeing the efficiency of bilingual processes.

In the public sector, the changes in the teaching profession have had negative effects on the development of an ethnoeducation policy. As Tomasevski (2004: 18) observes,

> The teaching profession was changed by Law 715 and the New Teaching Statute, with an increase in the school day and the number of students per teacher, and the tying of the financing of schools and teachers to the results of their students in examinations ...

In the past, indigenous teachers were exempt from the requirement of being trained teachers, as decreed in the General Education Law (1994), and these teachers were able to take part in in-service training courses, where they received a certification which was valid for a limited time. Nowadays, these teachers need to fulfil a series of requirements in order to teach in ethnoeducation programmes. They are selected according to their knowledge of the following: customs, degree of understanding of their culture, ability to articulate the knowledge of other cultures, as well as the knowledge and understanding of the community language and Spanish (Article 11). There is no overt interest in the pedagogical and sociolinguistic knowledge necessary to teach languages. Nor is there an understanding of what it means to work with oral languages which have no written tradition and which are being used in the school for the first time.

In indigenous education, the lack of appropriate pre-service and in-service teacher education courses, and the fact that many Indian teachers have not kept up with or have rejected their community traditions, has led to resistance to the cultural and linguistic demands involved in ethnoeducation programmes. The issue of the profile of indigenous teachers, their characteristics and leadership, as well as their cultural conflicts and classroom practices, warrants further study. Some communities, especially in the south of the country, have already begun to work on this, as can be seen in studies carried out by Bomba (2000) and Ramírez (2004).

In majority language contexts, the Colombian Labour Law (Article 74C1) specifies that a maximum of 20% of teachers in any school may be foreigners brought into the country for the purpose of teaching in the school; the rest must be local. This ruling may be modified, by applying for permission to bring in extra teachers up to a limit of approximately 30% of the total staff. However, expatriate teachers living and working in Colombia are classed as local residents and therefore the numbers of foreign nationals working at any one time may be much higher than the 20% stipulated by the law.

As a result of this situation, there are three different categories of teachers who work in most bilingual schools. First, there is the privileged class of foreign teachers contracted abroad, usually in USA or Britain, in the case of English–Spanish bilingual schools. Then, there are foreign residents in Colombia, and finally there are a large number of Colombian nationals. There is a corresponding language continuum which goes from monolingual foreign language speakers, through bilingual speakers, to monolingual Spanish speakers. This differential in language proficiency is reflected in the areas the teachers work in. Generally foreign staff and national bilingual teachers teach Foreign Languages, Science, Maths and Economics in the foreign language, while Colombian monolingual staff teach Spanish language and literature, Physical Education, Art, Music and Religion in the first language.

Although many schools see foreign language monolingualism among the staff as an advantage, in that the teachers will not be tempted to use Spanish in their classes, this can lead to difficulties of communication, especially with children who are in the initial stages of becoming bilingual. In general, school administrators value foreign language skills more highly in their staff than knowledge of the first language and this is often reflected in differential rates of pay.

According to the General Law of Education (1994), all Colombian staff need to have a recognised qualification in education (Article 198). Foreign staff, however, may be hired if they are qualified in areas other than education (Article 199). Many of the latter have training and experience in the teaching of English and other subjects to first language speakers. Relatively few, however, have been trained to deal with foreign language speakers of English, and while there is some in-service provision given, this is generally insufficient.

In the case of language teachers, some bilingual schools require proof of foreign language proficiency of potential bilingual Colombian staff, such as the Michigan Test or the TOEFL, but this depends on the individual establishment. Few schools seem interested in what teachers know about the theory and practice of bilingual education, according to reports from graduates from the Postgraduate Diploma Programme in Bilingual Education at Universidad del Valle (1997). The focus of most bilingual schools is on the development of foreign language proficiency in the students and this is assumed to depend largely upon the level of the teachers' foreign language proficiency. Thus, other educational and sociolinguistic factors are generally not rated very highly by school administrators, reflecting, to a certain extent, the situation of bilingual teachers in Indian communities.

Considering the experience of many bilingual schools which contract foreign staff, it is important that schools which intend to become bilingual consider the implications of hiring foreign staff, whose presence, because of superior rates of pay and conditions, may cause division in the institution. While foreign expertise is often highly valued by both parents and school administrators as a sign of school status, foreign teachers are, in general, a transient population, who often do not have time to identify with the institution or its wider aims. The financial burden involved in hiring foreign staff often means that there are not sufficient financial resources for the professional and language development of the Colombian teachers. Furthermore, this dependence on foreign expertise has the disadvantage of potentially perpetuating a mentality of underdevelopment, in that foreign staff are often considered the principal purveyors of new ideas and methodologies.

Towards a National Language Policy

Paradoxically, much of the success of the private bilingual schools in Colombia is that there is, as yet, no national bilingual education policy. While this situation leads to potential negative consequences with regard to consistency and coordination of bilingual provision at national level, it also allows schools the freedom to adapt features of established models to their own needs and philosophies and thus to cater more appropriately to the wishes of their students and parents. As noted by John Whitehead, British Council English Language Officer in Bogotá in 1991, 'the differences between a private bilingual school in Bogotá (the capital) where English is taught at pre-Kinder level and a state school in Villavicencio (a provincial city in the underdeveloped southern Department of Meta) . . . is huge' (personal communication). This flexibility is very much in accordance with current educational thinking in the country, as reflected in the General Education Law of 1994, which gave educational communities the autonomy to develop their own Institutional Educational Projects, taking into account Ministry guidelines.

However, there is a need in each institution for a coherent school bilingual policy, which is incorporated into the Institutional Educational Project, where language distribution throughout the curriculum is justified both on academic and contextual grounds, and where the treatment of cultural aspects, from a multicultural, bicultural or intercultural perspective, is contemplated. As yet, very few bilingual institutions in Colombia have policy documents of this kind. There is, however, a recent research study, financed by the Ministry of Education and carried out by Universidad de los Andes in Bogotá, aimed at drawing up guidelines to ensure appropriate development of linguistic, cultural and educational aspects of bilingual school programmes in majority language contexts (de Mejía *et al.*, 2006b).

Although in majority language educational contexts the absence of a national policy involving all languages in play and the 'flexibility' of institutional documents may be seen as a relative advantage, which has lead to some productive experimentation, in minority contexts this flexibility, as well as the lack of follow-up, has helped produce some innovations, but has had negative results, in the long term, as ethnoeducation programmes need special treatment, or positive discrimination, to compensate for the linguistic fragility of minority contexts.

When there is no strong Indian organisation which can provide expert support and financing, the usual practice has been to give a space in the curriculum to ethnoeducation themes and leave the responsibility to the bilingual teacher, on the pretext that knowing the language and being a member of the ethnic group will be enough to guarantee that s/he will be able to innovate, research and transform contents and practices.[29] The lack of visible results in the teaching of the indigenous language in the school has led some parents to request the return of Spanish native-speaking teachers and to reject the ethnoeducation programmes which they used to defend.

Twenty years after the beginning of ethnoeducation programmes, the main achievements of this initiative are: the legal framework, programmes of teacher training, the contributions of the universities, research projects and the recognition by some Indian organisations of ethnoeducation as an educational priority (Cortés Lombana, 2000).

However, the State is the only organisation which can assume the task of putting the principles outlined in the Political Constitution into effect, and in order to do this, the State needs to be committed to the project and not leave it to private initiatives or to efforts of minority communities which are marginalised. Some notable exceptions are certain communities in the Andean and in the Amazon regions which have set up their own educational programmes with international financing and/or the support of NGOs, or with their own resources from government transferences. However, in general, private initiatives that have been successful in the majority language contexts have not worked successfully in minority bilingual education programmes.

That it is possible for the State to give serious support to minority group initiatives is proved by the example in Brazil of the 'National Indian Reference Curriculum' (MEC, 1998), which in more than 300 pages summarises pilot initiatives of indigenous education in all regions of the country and covering a wide range of topics. The problems and possibilities of work on Indian languages in different sociolinguistic contexts are treated in great detail. Although the linguistic diversity of Brazil is much greater than in Colombia and the number of indigenous inhabitants much lower, today, national efforts in this country to improve indigenous education are far more systematic than in Colombia.

In our view, quality bilingual education is possible for all types of educational institutions if they are not divided into first- and second-class establishments. The users of this ideal equitable scenario would be, in the first instance, speakers of Spanish who want to learn foreign languages (English, German, French, Japanese, Chinese, Arabic or Portuguese[30]) in order to improve their access to work in the globalised world. There would also be speakers of ethnic community languages, and speakers of Portuguese in border areas, who want to learn Spanish as a means of escaping from their marginalised existence and in order to increase their possibilities of social mobility. In addition, this would also involve speakers of a little spoken Indian language who are anxious to learn a more prestigious indigenous language, as well as speakers of 'prestige' languages who wish to learn an Indian or Creole language to enrich their intercultural and cognitive experience.

In this ideal world, bilingual education would not have any detrimental effects. Instead, there would be a focus on enrichment bilingualism (Hornberger, 1991) to ensure that Spanish is not learnt at the cost of ethnic community languages. The teaching of English would not displace the learning of Spanish, or Portuguese in the border areas, nor would the learning of the dominant Indian language in multilingual contexts prevent the learning of other, smaller indigenous languages.

Contributions and Gaps in Sociolinguistic and Ethnographic Research: The Role of Colombian Universities

Ethnographic classroom research and educational environmental research are important areas of development in multidisciplinary team work. In majority language contexts there have been studies carried out which show the achievements as well as the difficulties of ethnographic research in school and classrooms contexts (see studies by Araújo & Corominas, 1996; de Mejía, 1994; de Mejía & Tejada, 2001; de Mejía *et al.*, 2003, 2006a). However, there is also a need to strengthen research and teacher education in sociolinguistic issues arising from a vision of bilingualism as a sociological and cultural phenomenon.

A key condition for the development of successful and effective bilingual education programmes in Colombia, which has been recognised more clearly in the state sector than in the private domain, is the need for appropriate teacher training and development in this area. The traditional divide between language teachers and subject specialists needs to be bridged, either by team teaching arrangements or by qualifying bilingual teachers who are subject specialists and therefore able to teach content areas in two or more languages and who have an understanding of the basic tenets of bilingual education. As yet, bilingual teacher training and development programmes are in their infancy in Colombia, although the Postgraduate Diploma in Bilingual Education run by Universidad del Valle in Cali provides in-service training for teachers who are working in bilingual contexts.

In an attempt to help solve some of these difficulties, several Colombian universities have designed classroom-based, semi-distance and distance learning programmes aimed at training Indian teachers to work in community bilingual education initiatives. Mahecha (2002) refers to the opening of six teacher training programmes in ethnoeducation, or in similar areas, in Colombia between 1992 and 2000: Universidad de la Amazonia in Florencia,[31] a pioneering programme opened in 1992; Universidad del Cauca, and Universidad de la Guajira in the north of the country, in 1995; in 1997 la Universidad Tecnológica de Pereira; in 1998 la Universidad Pedagógica y Tecnológica de Colombia in Tunja developed programmes for the south-eastern Departments of Guainía and Vichada, as the result of an agreement with the Etnollano Foundation. In 2000, the National Open University (UNAD) began another programme in the isolated region of Guainía.

These programmes are aimed at training Indian community leaders and teachers. Private Roman Catholic universities, such as the la Universidad Pontificia Bolivariana in Medellín and the associated Anthropological Missionary Institute, have been organising distance learning teacher training programmes for indigenous teachers since 1994.

The General Education Law (1994) made it obligatory for teachers to be officially certified, and as a result, over the last six years, there have been numerous initiatives on the part of private universities to set up in-service distance professional development programmes for indigenous teachers, particularly in the Amazon region and other remote areas. However, in many of these programmes there is very little reference to ethnoeducation[32] issues.

Enciso *et al.* (1996) are among the few who have produced official documents, with the help of an agreement with the German GTZ organisation,[33] which have helped to diagnose the current situation by means of a pilot study. Other joint attempts by the Ministry of Education and indigenous organisations to produce diagnostic studies have not prospered, due to the incidence of the undeclared civil war in indigenous regions, as well as internal political problems. This has caused the national Indian organisations that have power to negotiate to turn their attention to other urgent issues. Tomasevski (2004: 19) maintains that,

> ... our knowledge is inversely correlated to the importance of the object under study. We know a lot about educational policy and legal requirements, but we know less about the teaching process and even less about the learning process ...[34]

All sectors would benefit from a close articulation between academic programmes concerned with education, independently of whether they are concerned with the teaching of Spanish, minority languages or foreign languages. If we are interested in a real sociolinguistic perspective, all these contexts form part of the issues involved in language and cultural policy.

The lack of sociolinguistic research is well documented in majority language contexts and is serious in minority contexts. Much of what happens in bilingual or multilingual classrooms and in the language communities is still a mystery and it is for this reason that the planning of successful initiatives is so difficult. In general, the processes studied up to now from a sociolinguistic perspective show a very close connection between the learning and attitudes towards languages and the conditions of conflict or harmony present in the societies and the cultures involved.

If we can learn anything from Indian education and the perplexing questions posed by the progressive abandonment of native languages by young indigenous people, or the almost miraculous conservation of these languages by some sectors of these minority communities, it is that it is not possible to separate pedagogical concerns from identity politics. It is not a question of finding a 'recipe' or a successful methodology. Bilingualism in Latin America is conflictive, whether we refer to the compulsive hispanisation (or lusitanisation) of the Indians and the Afro-Colombians, or whether we talk of the increasing influence of English as a language of prestige or discrimination for access to jobs and higher education opportunities and, in the long term, as a threat to the linguistic and cultural identity of the Spanish and Portuguese heritage.

Conclusions

It is important to recognise that as bilingual education programmes for majority and minority language speakers are concerned with language and cultural contact at regional, national or international level, it is necessary to develop positive attitudes towards difference and diversity among those involved in these programmes. Thus, we think it is time to remove minority education from the anthropological reserve, which may end up as a ghetto, and position it in the mainstream. It is to be hoped that there will be more equity between the educational provision offered to the majority urban elite bilingual programmes and those available to the rural ethnic minorities. As Hamel (this volume) says, the two systems and their actors need to get in contact in order to jointly construct an integrated field which is valid for a multicultural and plurilingual nation. However, as we have illustrated above, the lack of a common platform where these issues may be discussed has led to separate, atomised visions of what bilingual education is or should be. We maintain that there is an urgent need for a forum to discuss common concerns of research, policy and practice in bilingual education in Colombia and to promote joint initiatives between the various actors involved.

In this respect, it is useful to refer to the words of Canagarajah (2005: 195), who warns us that commonly perceived tensions between language policies and practices indicate that, 'language planning involves a constant negotiation of the interests of different social groups and the changing priorities of a community'. This author suggests that we are now moving towards 'a more localised orientation that takes ... tensions, ambiguities and paradoxes seriously to construct policies from the ground up, along micro social domains'.

We need to recognise that local sociolinguistic, ethnographic analyses carried out in the context of situation are vital to the effective implementation of any modality of bilingual education. As Baetens Beardsmore (1993: 140) acknowledges, it is important not to adopt 'any single model, no matter how well-tried, without the necessary modifications to specific local circumstances ... merely because the research background has proved (its) effectiveness in the context for which (it was) developed'. This is especially true if we remember the enormous complexity and diversity of sociolinguistic and historical situations involved in attempts to 'recover' native languages, in particular the case of languages spoken by a very small number of inhabitants.

The tensions noted in bilingual education constitute an opportunity for reflection in order to build bridges. As we have indicated, there is a great contrast in conceptions of the interrelation between language, culture and identity. In majority language contexts there is a tendency to emphasise instrumental visions, which often underestimate the complexity of these connections, while in minority contexts the topic of culture tends to be the centre of attention and there is less concern with pedagogical aspects related to efficient processes of teaching and learning of languages. From this point of view, each sector would benefit from a dialogue directed towards the appropriate valuing of the relationship between language and culture. It is also important to recognise that pedagogical understanding is a key means of helping in the revitalisation of vanishing languages. This interchange would constitute a first point of contact between these two traditions of bilingual education in Colombia.

The State cannot relinquish its responsibility for the protection of the constitutional rights of the ethnic minorities, nor can it leave the development of a national language policy and regional educational and language policies regarding all the languages present in the country to the vagaries of private initiatives. A national language policy needs to be constructed from the grassroots upwards, involving local and community organisations, and leading to effective actions and financial solutions. The pilot projects that have been carried out by universities, private institutions, NGOs and indigenous organisations are a point of departure toward this aim.

There are few actors currently involved in bilingual education in the country. In the future it will be necessary to involve all Colombians and to help them to understand that bilingual education needs to be seen from an integral viewpoint, closely bound up with cultural issues. The widening of linguistic and cultural options in equitable fashion is a great challenge. It is as important to look outwards as well as inwards, taking into account the need to belong to a globalised world which is full of local complexities.

Notes

1. There is, of course, a third space, not mentioned by Hamel – bilingual education programmes designed for the Deaf, involving Colombian Sign Language and Spanish.
2. 'Los dos sistemas se encuentran en los polos opuestos de la escala de desigualdad social extrema que caracteriza a nuestros países latinoamericanos, y sus actores casi nunca cruzan palabras o caminos.' Author translation of this and subsequent quotations in Spanish in the original.
3. En Colombia el concepto de 'educación bilingüe' hace referencia a dos situaciones diferentes. En primer lugar, la educación bilingüe y bicultural – llamada también etnoeducación – dirigida a las minorías étnicas (...) se trata aquí de la enseñanza de la lengua nacional mayoritaria – el español – a niños hablantes de idiomas de minorías étnicas, paralelamente al cultivo escolar de estos vernáculos. El contexto de esta modalidad es el de una base social más o menos amplia, en Colombia, tanto para la lengua mayoritaria como para la minoritaria.
4. La situación (...) es la de niños y jóvenes que son hablantes de la lengua mayoritaria y a quienes se les enseña intensivamente una lengua extranjera (...) que es también el vehículo total o parcial de la instrucción general. Pero esta lengua extranjera no tiene una base social en el país: es decir, no es el idioma de una parte de la sociedad colombiana.
5. ... salvo contadas excepciones – experiencias piloto de educación bilingüe e intercultural en regiones indígenas y algunos extranjeros en las principales ciudades del país, – la educación básica y media en Colombia se desarrolla con base en el español, es decir, con base en el manejo y uso del español como lengua materna del 93% de la población colombiana. Por lo tanto, no es posible hablar de bilingüismo en Colombia como problema generalizado.
6. Pocos son los nacionales que se han detenido a meditar cómo nuestra realidad social se ha caracterizado por un acentuado plurilingüismo y una pluralidad cultural, tanto en el pasado como en el presente. Esta singularidad, no puede continuar siendo objeto exclusivo de uno o dos estudiosos (...) debe trascender a las esferas oficiales (...) para que tenga un reconocimiento cada vez más claro y efectivo y constituya un elemento definido dentro de los marcos de su identidad cultural.
7. The definition of ethnoeducation most commonly referred to comes from the Colombian Political Constitution (1991, Art. 55), which states that 'Education for ethnic groups is offered to the groups and communities who are part of the Nationality and who possess their own autochthonous culture, language, traditions and privilege. This education should be linked to the environment, social and cultural processes, with appropriate respect for their beliefs and traditions.' ('Se entiende por educación para grupos étnicos la que se ofrece a grupos o comunidades que integran la nacionalidad y que poseen una cultura, una lengua, unas tradiciones y unos fueros propios y autóctonos. Esta educación debe estar ligada al ambiente, al proceso productivo, al proceso social y cultural, con el debido respecto a sus creencias y tradiciones.')

8. Or when there is the possibility of having intercultural education for minority groups without bilingualism, as happens with various indigenous communities whose first language today is Spanish, and who are recognised as indigenous people because of their history, their traditional territory and some cultural practices.
9. Revalorar, en un programa educativo inter-cultural que reúne indígenas y no-indígenas, la herencia cultural de los pueblos indígenas en toda su diversidad 'étnica', cuando ésta se practica en condiciones de asimetría – dominación/sumisión – en las relaciones entre las dos partes a las que el término inter- alude, las sociedades indígenas y la sociedad envolvente, exige encarar las condiciones afectivas y cognitivas desde las que ambos tipos de actores, los indígenas y los no-indígenas, actúan y se expresan.
10. *The Summer Institute of Linguistics* is a North American missionary organisation of bible translation, which has intervened in minority languages all over the world. The organisation develops bilingual education programmes and has advised ministries of education in South America. Some of its scientific achievements have been recognised, however the institute has received frequent and constant questioning because of its proselytising activities. The organisation's web page is www.sil.org.
11. In reality, there are few areas where only two languages are used: one a minority indigenous or Creole language and the other a majority or dominant language, Spanish.
12. This is a large collective house, which is the traditional dwelling of some Amazonian Indian groups.
13. These sociolinguistic facts are extremely complex. See Gómez-Imbert (1991) for more information.
14. Another minority community that has begun processes of visibilisation and organisation is the gypsy community or the 'Rom community', which shares the situation of economic marginalisation.
15. A diferencia de muchos lugares del Caribe (Jamaica, Trinidad, Grenada, Guyana) donde coexisten la lengua inglesa – bajo la forma de inglés estándar caribeño – para efectos de la educación y las formalidades del Estado, y la lengua criolla para la comunicación cotidiana, en Providencia el espacio de la lengua inglesa ha sido gradualmente ocupado por la lengua española. Es probable, entonces, que esta falta de contacto entre la lengua criolla y su lengua lexificadora facilita aún más la interacción entre la lengua criolla y la lengua española.
16. diseñar y llevar a cabo una enseñanza del español que logre sus objetivos básicos – entre ellos, el manejo lingüísticamente correcto y socialmente apropiado de la lengua – y al mismo tiempo esté en armonía con la época en que vivimos: la 'sociedad de la información', el ciberespacio, la globalización.
17. Una visión ... que da cabida y promueve todas las manifestaciones culturales. Su desarrollo requiere una apertura hacia los aportes de la lengua estudiada y exige la garantía del conocimiento y apropiación de nuestra lengua y cultura.
18. Taken from the Report to the United Nations on the right to education. The report questions the fact that educational provision is not free, that there is a very low budget for education, there is emphasis on 'rationalising' policies and the reduction of expenditure, as well as educational and social exclusion and death threats made to teachers and trade union members in the educational sector.

19. La educación como un derecho cultural exige la afirmación de los derechos colectivos junto con los individuales (...) Una escolarización obligatoria, impuesta, puede ser violación de los derechos humanos por no cumplir con los criterios de aceptabilidad y adaptabilidad (...) La 'colombianidad' requiere combinar atención a la diversidad con aportes a la construcción de la identidad nacional.
20. These boarding schools were generally educational institutions run by Roman Catholic religious communities where students from different ethnic backgrounds and languages had to live together permanently during the school year. The language of communication was Spanish. Due to the high costs and the long distances to travel to and from their homes in the indigenous territories, students usually spent several years without seeing their families, until they finished their studies.
21. Although there are cases of temporary refusal of mainstream education, in general the communities cannot opt out of a system which guarantees access to society and the dominant languages.
22. This vision involves local knowledge, the construction of reality and the process of socialisation. The 'traditional' courses are not compartmentalised and systematised knowledge, but are based on a body of contextualised practices.
23. ... la búsqueda lingüística es inmediatamente una restauración ritual, en el nivel colectivo (...) el proyecto de recuperación lingüística cobra el carácter de proyecto político-ritual. La búsqueda de los vínculos con el pasado (...) es peligrosa y compleja (...) 'Recuperación' no puede ser (...) una simple fidelidad al pasado, una reconstrucción del código lingüistico, una réplica de los rituales. Recuperación significa primero que todo recreación simbólica ... No está en las normas de un lenguaje, de unas formas de cultura sino en la transformación de esas normas para que puedan volver a crear los objetos de la cultura – los bailes, el lenguaje mismo – y convocar en términos de las nuevas creaciones.
24. In Universidad Nacional and in other universities there are elective or optional courses on Indian language and culture or on indigenous knowledge with Indian teachers. Some private schools in Bogotá have also started to include pioneering curricular and extracurricular activities, such as courses on Indian languages and culture and field trips to Indian territories, hiring Indians as teachers or experts.
25. From the middle of the 20th century onwards, the rural areas of Colombia have suffered the effects of an undeclared civil war between the guerrilla movement, the army and paramilitary groups. Peasants and indigenous people constitute part of the displaced population, which according to Tomasevski (2004: 14) 'is estimated at 2.9 million people who have been forcibly displaced since 1985, and there are at least one million displaced school age children'.
26. En Colombia, la inversión pública en educación es igual que la privada, ambas representan cerca del 4% del PIB. Así pues, hay dos sistemas educativos paralelos en Colombia: educación pobre para los pobres y educación privada costosa para los ricos. Cerca del 30% de los alumnos están en la escuela privada en la primaria, 45% en la secundaria y 75% en la educación superior. (...)
27. As a result of decentralisation, the indigenous authorities directly manage state resources for investment. Due to the urgent need to respond to educational lack of resources or because of the impossibility of coming to an

agreement with local government officials, the Indians have set aside part of this money for the payment of teachers and the provision of resources for schools.

28. las políticas educativas del Gobierno debilitan el derecho a la educación por la falta de la garantía de la educación pública gratuita para la niñez en edad de escolarización obligatoria, por lo menos. La Relatora Especial estima importante destacar, como lo hace en cada informe anual, la diferencia entre la educación como mercancía y la educación como derecho humano.
29. These developments have been noted in the Tikuna Indian region of the Colombian Amazon area, in schools administered in the past by the Catholic Church and now by the local authorities.
30. Nowadays, the Brazilians are interested in learning Spanish as part of a national campaign, but there is no reciprocal interest in learning Portuguese in the rest of Spanish-speaking America.
31. Florencia is situated in the Andean mountains and is connected by road with the rest of the country. Communications between this area of access to the Amazon region and the Eastern areas are difficult, and are usually by means of long and uncertain river journeys. There are air connections with the rest of the country, but flights to the Amazon and Orinoco regions are infrequent, so that to travel to Leticia, Florencia and Mitú (the largest towns in this area) it is usually quicker to travel via Bogotá.
32. The control which the Ministry of Education should exercise over the programmes has not, in fact, been consistent. This is another example of the tendency to leave matters of national interest in the hands of private bodies. Indigenous teachers have to pay expensive registration fees to be able to be accredited as professional teachers, as no public institution offers general teacher education programmes leading to professional qualifications. This is different from what happens in the Amazon region of Brazil, where the the State made it obligatory for indigenous teachers to have a professional qualification, but provided the regional public universities with the necessary financial support to carry out these teacher education programmes.
33. German Technical Cooperation.
34. ... nuestro conocimiento es inversamente correlativo a la importancia del objeto de estudio. Sabemos bastante de las políticas educativas y de las leyes, pero sabemos menos acerca del proceso de enseñanza y menos aún sobre proceso de aprendizaje ...

References

Abouchaar, A. and Moya, S. (2005) Dominio de la lengua española entre estudiantes del grado quinto en la Isla de Providencia. In *Cuadernos del Centro de Estudios Sociales*, C.E.S. 9 (pp. 8–12). Bogotá: Universidad Nacional de Colombia.

Abouchaar, A., Hooker, Y. and Robinson, B. (2002) Estudio lingüístico para la implementación del programa de educación bilingüe en el municipio de Providencia y Santa Catalina. Número especial de *Cuadernos del Caribe N° 3*. San Andrés Islas: Universidad Nacional de Colombia.

Alarcón, D. (2001) Diagnóstico sociolingüístico del Amazonas, La Pedrera. M.A. thesis, Universidad Nacional de Colombia.

Appel, R. and Muysken, P. (1987) *Language Contact and Bilingualism.* London: Edward Arnold.

Araújo, M.C. and Corominas, Y. (1996) Procesos de adquisición del Inglés como segunda lengua en niños de 5 a 6 años, de colegios bilingües de la ciudad de Cali. M.A. Thesis, Universidad del Valle.

Aristizábal, S. (2000) Aproximaciones conceptuales a los modelos de conocimiento local. In *Memorias del Congreso de Etnoeducación*. Bogotá: Universidad del Cauca, Instituto Caro y Cuervo, CCELA. Universidad de Los Andes.

Baetens Beardsmore, H. (ed.) (1993) *European Models of Bilingual Education*. Clevedon: Multilingual Matters.

Bomba, J.D. (2000) Aspectos del uso del Nasa Yuwe y del Castellano en una escuela oficial en el Resguardo de San Lorenzo de Caldono, Cauca. Unpublished Monograph, Universidad del Valle.

British Council (1989) *A Survey of English Language Teaching and Learning in Colombia: A Guide to the Market*. London: English Language Promotion Unit.

Canagarajah, S.A. (2005) *Reclaiming the Local in Language Planning and Policy*. Mahwah, NJ: Lawrence Erlbaum Associates Publishers.

Cortés Lombana, P. (2000) Introducción. In *Memorias del Congreso de Etnoeducación*. Bogotá: Universidad del Cauca-Instituto Caro y Cuervo, CCELA. Universidad de Los Andes.

Crystal, D. (2000) *La Muerte de las Lenguas*. Cambridge: Cambridge University Press.

de Mejía, A.M. (1994) Bilingual teaching–learning events in early immersion classes; A case study in Cali, Colombia. Unpublished PhD thesis, Lancaster University.

de Mejía, A.M. (1996) Educación bilingüe: Consideraciones para programas bilingües en Colombia. *El Bilingüismo de los Sordos* 1 (2), 21–25.

de Mejía, A.M. (1998) Educación bilingüe en Colombia en contextos lingüísticos mayoritarios: Hacía una caracterización del campo. *Lenguaje* 26, 1–12.

de Mejía, A.M. (2002) *Power, Prestige and Bilingualism. International Perspectives on Elite Bilingual Education*. Clevedon: Multilingual Matters.

de Mejía, A.M. (2005) Bilingual education in Colombia: Towards an integrated perspective. In A.M. de Mejía (ed.) *Bilingual Education in South America* (pp. 48–64). Clevedon: Multilingual Matters.

de Mejía, A.M. and Tejada, H. (2001) Informe: Construcción de modalidades educativas bilingües en colegios monolingües de Cali. Gimnasio La Colina. Unpublished Research Report, Universidad del Valle, Cali.

de Mejía, A.M., Tejada, H. and Colmenares, S. (2003) Informe: Construcción de modalidades educativas bilingües en colegios monolingües de Cali. Colegio Sagrado Corazón de Jesús, Valle de Lilí. Unpublished Research Report, Universidad del Valle, Cali.

de Mejía, A.M., Tejada, H. and Colmenares, S. (2006a) *Empowerment. Empoderamiento y Procesos de Construcción Curricular Bilingüe*. Cali: Universidad del Valle.

de Mejía, A.M., Ordoñez, C.L. and Fonseca, L. (2006b) *Estudio investigativo sobre el estado actual de la educación bilingüe (inglés-español) en Colombia. Informe de Investigación*. Bogotá: MEN/CIFE.

Dieck, M. (1998) Criollistica Afrocolombiana. In L.A. Maya (ed.) *Geografía Humana de Colombia: Los Afrocolombianos*. Bogotá: Instituto Colombiano de Cultura Hispánica.

Enciso, P., Serrano, J. and Nieto, J. (1996) *Evaluación de la Calidad de la Educación Indígena en Colombia*. Bogotá: Ministerio de Educación Nacional y Deustsche Gesellchaft Für Technisches Zusammenarbeiten (GTZ).

Fagua, D. (2004) Diagnóstico sociolingüístico del departamento del Amazonas, Los Lagos: contacto y cambio. Universidad Nacional de Colombia, Facultad de Ciencias Humanas, Serie Encuentros (Tesis laureadas), Bogotá.

Friedemann, N. and Patiño, C. (1983) *Lengua y Sociedad en el Palenque de San Basilio*. Bogotá: Instituto Caro y Cuervo.

Gasché, J. (2001) El difícil reto de una educación indígena amazónica: alcances y abandonos. Paper presented in *Seminario de Educación en Contextos Multiculturales*. Universidad Nacional de Colombia, Sede Amazonas. Leticia.

Gómez-Imbert, E. (1991) Force des langues vernaculaires en situation d'exogamie linguistique: le casu du Vaupés colombien (Nord-ouest amazonien). *Cahiers des Sciences Humaines* 27, 535–559.

Gómez-Imbert, E. (2000) Lenguas indígenas de la Amazonia septentrional de Colombia. In E. González and M.L. Rodríguez (eds) *Lenguas Indígenas de Colombia*. Bogotá: Instituto Caro y Cuervo.

Hamel, R.E. (1994) Linguistic rights for Indian peoples in Latin America. In T. Skutnabb-Kangas and R. Phillipson (eds) *Linguistic Human Rights. Overcoming Linguistic Discrimination*. Berlin and New York: Mouton de Gruyter.

Hornberger, N.H. (1991) Extending enrichment bilingual education: Revisiting typologies and redirecting policy. In O. García (ed.) *Bilingual Education: Focusschrift in Honor of Joshua A. Fishman* (Vol. 1). Amsterdam/Philadelphia: John Benjamins.

Iriarte, G. (1997) Bilingüismo y sociolingüística. *Bilingüismo, Función Cognoscitivo y Educación*. Bogotá: Fondo de Publicaciones del Gimnasio Moderno.

Jamioy, J.N. (1998) Proceso de educación en el pueblo Camsá. In M. Trillos (ed.) *Educación Endógena frente a Educación Formal*. Bogotá: Universidad de los Andes, Centro Colombiano de Estudios de Lenguas Aborígenes.

Landaburu, J. and Echeverri, J.A. (1995) Los Nonuya del Putumayo y su lengua: Huellas de su historia, circunstancias de un resurgir. In: *La Recuperación de Lenguas Nativas como Búsqueda de Identidad Étnica* (1st edn). Bogotá: Centro Ediciones CCELA-UNIANDES.

Mahecha, D. (2002) Informe de las actividades para la estructuración y alimentación de una base de información sobre las entidades que adelantan programas de educación formal y no formal con población indígena en el departamento del Amazonas, con énfasis en la docencia. Documento impreso presentado a la Universidad Nacional, Sede Leticia.

MEC, Ministerio da Educação o do Desporto (1998) *Referencial Curricular Nacional para as Escolas Indígenas*. Brasilia: MEC.

Montes, M.E., Sánchez, E., Santos, A., Rojas, P. and Ramírez, H. (2005) Bilingüismo y contacto de lenguas. Estudios de caso sobre lenguas indígenas (yagua, quechua de Lamas, dialectos tikuna, sikuani, guajiro). Unpublished Research Report, Universidad Nacional de Colombia.

O'Flynn de Chaves, C. (1998) El Criollo Sanandresano. In L.A. Maya (ed.) *Geografía Humana de Colombia: Los Afrocolombianos*. Bogotá: Instituto Colombiano de Cultura Hispánica.

Pappenheim, R. (2002) Una aproximación sociolingüística al manejo de situaciones de inequidad lingüística. Universidad de Viena (mimeo).

Patiño, C. (2004) ¿Educación bilingüe? *Vigía del Idioma*. Bogotá: Academia Colombiana de la Lengua, 6.

Pérez Tejedor, J.P. (2007) Informe preliminar sobre bilingüismo en San Basilio de Palenque. In A.M. de Mejía and S. Colmenares (eds) *Bialfabetismo. Lectura y Escritura en dos Lenguas en Colombia*. Cali: Universidad del Valle.

Pineda, R. (1997) Política lingüística en Colombia. In X. Pachón and F. Correa (eds) *Lenguas Amerindias. Condiciones Socio-lingüísticas en Colombia* (pp. 155–176). Bogotá: Instituto Colombiano de Antropología e Historia, ICANH, Instituto Caro y Cuervo, ICC.

Ramírez, T. (2004) Factores de identidad étnica y profesional que afectan las prácticas de los docentes de zonas indígenas en contextos multiculturales (Silvia y Toribío). Unpublished Research Report, Universidad del Cauca, Colombia, Grupo GIGEC.

Rey de Castro, R. and Garcia, D. (1997) *Landmark Review of the Use of Teaching and Learning of English in Latin America. Colombia.* London: British Council.

Rey, L.L. (2001) Diagnóstico sociolingüístico del Amazonas, La Chorrera. M.A. Thesis, Universidad Nacional de Colombia, Bogotá.

Rodríguez, S. (2004) Diagnóstico sociolingüístico del Amazonas, zona ribereña (Mocagua, La Libertad, Ronda). M.A. Thesis, Universidad Nacional de Colombia, Bogotá.

Tomasevski, K. (2004) *Los Derechos Económicos, Sociales y Culturales. El Derecho a la Educación.* Informe de la Relatora Especial. (Misión a Colombia del 1° A 10 de octubre de 2003). Consejo Económico y Social, Comisión de Derechos Humanos. Naciones Unidas. February, 2004.

Triana, Y. and Antorveza, H. (1997) Factores que condujeron a la desaparición de lenguas indígenas. In X. Pachón and F. Correa (eds) *Lenguas Amerindias. Condiciones Socio-lingüísticas en Colombia* (pp. 85–154). Bogotá: ICANH-ICC.

Trillos, M. (1998) Conclusiones. In M. Trillos (ed.) *Educación Endógena frente a Educación Formal.* Bogotá: Universidad de los Andes, Centro Colombiano de Estudios de Lenguas Aborígenes.

Zuluaga, O. (1996) *La Enseñanza de Lenguas Extranjeras en Colombia en 500 Años.* Popayan: Taller Editorial, Universidad del Cauca.

Chapter 5
Staff Profiles in Minority and Prestigious Bilingual Education Contexts in Argentina

CRISTINA BANFI and SILVIA RETTAROLI

Introduction

Any review of the current literature on bilingual education shows clearly that there is a wide variety of bilingual education programmes around the world (Baker, 2001; Brisk, 1998; Cummins, 2000b; Moran & Hakuta, 1995; Roberts, 1995). The studies in question typically explain who the programme is aimed at, how it was developed, what its scope is, what the languages in question are, the results of the programme, etc. In this chapter, we have decided to focus on the people in charge of implementing these programmes, i.e. the teachers. We propose a preliminary exploration of the profile of teachers working on different types of bilingual programmes in Argentina, in the conviction that the teachers are a key component in the design of any educational programme. However, even if this statement may seem a truism to most, it is not unusual, in our experience at least, for bilingual programmes to be designed and set up without clearly defining *a priori* what the profile of the teachers should be, or even whether the individuals with such a profile exist.

A second aim is to explore the possible overlaps in the needs of (in-service) training of teachers which may lend themselves to becoming opportunities for collaboration and synergy across different bilingual programmes. We believe that a prerequisite for this sort of cooperation to be feasible is greater clarity about what profile teachers are expected to have and how they are supposed to attain this profile.

We will firstly describe the bilingual programmes currently in place in Argentina, as a backdrop to presenting the profiles of teachers who work within them. We then move on to discuss the profiles of teachers currently teaching in this kind of programme in relation to what has been said in the literature as regards the competencies required of teachers in bilingual programmes.

To contextualise the programmes described in this chapter we will present, on the one hand, some general considerations regarding the nature of bilingual education programmes and, on the other, some background information related to the education system within which the programmes described are inserted, making special reference to the teacher training programmes in place.

Theoretically speaking we adopt the broad definition of bilingual education provided by García (1997: 405) 'bilingual education involves using two languages in instruction' and, more specifically 'bilingual education is defined as education that aims to promote bilingual (or multilingual) competence by using both (or all) languages as media of instruction for significant portions of the academic curriculum' (Genesee, 2004: 548).

As regards the typology of bilingual education programmes, we adopt the classification provided by Baker (2001), which categorises programmes into weak or strong forms of bilingual education and along different parameters, i.e. typical type of child involved, language of the classroom, societal and educational aims, language outcome aims. In these terms, we would like to show that the programmes found in this region range between the models that Baker labels as Transitional, Mainstream with foreign language teaching and Mainstream bilingual.

Many authors have postulated the linguistic, academic and cognitive advantages presented by bilingual education (Baker, 2002; Cummins, 2000b; Hakuta, 1990). However, as Baker (2002) points out, bilingual education is not simply an educational issue, but rather an issue with significant political implications and the fact that bilingual education may be considered to have positive features does not necessarily mean that it will enjoy strong support.

Teacher Education in Argentina Today

The 1990s was a decade of reform movements in education in Latin America (on the development of the process, see Braslavsky & Cosse, 2006). Some of the reasons that drove the reforms included dissatisfaction with certain aspects of the system as it stood, e.g. high student repetition and drop-out rates, low number of classroom hours per day, 'poor quality' provision with respect to the official curriculum, poorly qualified and poorly paid teaching staff, minimal in-service training provision, and social inequity in the provision of education. The reform included the passing of new laws, the decentralisation of education provision, evaluation initiatives, data collection on outcomes of education and an increase in the number of years of compulsory education (see Nickson, 2001). Many of these initiatives were partly a product of external pressures on the governments of Latin America, linked to the provision or the withdrawal of financial support.

A positive outcome of the most recent reforms in Argentina, and the region as a whole, has been the increase in enrolment in education over the past four decades. However, this process has gone hand in hand with a process of deterioration of the teaching profession. On the whole, teachers in the region are poorly trained and badly remunerated.[1] The low salaries and poor working conditions have also entailed increased difficulties in the recruitment of new teachers (see Cámpoli, 2004). This has created a vicious cycle in which talented secondary school graduates aspire to any profession other than teaching, and posts are filled by candidates who would not succeed in other academic pursuits (see Kisilevsky, 1999, cited in Cámpoli, 2004).

As regards initial teacher training, there has been little change in provision of different options, although much in the way of declarations, agreements and even changes in degree titles. In this sense, as Cámpoli (2004: 5) points out, it is imperative to make a distinction between what the norms say and what happens in reality. Teachers in Argentina are trained at Teacher Training Colleges, which are tertiary institutions, and at universities. Both types of institutions are found in the private and state sectors. With over 90 universities and more than 1100 teacher training institutions, the sector exhibits a level of complexity almost unrivalled in the rest of the system. For the most part, teacher training programmes are within the public sector and do not require students to pay any kind of fee. A characteristic of these programmes is their great diversity in terms of degrees, as well as the outcomes in terms of standards achieved by graduates, as explained in a recent study (see Cámpoli, 2004).

Currently, pre-school and primary school teachers graduate from tertiary training institutions or universities after three years of study. They are trained to teach Spanish Language, Mathematics, Science and Social Sciences. Secondary school teachers take four year courses that are subject-specific (Maths, Biology, Spanish, French, etc.) at teacher training colleges or universities. In all cases, trainees take subject-specific and pedagogical subjects and all programmes have a practicum component. It is also possible to work as a secondary school teacher after having obtained a degree (e.g. Law, Medicine, Veterinary Science, History, etc.) and, in some cases, taking a supplementary course that covers the pedagogical component. Training courses for foreign language teachers are available in major world languages (English, French, Italian, Portuguese and German) and consist of 3–4-year programmes (primary/secondary). During this period candidates take courses which are generally taught in the language in question and which can be grouped into the following areas: linguistic development, cultural background, general and specific pedagogy, practice and observation.[2]

The most recent wave of reform has had an impact in further diversifying the denomination of teaching degrees available, but has not done away with the traditional degrees, still in existence (see Cámpoli, 2004).

Bilingual Education in Argentina

Bearing these considerations in mind, we will now proceed with the description of the bilingual education programmes currently in place in Argentina.

In the process of exploring the programmes and profiles of the teachers on bilingual education programmes in Argentina we found that the sources of information were, in general, very limited in quantity and in depth. In many cases we were forced to resort to journalistic renderings of the introduction of the programmes due to lack of official reports or other documentation setting out programme aims and objectives, the resources available, the description of the sociolinguistic situation, etc. For this reason, we have also resorted to our own practical knowledge of the local context, having had close contact with many of the programmes under discussion.[3]

The programmes

As in most other contexts, in Argentina the label 'bilingual school' is applied to a broad range of programmes that often have little in common and that typically do not have much contact with each other. In this chapter we provide a description of the programmes referred to as 'bilingual' in the region. However, as we know, and as Cazden and Snow (1990) cited in Baker (2001) have pointed out, bilingual education is a 'simple label for a complex phenomenon'. We have, thus, decided to include all those programmes termed 'bilingual', either in popular parlance or in their official denomination and will attempt to shed light on what kind of bilingual programme we are referring to in each case and the extent to which they can be considered bilingual. We also use the term 'programme' in the broadest possible sense, to describe a set of actions intended to organise the provision of a certain educational experience in the context of a particular institution or set of institutions. For the sake of brevity, we refer to them as Bilingual Education Programmes.

We will discuss the following programmes (for a summary of the information presented for each programme, see Appendix 1):

- Intercultural Bilingual Education Programmes for Indigenous Children,
- Bilingual Education Programmes for Deaf Children,
- Bilingual Education Programmes in State Schools,
- Bilingual Education Programmes in Language Contact Situations, and
- Bilingual Education Programmes in Elite Schools.

We should clarify at this stage that these are not necessarily the labels used by each of these programmes, but rather broad denominations that we have considered helpful for current purposes. We have, however, attempted not to stray too far from names that would be recognisable or understandable in each context.

Intercultural Bilingual Education Programmes for Indigenous Children

In spite of the fact that the 1990s was a period of new projects[4] in the field of bilingual and intercultural education in Latin America, it was not until 2004 that Argentina started to implement a model of intercultural bilingual education[5] (IBE) aimed at revitalising indigenous knowledge, language and identity.

A number of very different programmes can be considered under the general label of bilingual education in indigenous languages, or 'intercultural bilingual education (IBE) programmes' as they are broadly known in the region (see MECyT, 2004; also the conferences organised since 1985 *Congreso Latinoamericano de Educación Intercultural Bilingüe*[6]). Although the label 'bilingual school/programme' is widely applied in common parlance to a number of different types of programmes, it is only this modality that is granted official recognition, as exemplified in the recently approved Law of National Education in Argentina.

At the level of principles, the rights of indigenous groups to be recognised and have their language and culture respected are enshrined in the Argentine National Constitution,[7] the Federal Law of Education passed in 1993 and the new Law of National Education passed in 2006, which supersedes the Federal Law.[8] However, in practical terms the perception of indigenous people, taken from the most recent census,[9] is that only a small proportion of indigenous children are being taught in the indigenous languages. One can conclude that very little has been done to design educational policies to satisfy the specific needs of indigenous communities.

The IBE programmes range from those that serve communities where the language in question is alive, systematised to some degree and widely used in the community (e.g. Mbya-Guaraní, Mapudungun/Mapuche, Quichua and Wichi, as is shown for example by Intiman and Quintrel, 2004, for Mapudungun, and Jara, 2004, for Wichi) to others where the language is not currently used by the communities, and where, in many cases, there are no speakers left. In the latter case, the programmes aim at developing cultural awareness in the children of the community of their ancestral traditions. Therefore, indigenous school populations range from children who speak only an indigenous language and who are confronted with Spanish for the first time when they start school, to children who speak Spanish at home and have never been in contact with the indigenous language. Geographically, these

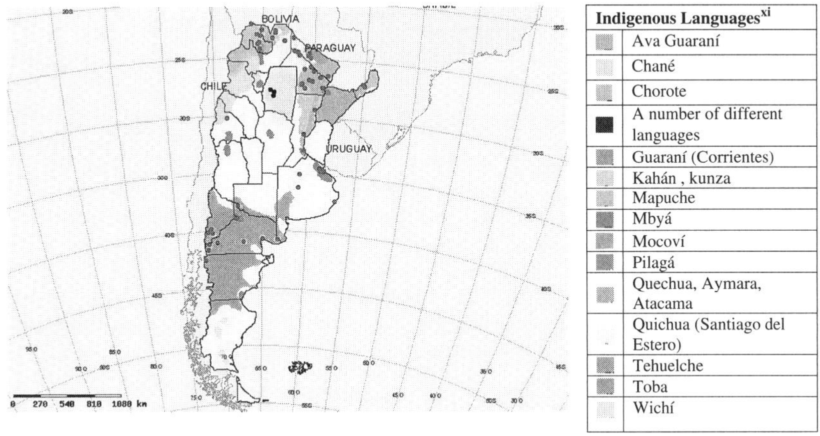

Figure 5.1 Map showing indigenous languages and IBE experiences
Source: Intercultural and Bilingual Education Map, Ministry of Education, www.mapaeducativo.edu.ar/pages/mapas/mecyt/?idatlas = 20. Accessed 16.3.07

programmes are usually found in the provinces where the indigenous communities have a numerically significant presence. The map below (Figure 5.1), produced by the Ministry of Education, shows the implementation of IBE in 2001.

In general, IBE programmes are found at pre-school and primary level in state schools, but rarely at secondary school level. One of the central aims of these programmes is to provide educational opportunities for these populations beyond the specific programme, i.e. insertion in the education system as a whole. As the broader education system is essentially monolingual in Spanish, this ultimately entails assimilation of the indigenous populations to the majority Spanish-speaking medium, if the pupils are to achieve educational success. Therefore, following Baker (2001), we may consider these programmes as Transitional.

Bilingual Education Programmes for Deaf Children

Bilingual education is upheld by many as the best option available for the education of the Deaf (see, for example, Bouvet, 1990; Grosjean, 2001; Mashie, 1995; Svartholm, 1993). Ideally, Deaf children develop Sign Language within early stimulation programmes and subsequently at school, where the curriculum is taught through the medium of Sign Language (Martin, 2001). Subsequently, the written form of the language spoken by the majority community is introduced (see McAnally *et al.*, 1999; Paul, 1998; Robertson, 2000).

In Argentina, programmes for Deaf children are found in a wide range of institutions such as:

- small urban institutions specifically for Deaf children;
- large schools for the Deaf whose origins date back to the oralist tradition;
- small groups of children integrated in ordinary schools with some kind of pull-out programme or with the aid of Sign Language interpreters; and
- Deaf children in special education schools that include children with different kinds of disabilities, etc.

These different programmes are found both in state and private institutions and the latter usually have access to government subsidies to cover part of their costs. This range of offers is compounded by the fact that there is no official provision of early stimulation programmes in sign language for Deaf babies, which clearly hinders their early development of Argentine Sign Language (*Lengua de Señas Argentina, LSA*). The situation of the children in programmes for the Deaf is often not ideal: most have had no access to LSA until they reach school and there, depending on the type of programme offered, they may have an opportunity of developing their sign language skills.

This means that there are various possible language scenarios when Deaf children arrive at school: some may have some sign language skills, particularly those who have genetic Deaf conditions and other Deaf relatives; others may have a smattering of Spanish, which is contingent on the level of hearing/deafness they have; and others may have no language at all, just rudimentary gestures used to communicate with their immediate family. Each institution is supposed to formulate their own *Proyecto Educativo Institucional (PEI)*,[10] taking into account factors such as those mentioned above. This accounts for the different organisational structures used, the timetables applied, the distribution of languages, etc. (Lapenda, personal communication, February 2007).

LSA has been used and continues to be used in classrooms to different extents, but its use has become more extended since the late 1980s and early 1990s, albeit in a rather 'intuitive' manner. There has been a decrease in the amount of translation between Spanish and LSA and more work has been carried out on the two languages as separate entities. This is all difficult to measure and assess as there are no official reports on the progress as yet, although there is a publication to appear under the auspices of the *Dirección de Educación Especial* (Lapenda, personal communication, February 2007).

One of the most important innovations recently introduced in schools in the Province of Buenos Aires is that the teaching of Spanish should be considered the teaching of a second or foreign language, not as a first language, in the case of Deaf children. In the province of Buenos Aires this notion was introduced as recently as 2005 and has entailed important changes, particularly with respect to the development of literacy skills in Deaf children (Lapenda, 2005).

Bilingual Education Programmes in State Schools

The early years of the 21st century have seen considerable development in the creation of bilingual state school programmes in the River Plate region, namely in the City of Buenos Aires.[11] As far as we are aware, these types of programmes are an innovation unique to the region, resulting from a conviction on the part of the education authorities that the educational system should provide the opportunity for the introduction of a foreign language to a population who would not otherwise have this possibility.

In Argentina the bilingual state school programme created in 2001 by the government of the City of Buenos Aires set out to provide foreign language tuition in the belief that the incorporation of a foreign language in the state-run schools, in particular those located in socially disadvantaged areas, would raise educational standards. Besides, there is an underlying assumption that introducing a foreign language at an early age, i.e. from the age of six, will help the pupils to find their way in different types of contexts, i.e. academically, in the job market, in life in general.[12]

Initially known as 'bilingual schools', the state schools that are participating in this programme in Buenos Aires are currently known as 'plurilingual schools'.[13] This was a government initiative with the support, and some funding, of foreign or international organisations such as The British Council,[14] and certain foreign embassies and publishing houses. The support involved is often in the form of resources and teacher training programmes. The plurilingual schools programme was implemented in schools in the city that have extended school days (*Escuelas de jornada completa*). Initially it was carried out in 12 schools: in six schools the foreign language taught was English; in two it was French; in another two, Portuguese; and in yet another two, Italian. Since then, the programme has grown in size and scope quite considerably, both through the increase in student numbers as the programme evolves in the first 12 schools, incorporating new cohorts, and by adding new schools, totalling 49 institutions in 2006 (see Figure 5.2 and Table 5.1 for details).

As part of this programme, the children are taught by two teachers. One of the teachers is the class teacher who teaches all subjects (Spanish, Science, Social Science and Mathematics) in Spanish. The other is the foreign language teacher who teaches the foreign language. Curricular content is not taught in the foreign language, therefore this programme should be more aptly considered an intensive foreign language programme rather than a bilingual education programme. According to

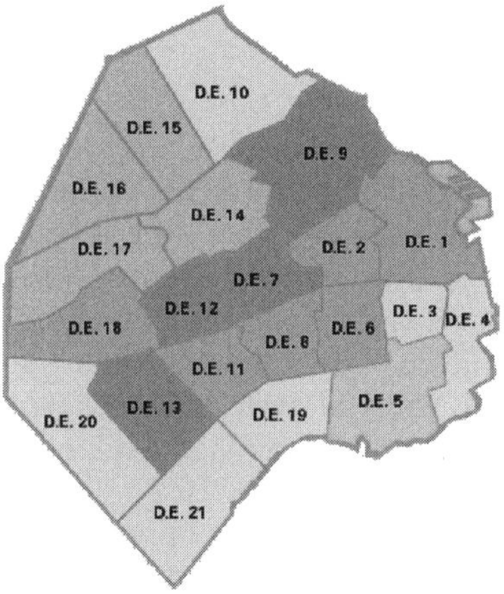

Figure 5.2 Map of the city of Buenos Aires showing the 21 School Districts (*DE-Distritos Escolares*). Data from 2006
Source: Escuelas Plurilingues, Ciudad Autónoma de Buenos Aires, www.buenosaires.gov.ar/areas/educacion/niveles/primaria/programas/bilingues/map_gif.php?menu_id = 11376. Accessed 17.3.07

Baker's (2001) typology, it should be considered a Mainstream programme with foreign language teaching.

Programmes such as the one described above can be implemented as initiatives or special programmes as the prerogative of the different jurisdictions (provinces and City of Buenos Aires) and, although other jurisdictions have expressed an interest in creating similar programmes, so far, no others have been started.

Bilingual Education Programme in a Language Contact Situation

The Brazilian–Argentine border regions, where natural boundaries such as rivers separate the respective communities, evidence a high degree of language contact. On the Brazilian side of the border, Spanish is seen as a foreign language or may even be considered a language of low prestige, as it is often associated with illegal commerce across the border. On the other hand, on the Argentine side of the border, Portuguese appears to have a greater and more positive influence. In the region there is a contact variety known as *portuñol*.

In 2001, Argentina and Brazil signed an agreement recognising two official languages in MERCOSUR, i.e. Spanish and Portuguese. In order to strengthen regional integration, a number of other cooperation agreements were signed which led to the creation of the *Programa Modelo de Enseñanza Común en Escuelas de Zonas de Frontera,*[15] a bilingual education programme which has set out to offer the Argentine children

Table 5.1 The districts of Buenos Aires where the bilingual schools are found. Data from 2006

	English	*French*	*Italian*	*Portuguese*
1	1		1	
2	1		1	
3	1			1
4	1		1	
5	1		1	
6	2	1		1
7	2	1		
8	1			1
9	1			
10	1			1
11	1			1
12	1		1	
13	1	1		
14	2	1	1	
15	1			
16	1			1
17	2	1	1	
18	1			1
19	2		1	1
20	1	1		
21	1			1
Total	26	6	8	9

Source: Escuelas Plurilingues, Ciudad Autónoma de Buenos Aires, www.buenosaires.gov.ar/areas/educacion/niveles/primaria/programas/bilingues/map_gif.php?menu_id = 11376. Accessed 17.3.07

in the region bordering Brazil the opportunity to learn Portuguese, while the Brazilian children have the chance of learning Spanish.

This programme was first introduced in 2005 in the provinces of Corrientes and Misiones, in the region bordering Brazil (see Armendariz

& Ruiz Montani, 2005, for a brief introduction to the programme). Besides Spanish and Portuguese and Portuñol, there are also some people who speak Guaraní.[16] This programme is now being implemented in the early stages of state-run primary schools in the region, and consists of the exchange of teachers who, literally, cross the border to teach in their twinned school in the other country. Table 5.2 shows which cities the schools participating in the project are located in.

According to Provincia de Misiones (2007), an important aim of the programme is to develop mutual understanding of the populations on both sides of the border, as well as additive bilingualism and biliteracy by means of bilateral intercultural curricular development. Among the other objectives are the teaching of Spanish and Portuguese in a standard variety which will allow the children to have access to the curricular contents (see Ortiz & Torres, 2006); the establishment of links with the children's families and with their communities to foster school–home connection; the act of relating with other bilingual programmes in the area (e.g. the Intercultural Bilingual Programme which promotes the teaching in Mbya Guaraní in Misiones) and last, but not least, the fostering of positive intercultural attitudes among the Argentine and the Brazilian pupils.

It is unclear so far whether curricular contents are actually taught as part of this programme. It would seem that the main aim of the programme is to provide tuition in the language of the neighbouring country and also provide an opportunity for intercultural exchange. If this is indeed the case, the programme should probably be considered Mainstream with foreign language tuition following Baker's (2001) typology.

Table 5.2 Names of the towns where the schools participating in the MECEF project are located

Province in Argentina	*Argentine city*	*Brazilian city*	*State in Brazil*
Misiones	Bernardo de Irigoyen	Dionisio Cerqueira	Santa Catarina
	Puerto Iguazú	Foz de Iguaçu	Paraná
Corrientes	Paso de los Libres	Uruguaiana	Rio Grande do Sul
	Santo Tomé	Sao Borja	
	La Cruz	Itaqui	

Bilingual Education Programmes in Elite Schools

The label 'bilingual school' is most widely applied to a large number of elite schools in Argentina, some of which date back to the 19th century. In this section, we follow de Mejía (2002: 45), when she defines elite or prestigious bilingual education as 'the whole range of programmes that provide bilingual education to highly educated, higher socio-economic status, usually majority-language speaking groups'. As de Mejía points out, even though the term 'elite' has negative associations, this type of programme makes 'a unique and valuable contribution to bilingualism in many parts of the world'.

As discussed in Banfi and Day (2005), the precursors among this group in Argentina originated as institutions set up by the different immigrant communities and have grown from that early stage to include children who have no ethnic connection with that immigrant group. Demographics have also meant that the vast majority of the children who attend these institutions speak Spanish at home and come into contact with the second language when they first start school. This type of school, particularly the Spanish–English bilingual schools, has grown considerably in number, and they have become far more international and less linked to a particular country. These are private institutions whose students come from the upper, upper-middle and middle classes. In this sense, and probably to a greater extent than any of the other programmes described, caveats in terms of self-selection factors apply, as indicated by Genesee (2004).

There are Spanish–English, –French, –German, –Italian bilingual schools that typically deliver a partial immersion bilingual programme (although this is rarely labelled as such by the institutions themselves). There is no control or regulation over the use of the label 'bilingual', so a large number of schools use the name quite liberally, as it has considerable appeal for prospective parents. Banfi and Day (2005) refer to the schools in this sector as 'Global Language Schools' and estimated the total number to be somewhere around 200, with around 120–150 in the growing Spanish–English subsector.

These programmes start as early as preschool and continue through to the end of secondary school. All content areas in the school curriculum are usually taught both in Spanish and in the foreign language. They comply with the local official requirements and the foreign curriculum is usually guided by an international or foreign standard and (some of) the students obtain the international qualifications associated with these (e.g. International Baccalaureat, IGCSE-A-levels, French *Baccalauréat, Abitur, Maturitá*).

There are also schools linked to the Jewish, Armenian, Japanese and Korean communities which teach Hebrew, Armenian, Japanese and Korean. Many of them present themselves as trilingual (i.e. teaching

Spanish, the language in question and English).[17] These schools do not have partial immersion programmes as such but, instead, teach the languages in question as a means of accessing the cultures involved.[18] They are often linked to ethnic communities.

If we apply Baker's (2001) typology to this type of school, we conclude that this is a case of Mainstream bilingual education.

The Teachers

In this section we shall briefly describe the teacher profiles of those in charge of the different programmes with the aim of getting closer to defining their professional identity.

In spite of the fact that the last decade has witnessed the creation of a number of Intercultural Bilingual Education Programmes for Indigenous Children in a few provinces, there is a growing concern about the lack of expertise among the teachers in charge of implementing these programmes (Hirsch, 2003). They are preschool and primary school teachers with no specific training for the context or in the language beyond their own interest and motivation (see Gualdieri, 2004).[19] Aranda *et al.* (2004: 46) clearly state, '... the teachers do not speak the mother tongues of the indigenous populations which means that communication problems constitute the main cause of pupil dropout.'

A figure that is supposed to fill the gap in communication between the teacher and the pupils is that of the indigenous language assistant. More often than not, these assistants do not have any preparation for this role beyond the most basic, often unsuccessful, schooling. Some authors, such as Aranda *et al.* (2004), go as far as saying that there are practically no properly trained and appointed bilingual teaching assistants.

There is only one teacher training college that provides initial teacher training for intercultural bilingual teachers.[20] There are a few other colleges that train teachers for preschool or primary, which have included in their curricula one or two subjects to raise awareness about intercultural matters (see Acuña, 2003). These in-service courses rarely take into account diversity in the different sociolinguistic contexts and neither do they delve into the study of the indigenous languages' semantics, phonology or syntax (see Hirsch, 2003).

Most practising teachers on Bilingual Education Programmes for Deaf Children have not had any courses in LSA as part of their formal training. Even in the late 1980s, the use of LSA was not positively regarded at teacher training institutions (Lapenda, February 2007). The training of Special Needs Teachers (*Profesor en Educación Especial*) used to be generic for different kinds of disabilities and have a paramedical bias. This has changed in recent years, with a more pedagogical approach characterising the training programmes. The current teacher training programme for teachers of the deaf in the Province of Buenos Aires, *Profesor en Educación Especial en Discapacidad Auditiva*,[21] does include LSA classes and courses on how to teach language and sign language, as well as courses in linguistics and sociolinguistics, but as only a few cohorts of teachers have completed this programme, it is difficult to assess what impact this training will have on the ground.

One innovation that has much improved the situation for Deaf children in schools has been the presence of Deaf adults, who play the role of language informants as well as adult role models for the children, who have few opportunities for contact with Deaf adults in their daily life. Their role is parallel to that of the indigenous language assistants and their function can vary considerably depending on personality and other factors. These initiatives are far from comprehensive in the system as a whole and are usually supported and financed by the local community. In some contexts, interpreters are available to interpret lessons for deaf children, particularly at secondary school level. However, and despite advances in this area, the educational outcomes of Deaf children are far from what could potentially be expected.

In the plurilingual schools of Buenos Aires, in the Bilingual Education Programmes in State Schools discussed in this paper, the class teacher is a qualified primary teacher, whereas the foreign language teacher is a qualified foreign language teacher in the relevant language. Before starting to teach on the programme, the foreign language teachers must attend a one-month training course which introduces them to the plurilingual modality. The training course consists of face-to-face meetings with teacher trainers, with tutors, class observations and a formal evaluation to be carried out individually in writing.[22] As far as we are aware, the primary school teachers, who teach in Spanish, do not receive any specific training to teach on this programme. The programme aims at establishing coordination between staff members teaching in the different languages; however, AGCBA (2004) reports that there is no evidence of such coordination in practice.

The teachers involved in the Bilingual Education Programme in a Language Contact Situation (between Argentina and Brazil) are primary school teachers. In their own countries, each teacher teaches the prescribed curriculum to their pupils in the teacher's own language, i.e. Spanish and Portuguese respectively. When they cross the border, the Argentine teacher teaches Spanish to the Brazilian pupils and the Brazilian teacher teaches Portuguese to the Argentine children. According to Ortiz and Torres (2006) this programme promotes the teaching of Spanish and Portuguese by primary school teachers, rather than by foreign language teachers. However, in neither country are these teachers trained to teach a L2 before participating in the programmes.

The teachers who teach in Bilingual Education Programmes in Elite Schools vary as much as the existing schools and programmes. Below, we present a description of some of the profiles which characterise most teachers within this sector. As in every case, exceptions to the rule can be found.

A few schools, usually the oldest and largest ones, have a small number of contract staff who are either provided by the government that partially supports the institution[23] or via private contracts. These teachers are typically native speakers of the foreign language in question, who hold teaching degrees in their country of origin. According to the regulations, teachers teaching a given subject in the foreign language and within an officially recognised bilingual programme should hold a degree in the subject, as well as being able to accredit a degree of proficiency in the foreign language. In this subgroup of teachers we find Mathematics, Physics and History teachers, but also veterinarians who teach Biology, lawyers who teach History and engineers who teach Maths. These teachers have usually learned the language they teach in as a consequence of having attended one of these bilingual schools themselves and/or because they are part of the relevant community.

Another group of teachers typically found within these schools are local foreign language teachers, who teach the language in question or an assortment of subjects that may or may not have been part of their initial training. Some examples include: Literature, History and Geography. Other subjects occasionally taught by foreign language teachers include: Business Studies, Economics and, more rarely, the Sciences. Another segment of the teaching population that can be found in a number of elite bilingual schools are individuals who do not hold official qualifications as a teacher, but who are typically alumnae of the school, a native speaker of the language by virtue of being a member of the relevant community. Finally, there is the group of teachers who teach the subjects taught in Spanish, i.e. those that are part of the official requirements, and who make up approximately half the teaching staff of each school. They are usually locally qualified teachers in their subject of expertise and usually only speak a little of the foreign language taught in the school.

Areas of Convergence across Bilingual Programmes

Having described the different bilingual programmes in existence in Argentina in some detail and the profiles of teachers involved in them, we will now look at those areas that can help towards analysing possible points in common between minority and prestigious bilingual programmes. To this end, we will firstly look into the relative power relation of the languages involved in the different programmes, as this has a clear impact in the practice of the programmes. We will then concentrate on the areas of knowledge that teachers and other staff members on bilingual programmes require. Our interest in these stems from the fact that we believe that the induction into these areas through teacher training and development are an ideal arena for possible synergy actions across the different types of programmes.

Languages of power and the power of languages

The descriptions above call for the review of certain sociolinguistic factors that have an unavoidable impact on the implementation of the different kinds of programmes described.

An initial distinction that we need to draw is that of the situation of minority and endangered languages, on the one hand, and of majority or global languages, on the other (on the education of minority language students, see Baker, 2000; Cummins, 2000a; Skutnabb-Kangas, 2000; on that of majority language students, see Genesee, 2004). If we classify the programmes described above along these lines, we see that the indigenous language programmes, and the bilingual programmes for Deaf children, fall in the former category, whereas all the other programmes fall in the latter.

Even though indigenous languages have received constitutional and legal recognition, they have not, as in other countries of the region, been awarded official status. The case of Argentine Sign Language is even less auspicious, with only some recognition at the provincial level. As Dorian (2004: 437) states, 'the consequences, for speakers of languages without official status, amount to a sharp power differential, both linguistic and social', and this is clearly reflected in the status and possibilities of the bilingual programmes aimed at the different populations. In these cases, together with the central aims of the bilingual programmes, whether stated explicitly or implicitly, it is the learning of Spanish and the development of literacy in this language. Although certain authors, for example, Gualdieri (2004), indicate that bilingualism and biliteracy should be the desired aims, practitioners still consider the *castellanización*[24] of the pupils in question a successful outcome (see Jara, 2004). Cazden (1992), as reported in Faltis (2002: 282), points out that 'schools that operate from this assimilationist perspective typically have very few literacy materials available in the bilingual learners' native languages, and teachers tend to have low levels of proficiency in the students' native languages', situations which, as we have described, are instantiated in both the case of indigenous and sign languages. In both these types of programmes it is unclear whether the language experiences in the two languages are differentiated in the classroom, given the fact that there is a single teacher and a language assistant in the best of cases. If we agree with Bialystok (2004: 596) that there is a 'necessity of having experiences in each of the languages separately to develop specific skills in those languages', this is clearly an unsatisfactory state of affairs.

In the case of Deaf students, great emphasis is also placed on the development of literacy skills in Spanish, as well as the development of skills such as lip-reading, and the maximisation of hearing skills where there is residual hearing. In recent years, though, more interest has been allocated to the development of sign language as a language in its own right, not just as a transitional means of communication, but also as a means of transmitting curricular contents. However, provision is limited and not systemwide. This means that there is a clear danger in these cases that the children's mother tongue (or most accessible language) will have limited or no development in the school context (and probably anywhere else), thus posing a major threat to its future for the individual as well as the community.[25] Taking these factors into account, these programmes should probably be characterised as Transitional according to Baker (2001), a weak form of bilingual education that generally leads to relative monolingualism rather than bilingualism.

In contrast with this situation, the other three types of programmes described i.e. Bilingual Programmes in Language Contact situation, Bilingual Programmes in State Schools and in Elite Schools, can be said to aim at providing educational enrichment for majority children, by helping them to develop second or foreign language skills in languages that have international and/or regional recognition and political and economic relevance (see Baker, 2002). This has practical implications in terms of the availability of trained teachers, teaching materials, etc. It is rarely, if ever, the case that the children's native language is in any way threatened by this type of programme,[26] not only because there is explicit support for it within the programme itself, but, mainly, because we are talking about a language which is a global language in itself, i.e. Spanish. Perhaps even more importantly, it is the sociocultural recognition of such programmes as something to aspire to that lends them firstly, prestige and, subsequently, additional resources. The languages in question are not invested with official status in the country, but are official languages of many other (powerful) countries around the world. One of them, i.e. Portuguese, does have official language status at the regional level through Mercosur.[27] Further recognition is accorded to these languages in terms of their long-standing educational tradition. Foreign language teachers have been trained in Argentina since the early 20th century (see Banfi & Moyano, 2003). In those days, teachers were trained to teach English, French, German and Italian.[28] Later, Portuguese was added.

It is obvious from these examples that, as Faltis (2002: 285–286) points out, 'the languages of bilingual learners are not neutral. Societal and community forces, as well as teacher's ideologies about language and learning, carry with them socio-historical dimensions about the usefulness and power of a bilingual learner's two languages.'

Summarising, and applying Baker's typology to the programmes described for Argentina, we can postulate the categorisations as shown in Table 5.3.

The Profiles of Teachers in Bilingual Education Programmes: Some Propositions for Teacher Education

Different authors have indicated that teachers in Bilingual Education Programmes need appropriate teaching certificates or credentials, including bilingual and/or EFL credentials, appropriate content knowledge, classroom management skills, suitable instructional strategies and training in bilingual education (Cloud *et al.*, 2000; Lindholm-Leary, 2005; Met & Lorenz, 1997). Lack of background in bilingualism and in bilingual education, a very common feature of bilingual education worldwide, can lead to the poor development of programme structure, curriculum and instructional strategy choices (Lindholm-Leary, 2005).

According to Baker (1995: 203), 'one problem in bilingual education is that there is little teacher training for working in bilingual schools and bilingual classrooms. In the majority of teacher training courses, even in bilingual countries, there are few courses that prepare teachers for educating bilingual children.' This situation is exemplified in the programmes described in this chapter. With the exception of the CIFMA programme for the training of intercultural bilingual teachers for indigenous language contexts, there are no specific initial teacher training programmes in Argentina that train teachers to teach in Bilingual Education Programmes.[29] Generally speaking, teachers teaching within bilingual education programmes hold an initial teacher training qualification and subsequently engage in some kind of in-service professional development activity that is more or less specifically linked to the bilingual nature of the programme they teach in. These activities may be provided by those responsible for the programme (the government or the private school) or other organisations.[30] There is wide variation as to whether the activities are compulsory or optional for teachers and, in many cases, the teachers take part in these activities in their own time and at their own expense.[31]

The question one should ask oneself, of course, is: what is the specific training that teachers in bilingual education programmes require to be able to perform their task competently? Shulman (1987: 8) proposes that the knowledge base of teachers, all teachers, includes seven basic components: content knowledge, general pedagogical knowledge, curriculum knowledge, pedagogical-content knowledge, knowledge of learners and their characteristics, knowledge of educational contexts and

Table 5.3 The application of Baker's typology to the programmes under study

Bilingual programmes in Argentina	*Type of programme*	*Typical type of child*	*Language of the classroom*	*Societal and educational aim*	*Aim in language outcome*	*Weak/strong form*
Intercultural Bilingual Education Programmes for Indigenous Children, Bilingual Education Programmes for Deaf Children	Transitional	Language minority	Moves from minority to majority language	Assimilation	Relative monolingualism	Weak
Bilingual Education Programmes in State Schools, Bilingual Education Programmes in Language Contact Situations	Mainstream with foreign language teaching	Language majority	Majority language with L2/FL lessons	Limited enrichment	Limited bilingualism	Weak
Bilingual Education Programmes in Elite Schools (BEPES)	Mainstream bilingual	Language majority	Two majority languages	Maintenance, pluralism and enrichment	Bilingualism and biliteracy	Strong

knowledge of educational ends. According to CAL (1974), the ideal bilingual teacher should have competencies and knowledge in the following areas: personal qualities, language proficiency, linguistics, culture, instructional methods, curriculum utilisation and adaptation, assessment, school–community relations and supervised teaching. Obviously, these areas of expertise are applicable to teachers in all kinds of programmes, not just those that are bilingual in nature; however, the specificity of the context should have an impact in every one of the areas mentioned.

Teaching in a bilingual programme requires specialist training in immersion pedagogy, curriculum, materials and resources, and L2 and target language assessment. This must include pre-service and ongoing in-service in: bilingual theory and research, the bilingual programme model the school follows, second language acquisition and development, instructional strategies in second language development, multicultural training and cooperative learning strategies, among others (May *et al.*, 2004).

Subsuming, and somewhat simplifying these areas, we would like to propose the following five areas of knowledge base for teaching in bilingual programmes. We believe that these teachers should have knowledge of and competencies in:

- the languages involved in the programme,
- the cultures involved in the programme,
- the content to be taught,
- pedagogical knowledge, and
- bilingualism and bilingual education.

In the following sections we will discuss each one of these areas in turn.

Language competence of the teaching staff

In bilingual programmes, it is desirable that teachers should at least have a high level of the language they are expected to teach in and some knowledge of the other language. The idea that two sets of monolingual teachers should teach within bilingual programmes, assuming that they are, individually, better models of native speakers, ignores the fact that the pupils are bilingual and that there is much to be gained from drawing comparisons and making links between the two languages. Besides, this idea of the two co-existing monolingual worlds does not allow for much interaction or collaboration between staff members.

The proficient use of the two languages in question is hardly even seen as an issue with regard to staffing in any of the bilingual programmes described in this paper (for a detailed summary of the situation in each programme described in this paper, see Appendix 2). This often leads to a situation in which two sets of monolingual speakers co-exist in many of the bilingual programmes described. This is the case in Bilingual Education Programmes for Indigenous Language Children, Bilingual Education Programmes for Deaf Children[32] and contract teachers in Bilingual Education Programmes in Elite Schools. Alternatively, there is the case where one set of teachers is monolingual and the other is bilingual, but is strongly identified with one of the languages, thus still creating a two-camp school. This is the case with Bilingual Education Programmes in State Schools, Bilingual Education Programmes in Contact Situations and Bilingual Education Programmes in Elite Schools.

Metalinguistic awareness

Genesee (2004: 571) points out that 'while functional use of the target language is generally effective at promoting L2 proficiency, instructional strategies that systematically raise awareness of and create opportunities for students to learn specific linguistic forms that serve their communicative needs and goals can extend L2 learning.' For this type of strategy to be used, teachers need to develop awareness of language processes themselves. As many studies have recently shown, it is not sufficient for teachers to have a proficient use of the languages in question. They should also be capable of metalinguistic reflection in order to interpret the process their pupils go through and be able to guide them appropriately (see Adger *et al.*, 2002 and Fillmore & Snow, 2000 on what teachers need to know about language). According to Cummins (2000a), it is of utmost importance when teaching specific aspects of academic registers in both languages and when promoting students' awareness of language and how it works.

Teachers who teach in Spanish have generally had some metalinguistic reflection in their training in teaching Spanish as a first language. As regards the other languages involved in these programmes, very few of the teachers involved have had metalinguistic reflection as part of their initial training. For a detailed summary of the language and metalinguistic skills of the different teachers involved in all the programmes, see Appendix 2.

Bearing in mind the above, it is our recommendation that all teachers in Bilingual Education Programmes should have access to developing metalinguistic awareness as part of their initial, pre- or in-service training.

The cultural dimension

If we agree with Baker (2001) that bilingual programmes should aspire to develop bicultural competencies in pupils, the teachers who teach them should be familiar with the cultures involved, as well as incorporating intercultural reflection in their teaching.

From an anthropological or sociological perspective, culture can be defined as the attitudes, habits and daily activities of a people, their ways of thinking, their values, their frames of reference (Valette, 1986). Within this broad interpretation of the notion of culture in relation to education, we believe that teachers who teach within bilingual/bicultural programmes should develop awareness of the following cultures interacting as part of the programmes:

- the culture of the students (which may be different from that of the teacher(s)),
- the culture of the teachers (which may be different as well from that of the students),
- the cultures of the speakers of each language involved,
- the relation between language and culture, and
- the school culture.

There is usually an assumption that students and teachers share the same culture. The lack of recognition that cultural backgrounds may well be very different often leads to miscommunication and misunderstanding. Specific reflection and comparison of the cultures associated with the native language of the students and the second language learnt in the school context should lead to fruitful learning opportunities. For the teachers to be able to generate situations where this occurs, they should themselves have had access to intercultural reflection instances. Ipiña Melgar (1997), in his analysis of IBE, believes that personal as well as professional development is called for, to enhance the teacher's intercultural understanding. A further element to take into account is that of the contrast between the school and the pupil's culture, which is present in every educational situation, but particularly poignant in the case of minorities and bilingual education.

Knowledge about the different cultures that interact in bilingual education classrooms seems to be lacking in the different groups of teachers who are implementing this type of programme in Argentina. Traditionally, in foreign language initial teacher training courses, the 'culture' element included the learning of geography, history, the social sciences and the arts of the foreign language culture.[33] In the case of mainstream pre-school, primary or secondary teacher training, however, little, if any, reference is made to cultural notions along the lines proposed above.

The content to be taught

The content to be taught in a particular educational programme is intrinsically bound up with the culture of that programme, i.e. what is relevant to one society, and therefore worth including in the school curriculum, and which may or may not be relevant to another society.

A Bilingual Education Programme should take this duality into consideration both in its design and the training of its teachers. If teachers are not familiar with the content and the outlook dominant in the particular society, they can hardly be expected to teach it. A topic such as 'the environment' will be dealt with in very different ways in different societies. Another clear case in point is the teaching of history from a particular standpoint. Even in subjects as 'objective' as mathematics, the outlooks, contents and techniques used may differ from one society to another.

In the case of the teachers in charge of the IBE programme, they should be able to handle anthropological concepts, such as cultural change, racism, prejudice and discrimination, and gender in education. The knowledge of these concepts can help IBE teachers understand diversity and culture change and impart intercultural education. Another case in point is that of foreign language teachers who end up teaching content area subjects in elite Bilingual Education Programmes. Where it may well be true that they took history or geography courses as part of their training, this was generally not aimed at teaching the discipline. In the majority of the other programmes described, the teachers, being qualified teachers, handle the content of the areas to be taught, whether the subject area belongs to the Sciences, the Arts, Social Studies or any other. Thus, they often lack knowledge of the discourse, the text types and probably the specialised language used by the speakers of the other language when studying the areas taught. This is the case of the teachers who teach in the MECEF schools; and, to a lesser extent, the teachers in elite schools and in plurilingual schools in the City of Buenos Aires. The IBE teachers do not usually teach subject area content in the indigenous language and, thus, do not need specific training in these areas. In the case of teachers who teach Deaf pupils, there is little awareness of the need for specificity of Sign Language discourse when dealing with different disciplines.

Pedagogical knowledge

Teaching in a bilingual education programme has some elements in common with other kinds of teaching. In fact, bilingual education, as is the case of general education, is likely to succeed when quality of instruction is assured on a day-to-day basis, including quality of materials among others (Genesee, 2004). However, there are also certain specificities that impact on the way the teaching is carried out.

The possibilities for integration and collaboration of the different teachers involved, the use of materials in one language and the other are all areas worth exploring by teachers. Skills related to materials design should also be an important component of the profile of teachers in Bilingual Education Programmes, given the dearth of such materials and the general reliance on teachers to create their own materials. Pedagogical orientation has a crucial role to play in bilingual education. As Faltis (2002: 283) puts it, 'Within both assimilation- and cultural pluralist-oriented bilingual classroom settings, [...] a teacher's pedagogical orientation and the way he or she uses language in the classroom can also have a bearing on how, and how well, learners become bilingual.'

The teachers in the programmes described in this chapter, being qualified teachers, have the necessary pedagogical knowledge to work as teachers in any type of context. Yet there seems to be a gap in their knowledge as regards the specificities mentioned above in relation, for example, to the design of teaching materials for the teaching of contents in a language other than the students' or the teachers' mother tongue. The absence of skills related to materials design when faced with a L2 learning process makes these teachers' work difficult, especially when there is no material available. This is particularly striking in the case of programmes such as those for indigenous and deaf children and the language contact programmes, where no specific materials are available. In most of the other programmes, even though there may not be specific materials, there are many resources teachers can turn to and adapt without too much difficulty if they have the training and skills necessary for this task.

Bilingualism and bilingual education

Given that there are no specific actions related to the training and professional development of teachers in Bilingual Education Programmes, it is not surprising that the overwhelming majority of them do not have any kind of training in bilingualism and bilingual education.

We maintain that it is important for teachers to have knowledge of bilingualism at the individual and social levels so that they may be able to understand the process that their pupils are going through in their development as bilingual individuals, as well as reflecting on their own reality as bilinguals. On the other hand, in order for them to understand the kind of programme they are teaching in, its aims and outcomes, they need to be familiar with studies of bilingual education.

A basic course on bilingualism which encompasses linguistics, psycholinguistics and sociolinguistics perspectives may give those teachers teaching in Bilingual Education Programmes the opportunity to explore the linguistic, social and cognitive implications of bilingualism in the individual and in the social groups where the languages in question are spoken. By dealing with issues concerning the kinds of representations and processes that bilingual speakers use in order to produce and comprehend different languages (Dewaele, 2003), the teachers will be able to examine bilingualism and bilingual education from the perspectives of second language acquisition and sociocultural theory. Moreover, a course on bilingual education can help the teachers focus on issues of second language acquisition including pedagogy and research, intercultural communication, alternative research methodologies and educational foundations.

In Argentina, in spite of the fact that there are pre-service and in-service professional development courses for teachers implementing the bilingual programme in state-run schools in the City of Buenos Aires and for bilingual teachers in elite schools, this component is almost completely absent in the bilingual programmes for indigenous and deaf children. And although there have been attempts at organising teacher development seminars for the teachers participating in the bilingual programmes in language contact situations, there are no records of any systematic in-service programme.

Table 5.4 summarises the information provided above about each type of bilingual education programme and how the teacher profiles relate to the five proposed areas of base knowledge. We can draw the following conclusions from what is shown in the table:

- There is a glaring absence or limitation of (indigenous/sign) language skills in teachers of indigenous and Deaf students. This is a situation that has changed somewhat over the last decade, in the case of sign language at least, if we take into account the recognition that this knowledge has been given officially, by including sign language as part of the teacher training curriculum and in-service teacher development activities. However, there is much to be done in both these sectors if teachers are to acquire language levels appropriate to teaching within Bilingual Education Programmes.
- Most teachers teaching on Bilingual Education Programmes need to develop metalinguistic awareness. In some cases, they need to supplement the linguistic awareness they already possess.
- In general, we observe that there is very little background in the areas of language and language teaching awareness or intercultural communication. This stems partly from the fact that the initial training of these teachers does not include this component. This situation could then be remedied at that stage or, more realistically, as part of in-service training.
- There is an across-the-board lack of knowledge of bilingualism and bilingual education. This is perhaps the most glaring absence. Furthermore, the most paradoxical aspect of this absence is the lack of awareness of the need for this sort of background in both teachers and education administrators.
- Both pre-service and in-service provision need to be significantly extended and resourced nationally as part of a coordinated policy approach to bilingual education.

Table 5.4 Summary of how the five areas of knowledge base apply to the profiles of teachers on the programmes under analysis

	Intercultural Bilingual Education Programmes for Indigenous Children	*Bilingual Education Programmes for Deaf Children*	*Bilingual Education Programmes in State Schools*	*Bilingual Education Programmes in Language Contact Situations*	*Bilingual Education Programmes in Elite Schools*
Languages[a]	Spanish	Spanish	(a) Spanish[b]	(a) Spanish[c]	(a) Spanish
		LSA[d]	(b) FL[e]	(b) Portuguese	(b) FL
					(c) None[f]
Cultures	No	No	(a) No	No	Yes/no
			(b) Yes/no		
Content (i.e. what to teach)	Yes	(Yes)[g]	Yes	Yes	Yes
Pedagogical (i.e. how to teach)[h]	Yes	Yes	Yes	Yes	Yes
Bilingualism & Bilingual Education	No	No	No	No	No

[a]In this row, we state the language that the teachers have been trained to teach, i.e. the language in which they have had metalinguistic training
[b]Where two teachers teach on the programme, and their skills differ, we indicate them separately
[c]In this case, we are referring to two groups of teachers, one who teach in Spanish and the other in Portuguese
[d]Only in recent years
[e]Foreign language teachers who teach in English, French, Italian or Portuguese. When we say 'foreign' language, we mean that it is foreign to the students, not necessarily the teachers
[f]Typically, foreign or contract staff have had no metalinguistic reflection on their own language, beyond their own school experience
[g]A considerable portion of the training of special education teachers is devoted to rehabilitation rather than the contents that are to be taught
[h]In this section, when we say that teachers have received training in how to teach, what we mean is that they have been taught how to teach in some idealised neutral context, certainly not in a context as particular as that of bilingual education

Recommendations and Conclusions

It is clear that many aspects of the training of teachers will need to be programme- or language-specific. An obvious case in point is the development of linguistic or cultural skills. In other areas, we find more general needs that could be catered for jointly or collaboratively. More to the point, the cross-programme cooperation and collaboration in teacher development activities could greatly enhance these experiences. Besides, in a broader policy sense, this sort of collaboration would be greatly facilitated by the official recognition of the existence of all the programmes described here as bilingual education programmes. This would allow for them to have equivalent standing and permit the finding of points of contact for collaboration.

While there are many reasons why the cooperation across these different programmes may seem a positive and reasonable endeavour, there are also many factors that hinder this form of cooperation. Most of these stem from the different, and often mutually exclusive, sectors in which the programmes originate and the consequently distinct institutional cultures that they are immersed in and, in turn, generate. The student populations they serve do not, for the most part, overlap, and neither do the teacher populations. The locations of the institutions where these programmes are implemented are also different and often far apart. Their separate traditions and, for the most part, total lack of contact, also generate mutual mistrust and prejudice. If we add to this the fact that some forms of bilingual education are officially recognised, while others are not, we understand why very little opportunity for collaboration is found.

In sum, these factors, taken as a whole, make it very difficult for instances of mutual cooperation to exist. It would require an enlightened, centrally coordinated initiative, possibly on the part of the national Ministry of Education, to bring these programmes together and encourage different forms of cooperation.

In this context, a number of options are available. Firstly, an explicit acknowledgement of the existence of bilingual education as an encompassing term that would be helpful in providing some common ground and theoretical support for all these different programmes. Secondly, it is of crucial importance that the actual programmes in existence be studied and documented to be able to understand the similarities and differences across them more clearly. This would in turn lead to empirically defining general and particular bilingual teacher profiles, including shared and specific needs of teachers in different types of programmes. It would seem to us, given the reality of such varied circumstances and training backgrounds, that the profiles should ideally be defined in terms of competencies or knowledge areas rather than specific qualifications, which may turn out to be more limiting. Given all these conditions, we believe that the stage would be set to explore the possibilities for tapping into the potential for collaboration in teacher development and research.

A promising initiative in this respect was the *I Congreso del MERCOSUR: Interculturalidad y Bilingüismo en Educación*,[34] held in the city of Posadas, Misiones in September 2005. The province of Misiones is a prime example of language contact (90% of its borders link it with Paraguay and Brazil) and it is also host to one of the strongest indigenous language groups, the Mbya-Guaraní. The participants in the conference included academics and government officials with interests in the indigenous language programmes, foreign and first languages, as well as the neighbouring countries, Paraguay and Brazil. There were no representatives present, however, of bilingual education of Deaf children, as well as those working in the area of elite bilingual programmes. This may be a reflection of how incipient these areas are as subject of research studies and, thus, the number of specialists is probably more limited. Also, the long-standing tradition that views the schooling of deaf children in terms of rehabilitation and as a medical rather than an educational endeavour may have an impact in keeping this groups of teachers marginalised from exchanges related to bilingual education. It is hoped that this situation will be remedied in the near future, that this sort of initiative will have continuity and, crucially, that it will have a positive impact on the ground and not remain at the level of theoretical or ministerial discussion. Another auspicious event was the Seminar organised by the national Ministry of Education in Argentina with reference to the language contact programme in Misiones and Corrientes. Representatives of the state bilingual schools and elite bilingual schools were also invited.[35]

At the level of professional development activities for teachers involved in Bilingual Education Programmes, the planning of such activities should take into account the general and specific needs of the populations in question. Where the needs are general, joint activities could be organised, whereas more specific needs would have to be dealt with at the programme, or even school, level.

One general conclusion we have come to is that in our context, as in many others, not everything that calls itself, or is called 'bilingual education' is such, if measured against definitions such as García (1997) and Genesee (2004). The label 'bilingual' is a popular one, particularly among politicians, for a number of different reasons. It can be used to present a programme as equivalent to those accessible to elite groups, within a state institution and accessible to disadvantaged children. It conjures up among parents, and the public in general, the notion of extremely proficient command of a foreign language, even an intuitive notion of balanced bilingualism. It is also widely used as a powerful marketing tool by numerous educational institutions. It is applied to contexts where there are (some) bilingual speakers present, or even where there are monolingual speakers of two languages (indigenous programmes).

This review of the different types of bilingual programme available in Argentina today has led us to conclude that the most realistic way of achieving the profiles of teachers required of the different Bilingual Education Programmes is to develop pre- and in-service programmes that aim at supplementing the initial qualifications that teachers bring to the programme they work in. We do not believe it is realistic to advocate programme-specific initial teacher training programmes. On the other hand, we believe that all actors involved in any kind of bilingual programme should have access to the possibility of reflecting on the theoretical notions underlying the five areas of knowledge. In other words, this should not be limited to teachers but also include those responsible for these programmes at other levels, such as school heads, supervisors and education authorities, at the appropriate level in each case.

Acknowledgements

This chapter was presented as part of the Colloquium 'Integrated Perspectives Towards Bilingual Education: Bridging the Gap Between Prestigious Bilingualism and the Bilingualism of Minorities' at the International Symposium on Bilingualism ISB5 in Barcelona on 22 March 2005. We would like to thank the audience there, our co-panelists and, particularly, the colloquium chairs and editors of this volume, Drs Christine Hélot and Anne-Marie Truscott de Mejía.

Notes

1. IIPE-UNESCO conducted a survey of teachers in Argentina. The analysis can be found in Tenti Fanfani *et al.* (2000).
2. For examples of foreign language teacher curricula, see http://institutojvgonzalez.buenosaires.edu.ar/ingles/plan.html and http://www.lenguasvivasjrf.edu.ar/shop/index.asp. Accessed 24.3.07.
3. Both authors have designed and implemented teacher training programmes for teachers in bilingual education programmes in elite schools; they were responsible for coordinating the evaluation of the *Impact of the English Partial Immersion Bilingual Programme in Uruguay* (2005–2006). Cristina Banfi is co-author of a signing book for teachers and parents of Deaf children and has conducted teacher development courses on LSA and presented papers on the indigenous language situation in Argentina (see Banfi, 1995). Both authors participated in the Bilingual Programme in Language Contact Situations Technical Seminar organised by the National Ministry of Education in 2006.
4. The *Programa de Formación en Educación Intercultural Bilingue para los Países Andinos* (PROEIB, National Programme of Bilingual Intercultural Education),

the Mayan schools of Guatemala, the intercultural 'pilot schools' in Mapuche territories in Chile and the Zapatista academies of indigenous languages in Mexico. For further information see http://coleccion.educ.ar/coleccion/CD9/contenidos/index.html (accessed 22.3.07).

5. PNEIB, *Programa Nacional de Educación Intercultural Bilingüe*[5] proposed by the National Ministry of Education (National Programme of Bilingual Intercultural Education). For further information see http://coleccion.educ.ar/coleccion/CD9/contenidos/index.html (Access: 22/03/07).
6. *Latin American Conference on Intercultural Bilingual Education.* The first of these conferences was held in Guatemala in 1995, the second in Cochabamba, Bolivia, the following year (for further information about the second conference, see http://www.rieoei.org/oeivirt/rie13a11.pdf). The most recent one, the 7th, was held in Cochabamba, Bolivia in October 2006 (see http://viieib.proeibandes.org for further information about it).
7. Chapter IV, Sec. 75, Point 17. www.argentina.gov.ar/argentina/portal/documentos/constitucion_ingles.pdf (accessed 16.3.07).
8. For the text of the law, see www.me.gov.ar; for the debate http://debate-educacion.educ.ar/ley. The section on the rights of indigenous populations is Chapter XI, http://debate-educacion.educ.ar/ley/ley_educacion_nacional.pdf (accessed 16.3.07).
9. Complementary Survey of Indigenous Peoples. For more details, see http://www.indec.mecon.ar/encampo/indigenas.asp (accessed 16.3.07).
10. Educational Institutional Project. This applies to all institutions in the system.
11. Bilingual programmes of this sort have also been developed in the region, specifically in Uruguay, but a discussion of these exceeds the possibilities of this paper. For further information, refer to the site of the Ministry of Education: http://www.mecaep.edu.uy/home.aspx (see Escuelas de Tiempo Completo, Programa de Educación Bilingüe) (accessed 16.3.07).
12. See http://www.registrocivil.gov.ar/areas/educacion/cepa/pluriint2008.php (accessed 16.3.07).
13. The programme was created by means of Resolution 786/01 on 17 May 2001. Interestingly, as the AGCBA (2004) report indicates, the resolution came after months of the actual implementation of the programme. The programme's full name was initially *Programa Escuelas Bilingües de la Ciudad de Buenos Aires*, and, since 2002 it has been *Programa Escuelas de Modalidad Plurilingüe con Intensificación en Lenguas Materna y Extranjera.* For further information on the programme, see www.buenosaires.gov.ar/areas/educacion/niveles/primaria/programas/bilingues/index.php (accessed 16.3.07).
14. The British Council is effectively the cultural arm of the British Embassy. It is involved in supporting the programme in the City of Buenos Aires.
15. This can be translated as 'Common Teaching Model in Schools in Bordering Regions'. See further information in the Ministry of Misiones website www.mcye.misiones.gov.ar/index.php?option=com_content&task=view&id=80&Itemid=110 (accessed 17.3.07).
16. Guaraní and Spanish are official languages in neighbouring Paraguay.
17. Some schools, such as Colegio Tarbut (www.tarbut.net, accessed 16.3.07), present themselves as trilingual schools as they teach a partial immersion programme in Spanish and English and also Hebrew.
18. The Nichia Gakuin Argentine–Japanese school may be an exception to this rule, and may be more aptly classified with the Global Language Schools. For further information, see www.nichiagakuin.com (accessed 16.3.07).

19. As Escobar (2004: 644) points out, whereas '... in colonial times, bilingualism was bi-directional, since merchants and priests (who in the early colonial period were present in high numbers) learned the indigenous languages of the region they worked in, and some indigenous elite in turn learned Spanish. By contrast, in modern times bilingualism is mostly unidirectional, from the indigenous language towards Spanish, although different degrees of Spanish are evident.' In educational terms, what we can say is that the majority of teachers appointed to teach in these programmes do not speak the language of the community.
20. According to Resolución 63/97 of the *Consejo Federal de Cultura y Educación*, three types of degrees can be offered: *Profesor Intercultural Bilingüe Modalidad Aborigen para la educación Inicial*, *Profesor Intercultural Bilingüe Modalidad Aborigen para el Primero y el Segundo Ciclo de la Educación General Básica* or *Profesor Intercultural Bilingüe Modalidad Aborigen para el Tercer Ciclo de la Educación General Básica y de Educación Polimodal en ... (una disciplina específica)*. The second of these degrees is offered by the CIFMA teacher training college, Centro de Investigación y Formación para la Modalidad Aborigen, in Sáenz Peña, Chaco, see www.periodismosocial.org.ar/area_infancia_informes.cfm?ah=104 (accessed 22.3.07). On the most recent cohort of graduates, see www.chaco.gov.ar/prensachaco/publicacion/default.asp?IdNotaAPublicar=37606&FuncionARealizar=1&Dia=13&Mes=12&Anio=2006 (accessed 24.3.07).
21. For the full curricular design, see http://abc.gov.ar/Docentes/DisenioCurricular/default.cfm (accessed 16.3.07).
22. For further information, see www.registrocivil.gov.ar/areas/educacion/cepa/pluri1c2006.php (accessed 16.3.07).
23. See, for example, Lycée Franco-Argentin Jean Mermoz (www.lyceemermoz.edu.ar, accessed 16.3.07), Goethe Schule (www.goethe.edu.ar, accessed 16. 3.07).
24. *Castellanización* can be translated as 'becoming a speaker of Spanish', however, it has much broader social and sociolinguistic implications.
25. On dangers involving serious prevention or delay of cognitive growth potential see Branson and Miller (1998, 2000); Grosjean (2001), Jokinen (2000); Martin (2001); Reagan and Osborn (2002) and Skutnabb-Kangas (2000).
26. It is not the subject of this paper, but the fact is that there is no provision for the maintenance of the minority language of immigrant children within this system, a situation that would deserve a separate study in itself.
27. This official status is embedded in the Treaty of Asunción and the Protocol of Ouro Preto and included in the agreement for the mutual recognition of teaching degrees for the teaching of Spanish and Portuguese as foreign languages. www.mrree.gub.uy/Mercosur/ConsejoMercadoComun/Reunion28/AnexoII/ANEXO_DEC_9-05.htm (accessed 16.3.07).
28. See Argentina, Presidential decree (1904). See also Raufet (1962).
29. Precedents in such programmes do, however, exist. There was a programme based at the state-run teacher training college, E.N.S. 'Sofía Spannenberg' (formerly 'John F. Kennedy') that trained primary bilingual teachers in English and Spanish. This programme was discontinued in 1999 (www.spangenberg.edu.ar, accessed 16.3.07). Another such programme, also in Spanish and English, existed at St. Catherine's Teacher Training College, in the private sector in this case, but it has also been discontinued in the last few years.

30. On an example of this sort of provision by an association of schools, see Banfi (2006).
31. For the purposes of this chapter we would like to make the following distinctions, as they are not always clear, at least in our context. By Initial Teacher Training we understand the course of studies taken by teacher trainees which provides them with knowledge of the discipline content area(s) and other related areas, of General and Specific Pedagogy, Practice and Observation. In Argentina, these courses are delivered at Teacher Training Colleges (tertiary level institutions) or at universities and they last three to four years. By Pre-Service Teacher Training/Development, or Induction, we understand the type of training that qualified teachers take before starting to work on a new project or programme. These activities should be more specific than the initial teacher training courses themselves and provide teachers with the necessary information/knowledge about the project or programme. They are far from pervasive in institutions in Argentina, many of which operate a 'sink or swim' induction method. In-service teacher training/development and activities are set up so that teachers keep abreast of the latest trends in teaching and learning in the different areas. In some cases, the offer of INSET activities is provided by the education authorities of the relevant governmental agency, whereas in others it is the school or a group of schools that organise these activities. The offer is far from comprehensive and often rather haphazard. In this sense, we consider teacher training as a continuum, beginning with the initial training and continuing throughout the duration of the teacher's working life, as the notion of Continuing Professional Development, so in vogue nowadays, indicates.
32. As regards knowledge of LSA, many teachers have felt the need to learn this language to be able to do their jobs properly, doing so in their own free time and covering the cost themselves. More recently, LSA courses have been included in the teacher training curriculum and interpreting courses have also been created. There are also initiatives by government agencies to provide INSET for teachers currently working within the system. One case in point is the province of Buenos Aires, under the auspices of the *Dirección de Educación Especial* (Lapenda, February 2007).
33. For details of the subjects taken by foreign language teachers, see http://institutojvgonzalez.buenosaires.edu.ar/ingles/archivos/mapa_pi.pdf (accessed 24.3.07).
34. First Mercosur Conference: Interculturality and Bilingualism in Education.
35. 'Reunion de Consulta Tecnica sobre modelos de bilinguismo', 8 and 9 May 2006 in the context of the Intercultural Bilingual Programme for the Border Region.

References

Acuña, L. (2003) Lengua materna, lengua segunda y bilingüismo en la EIB. Paper presented at the Encuentro Nacional de Educación e Identidades: Los pueblos originarios y la escuela, Universidad Nacional de Luján. On WWW at http://www.ctera.org.ar/iipmv/areas/Identidades/Ponencias/Abstrac/29.doc. Accessed 16.3.07.

Adger, C.T., Snow, C.E. and Christian, D. (eds) (2002) *What Teachers Need to Know About Language*. McHenry, IL and Washington, DC: Delta Systems, and Center for Applied Linguistics.

AGCBA (2004) *Informe Final de Auditoría – Escuelas Bilingües – Auditoría de Gestión*. Buenos Aires: Auditoría General de la Ciudad de Buenos Aires. On WWW at www.agcba.gov.ar/docs/Info-557.pdf. Accessed 16.3.07.

Aranda, S., Rosario, A. and Zidarich, M. (2004) La Pareja Pedagógica: Un vínculo a construir. In Ministerio de Educación, Ciencia y Tecnología. *Educación Intercultural Bilingüe en Argentina*. Buenos Aires: MECyT.

Armendariz, A. and Ruiz Montani, C. (2005) *El Aprendizaje de Lenguas Extranjeras y las Tecnologías de la Información: Aprendizaje de Próxima Generación*. Buenos Aires: Lugar Editorial.

Baker, C. (1995) *A Parents' and Teachers' Guide to Bilingualism*. Clevedon: Multilingual Matters.

Baker, C. (2000) *A Parents' and Teachers' Guide to Bilingualism* (2nd edn). Clevedon: Multilingual Matters.

Baker, C. (2001) *Foundations of Bilingual Education and Bilingualism* (3rd edn). Clevedon: Multilingual Matters.

Baker, C. (2002) Bilingual education. In R.B. Kaplan (ed.) *The Oxford Handbook of Applied Linguistics*. Oxford: Oxford University Press.

Banfi, C. (1995) Indigenous languages in South America: An optimistic prognosis? Paper presented at the Fourth Postgraduate Linguistics Conference, University of Manchester, March 1995.

Banfi, C. (2006) Teaming Up: The advantages of pooling resources in Professional Development. *International Schools Journal* XXV (2).

Banfi, C. and Bianco, G. (2005) *Cuentos en Mano*. Video and printed material for teachers and parents of Deaf children. Buenos Aires: ADAS-Asociación de Artes y Señas.

Banfi, C. and Day, R. (2005) The evolution of bilingual schools in Argentina. In A-M. de Mejía (ed.) *Bilingual Education in South America*. Clevedon: Multilingual Matters.

Banfi, C. and Moyano, G. (2003) La tradición Argentina en formación docente en lenguas extranjeras. In M.I. Dorronzoro, M.S. González, E. Klett, M. Lucas, R. Pasquale and M. Vidal (eds) *Enseñanza de Lenguas Extranjeras en el Nivel Superior*. Balances y perspectivas en investigación y docencia. IX Jornadas de Enseñanza de Lenguas Extranjeras en el Nivel Superior. Universidad de Buenos Aires. Facultad de Filosofía y Letras. Dpto. de Lenguas Modernas. Buenos Aires: Araucaria Editora.

Bialystok, E. (2004) The impact of bilingualism on language and literacy development. In R.B. Kaplan (ed.) *The Oxford Handbook of Applied Linguistics*. Oxford: Oxford University Press.

Bouvet, D. (1990) *The Path to Language: Bilingual Education for Deaf Children*. Clevedon: Multilingual Matters.

Branson, J. and Miller, D. (1998) Nationalism and the linguistic rights of Deaf communities: Linguistic imperialism and the recognition and development of sign languages. *Journal of Sociolinguistics* 2 (1), 3–34.

Branson, J. and Miller, D. (2000) Maintaining, developing and sharing the knowledge and potential embedded in all our languages and cultures: On linguists as agents of epistemic violence. In R. Phillipson (ed.) *Rights to Language: Equity, Power and Education* (pp. 28–32). Lawrence Erlbaum Associates.

Braslavsky, C. and Cosse, G. (2006) Las actuales reformas educativas en América Latina: Cuatro actores, tres lógicas y ocho tensiones. *Revista Electrónica Iberoamericana sobre Calidad, Eficacia y Cambio en Educación* 4 (2e), 1–26. On WWW at www.rinace.net/arts/vol4num2e/art1.pdf. Accessed 19.3.07.

Brisk, M.E. (1998) *Bilingual Education from Compensatory to Quality Schooling*. Mahwah, NJ: Lawrence Erlbaum.

Cámpoli, O. (2004) *La formación docente en la República Argentina*. Buenos Aires: IESALC. On WWW at www.iesalc.unesco.org.ve/programas/formacion%20 docente/Formaci%C3%B3n%20docente%20Argentina.pdf. Accessed 19.3.07.

Cazden, C. (1992) *Language Minority Education in the United States: Implications of the Ramirez Report*. Santa Cruz, CA: National Center for Research on Cultural Diversity and Second Language Learning.

Center for Applied Linguistics (CAL) (1974) *Guidelines for the Preparation and Certification of Teachers for Bilingual/Bicultural Education*. Arlington, VA: Center for Applied Linguistics.

Cloud, N., Genesee, F. and Hamayan, E. (2000) *Dual Language Instruction*. Boston, MA: Heinle & Heinle.

Cummins, J. (2000a) *Language, Power and Pedagogy: Bilingual Children in the Crossfire*. Clevedon: Multilingual Matters.

Cummins, J. (2000b) Immersion education for the millennium: What we have learned from 30 years of research on second language immersion. On WWW at www.iteachilearn.com/cummins/immersion2000.html. Accessed 24.3.07.

de Mejía, A.M. (2002) *Power, Prestige and Bilingualism: International Perspectives on Elite Bilingual Education*. Clevedon: Multilingual Matters.

Dewaele J-M. (2003) Introduction: Opportunities and challenges of bilingualism. In L. Wei, J-M. Dewaele and A. Housen (eds) *Opportunities and Challenges of Bilingualism* (pp. 1–12). Berlin: Mouton De Gruyter.

Dorian, N. (2004) Minority and endangered languages. In T.K. Bhatia and W. Ritchie (eds) *The Handbook of Bilingualism*. Oxford: Blackwell.

Escobar, A.M. (2004) Bilingualism in Latin America. In R.B. Kaplan (ed.) *The Oxford Handbook of Applied Linguistics*. Oxford: Oxford University Press.

Faltis, C. (2002) Contexts for becoming bilingual learners in school settings. In R.B. Kaplan (ed.) *The Oxford Handbook of Applied Linguistics*. Oxford: Oxford University Press.

Fillmore, L.W. and Snow, C. (2000) *What Teachers Need to Know About Language*. Washington: Centre for Applied Linguistics. On WWW at http://faculty.tamu-commerce.edu/jthompson/Resources/FillmoreSnow2000.pdf. Accessed 16.3.07.

García, O. (1997) Bilingual education. In F. Coulmas (ed.) *The Handbook of Sociolinguistics*. Oxford: Blackwell.

Genesee, F. (2004) What do we know about bilingual education for majority-language students? In T. Bhatia and W. Ritchie (eds) *The Handbook of Bilingualism*. Oxford: Blackwell Publishing.

Grosjean, F. (2001) The right of the Deaf child to grow up bilingual. *Sign Language Studies* 1 (2), 110–114. On WWW at www.unine.ch/ltlp/pub/rightdeafchild_en.html. Accessed 15.3.03.

Gualdieri, B. (2004) El lenguaje de las experiencias. In Ministerio de Educación, Ciencia y Tecnología. *Educación Intercultural Bilingüe en Argentina*. Buenos Aires: MECyT.

Hakuta, K. (1990) Language and cognition in bilingual children. In A. Padilla, H. Fairchild and C. Valadez (eds) *Bilingual Education: Issues and Strategies* (pp. 47–59). Newbury Park: Sage Publications.

Hirsch S, (2003) Aportes a la formación docente en educación bilingüe intercultural: La capacitación para la docencia en comunidades guaraníes del norte salteño. Paper presented at Encuentro Nacional de Educación e Identidades: Los pueblos originarios y la escuela, Universidad Nacional de

Luján. On WWW at www.ctera.org.ar/iipmv/areas/Identidades/Ponencias/31.doc. Accessed 3.3.07.

Intiman, M. and Quintrel, A. (2004) Enseñanza de la lengua Mapuche. In Ministerio de Educación, Ciencia y Tecnología. *Educación Intercultural Bilingüe en Argentina*. Buenos Aires: MECyT.

Ipiña Melgar, E. (1997) Condiciones y perfil del docente de educación intercultural bilingüe. *Revista Iberoamericana de Educación* 13. On WWW at www.oei.es/oeivirt/rie13a04.htm. Accessed 3.3.07.

Jara, V. (2004) La implementación en la escuela de la lengua materna wichi. In Ministerio de Educación, Ciencia y Tecnología. *Educación Intercultural Bilingüe en Argentina*. Buenos Aires: MECyT.

Jokinen, M. (2000) The linguistic human rights of Sign language users. In R. Phillipson (ed.) *Rights to Language. Equity, Power and Education* (pp. 203–213). Mahwah, NJ: Lawrence Erlbaum.

Kisilevsky, M. (1999) Estudiantes de formación docente, universitarios y maestros, perfiles y circuitos. BID-FLACSO.

Lapenda, M.E. (2005) Enseñar a leer y escribir a niños sordos. *Novedades Educativas* 174 (June).

Lindholm-Leary, K.J. (2005) *Review of Research and Best Practices on Effective Features of Dual Language Education Programs*. San José: San José State University.

Martin, D.S. (2001) The English-only movement and sign language for deaf learners: An instructive parallel. *Sign Language Studies* 1 (2), 115–124.

Mashie, S. (1995) *Educating Deaf Children Bilingually*. Washington, D.C.: Gallaudet University.

May, S., Hill, S.R. and Tiakiwai, S. (2004) *Bilingual/Immersion Education: Indicators of Good Practice*. Final Report to the Ministry of Education. Hamilton: University of Waikato.

McAnally, P.L., Rose, S. and Quigley, S.P. (1999) *Reading Practices with Deaf Learners*. Austin, TX: Pro-Ed.

Met, M. and Lorenz, E.B. (1997) Lessons from U.S. immersion programs: Two decades of experience. In R.K. Johnson and M. Swain (eds) *Immersion Education: International Perspectives* (pp. 243–264). Cambridge: Cambridge University Press.

Ministerio de Educación, Ciencia y Tecnología (MECyT) (2004) *Educación Intercultural Bilingüe en Argentina*. Buenos Aires: MECyT.

Moran, C.E. and Hakuta, K. (1995). *Bilingual Education: Broadening Research Perspectives*. ERIC Reproduction Document ED382720. Washington, DC: Office of Educational Research and Improvement.

Nickson, A. (2001) Education reform in Latin America: Decentralization or restructuring? Paper presented at Conference on Exclusion and Engagement: Social Policy in Latin America, Institute for Latin American Studies, University of London. On WWW at www.idd.bham.ac.uk/research/publications/Staff/Education%20Reform%20in%20Latin%20America3.pdf. Accessed 19.3.07.

Ortiz, L. and Torres, C. (2006) La frontera como espacio redefinidor de identidades. *Ponencia en las Jornadas Interdisciplinarias Lenguas, Identidad e Ideologías*. Facultad de Filosofía y Letras de la UNT. On WWW at http://usuarios.arnet.com.ar/yanasu/Resumen%20Ortiz%20Mar%EDa%20Leticia-Torres%20Carlos%20Daniel.pdf. Accessed 19.3.07.

Paul, P.V. (1998) *Literacy and Deafness: The Development of Reading, Writing and Literate Thought*. Boston: Allyn and Bacon.

Provincia de Misiones (2007) Departamento de Educación Intercultural Bilingüe. Ministerio de Cultura y Educación de Misiones. On WWW at http://www.mcye.misiones.gov.ar/index.php?option=com_content&task=blogcategory&id=51&Itemid=110. Accessed 19.3.07.

Raufet, R. (1962) *La Enseñanza de las Lenguas Viva en la Argentina*. Catamarca: Instituto Nacional del Profesorado de Catamarca.

Reagan, T. and Osborn, T. (2002) *The Foreign Language Educator in Society: Towards a Critical Pedagogy*. Mahwah: Lawrence Erlbaum Associates.

Roberts, C.A. (1995) Bilingual education program models: A framework for understanding. *The Bilingual Education Research Journal* 19 (3/4), 369–378.

Robertson, L. (2000) *Literacy Learning for Children Who are Deaf or Hard of Hearing*. Washington, DC: AG Bell.

Shulman, L.S. (1987) Knowledge and teaching: Foundations of the new reform. *Harvard Educational Review* 57 (1), 1–22.

Skutnabb-Kangas, T. (2000) *Linguistic Genocide in Education – or Worldwide Diversity and Human Rights?* Mahwah, NJ: Lawrence Erlbaum.

Svartholm, K. (1993) Bilingual education for the deaf in Sweden. *Sign Language Studies* 81, 291–332.

Tenti Fanfani, E., López, N., Tedesco, J.C. and Urresti, M. (2000) Los docentes argentinos, Resultados de una encuesta nacional sobre la situación y la cultura de los docentes. Buenos Aires: IIPE-UNESCO. On WWW at www.iipe-buenosaires.org.ar/pdfs/los_docentes.pdf. Accessed 19.3.07.

Valette, R.M. (1986) The culture test. In J.M. Valdes (ed.) *Culture Bound: Bridging the Cultural Gap in Language Teaching*. New York: Cambridge University Press.

Appendix 1 Summary of the different types of Bilingual Education Programmes in Argentina

	Intercultural Bilingual Education Programmes for Indigenous Children	***Bilingual Education Programmes for Deaf Children***	***Bilingual Education Programmes in State Schools***	***Bilingual Education Programmes in Language Contact Situations***	***Bilingual Education Programmes in Elite Schools***
Population served	Indigenous, underprivileged	Deaf, often with added disabilities	Inner-city, underprivileged	Population in areas bordering with Brazil	Urban and suburban, privileged
Languages					
Home/L1	Indigenous language or Spanish	Spanish/null	Spanish	Portuguese, Spanish, *Portuñol*	Spanish
Instruction	Spanish	Spanish & LSA	Spanish & English, French, Italian or Portuguese		Spanish & English, French, Italian or German (to a lesser extent Hebrew, Armenian, Japanese, Korean[a])
Location of schools	Provinces. Rural areas, but increasingly, urban	Urban & suburban	City of Buenos Aires	Misiones and Corrientes (Argentina); border with Brazil	Large cities and suburbs

Appendix 1 *(Continued)*

	Intercultural Bilingual Education Programmes for Indigenous Children	***Bilingual Education Programmes for Deaf Children***	***Bilingual Education Programmes in State Schools***	***Bilingual Education Programmes in Language Contact Situations***	***Bilingual Education Programmes in Elite Schools***
Type of programme	State. Mostly KG & Primary. Transitional bilingual programme	State & Private. State Subsidies. Primary & secondary. Transitional bilingual programme	State – primary. Mainstream with Foreign Language in Buenos Aires	State. Primary, 1st form (2005). Mainstream with Foreign Language	Private. Fee-paying (high). All levels (K-12). Integrated curriculum. Partial early immersion. Mainstream bilingual
Curriculum/ curricula	City or Provincial curriculum	City or Provincial curriculum	City/National curriculum + intensive FL teaching	Provincial curriculum	City or Provincial curriculum + integrated with foreign/intern'l curriculum
Resources & sources	Very few resources. Developed by teachers. Provincial state	Very few resources. Developed by teachers	Reasonable. Embassies (Canada, Brazil, Italy, France & Portugal, The British Council); publishers	Information not available. Provincial state	Very good. Fees & foreign gov't subsidies & support[b]

Appendix 1 *(Continued)*

	Intercultural Bilingual Education Programmes for Indigenous Children	*Bilingual Education Programmes for Deaf Children*	*Bilingual Education Programmes in State Schools*	*Bilingual Education Programmes in Language Contact Situations*	*Bilingual Education Programmes in Elite Schools*
Since	Recent experiences	Since 1987	Since 2001	Founded 1.3.05	Oldest school founded in 1838
Schools	See experiences and schools included in: MECyT (2004)	e.g. CIBES	English (26), French (6), Italian (8), Portuguese (9). 2006 Data	e.g. Escuela 604 Bilingüe. Intercultural N° 1	English, French, Italian, German Schools (Hebrew, Armenian, Japanese, Korean schools)
Teaching staff	Primary school teachers, indigenous language assistants	Special needs teachers, primary & secondary school teachers, LSA speakers as assistants	Primary school teachers, foreign language teachers	Primary school teachers, foreign language teacher (Portuguese)	Primary & secondary school teachers, foreign language teachers, contract teachers

[a]Instruction in these languages is often limited to the teaching of the language itself and some courses on history/culture
[b]The government subsidies and support only apply to some cases, e.g. some French, German and Italian schools
[c]LSA knowledge acquired informally, if at all

Appendix 2 The languages involved in the programmes

Programme	*Teaching staff*	*Language competence*	*Language used in the classroom*	*Metalinguistic awareness as part of training*
Intercultural Bilingual Education Programmes for Indigenous Children	Form teacher	Spanish (L1)	Spanish	Spanish as L1
	Indigenous lg. Assistant	Indigenous language (L1) Spanish (L2)	Indigenous language Spanish for translat-ing	No
Bilingual Education Programmes for Deaf Children	Form teacher	Spanish (L1) Some LSA	Spanish Some LSA	Spanish as L1
	LSA assistant	LSA (L1?)	LSA	No
Bilingual Education Programmes in State Schools	Form teacher	Spanish (L1)	Spanish	Spanish as L1
	Foreign language teacher	Spanish (L1) FL-English, French, Italian or Portuguese (L2)	Foreign language	Spanish as L1 English, French, Italian or Portuguese as FL
Bilingual Education Programmes in Language Contact Situations (Argentine side)	Form teacher	Spanish (L1)	Spanish	Spanish as L1
	Portuguese lg. Teacher	Portuguese (L1)	Portuguese	Portuguese as L1

Appendix 2 (*Continued*)

Programme	*Teaching staff*	*Language competence*	*Language used in the classroom*	*Metalinguistic awareness as part of training*
Bilingual Education Programmes in Elite Schools	Contract teacher	Foreign Language (L1)	Foreign language	Foreign Language as L1
	Form teacher who teaches in the FL	Spanish (L1) Foreign Language (L2)	Foreign language	Spanish as L1
	Subject teacher who teaches in the FL	Spanish (L1) Foreign Language (L2)	Foreign language	No
	Form teacher who teaches in Spanish	Spanish (L1)	Spanish	Spanish as L1
	Subject teacher who teaches in Spanish	Spanish (L1)	Spanish	No (unless they teach Spanish language)
	Foreign language teacher	Spanish (L1) FL-English, French, German, Italian or Portuguese (L2)	Foreign language	English, French, German, Italian or Portuguese as FL

Part 2

Europe

Chapter 6

The National Languages Strategy in the UK: Are Minority Languages Still on the Margins?

JIM ANDERSON, CHARMIAN KENNER and EVE GREGORY

Introduction

The UK has an increasingly multilingual population; 10.5% of pupils in primary schools have a home language other than English and London schoolchildren speak over 300 languages between them (Baker & Eversley, 2000). However, children's bilingual abilities are marginalised in mainstream school settings. Government policy in the 1980s designated mother tongue teaching as the responsibility of minority language communities (Swann, 1985), and most classes take place in community language schools run by volunteers, operating in 'borrowed spaces' (Martin *et al.*, 2004) after school or at weekends.

Meanwhile, foreign language instruction, mainly in French, German or Spanish, has until recently been available only in secondary schools from age 11. However, the new National Languages Strategy opens a period of greater potential for language learning, particularly in primary school. Children will be offered the chance to learn another language from the age of seven, and in theory this can include languages spoken by minority communities. A second key strand of the strategy is the decision to expand the number of specialist language colleges. These are state secondary schools with a responsibility to diversify their language offer and to build links with the local community. A third strand is the Languages Ladder, a new assessment framework currently being developed for 26 languages, European and non-European, intended to provide recognition for language achievement at any age and across all levels.

What will these policy changes mean in practice? This chapter will first consider how minority languages in the UK are currently seen as lacking in value and status, and whether such attitudes may work against their integration into the curriculum. Recent policy attempts to break down the distinction between 'minority languages' and the more prestigious 'foreign languages' will be discussed, with 'cross-over languages' such as Spanish or Mandarin Chinese highlighting the contradictions inherent in such terminology.

Key strands within the National Languages Strategy will then be considered critically in relation to diversification, inclusion and overall coherence. For example, findings from National Languages Strategy pilot projects show that very few primary schools have yet included minority languages in their provision, suggesting an incoherence of discourse and practice around multilingualism at the national and local level.

Finally, we will present research findings showing how children benefit from learning in community language contexts. This suggests the advantages to be gained from bringing a range of languages and literacies into the mainstream curriculum. The chapter concludes with questions about how integration could be accomplished to aid the learning of both bilingual and monolingual children, without simply exploiting bilingual children's knowledge for the sake of others, and without losing the social and cultural ethos specific to community contexts.

Languages in the UK: An Invisible Variety

Post-war reconstruction in the UK was founded on the economic contribution of immigrant workers. Former colonies that had produced the wealth of the British Empire now became the source of labour for factories, hospitals and transport (Edwards, 2004). Most new arrivals came from the Caribbean or the Indian subcontinent, from the 1950s onwards, bringing with them a wide range of languages and literacies. However, these were ignored in mainstream education, although more favourable attitudes towards multiculturalism in the 1970s led to the following strongly worded statement in a Government report:

> No child should be expected to cast off the language and culture of the home as he crosses the school threshold and the curriculum should reflect those aspects of his life. (Bullock, 1975: 543)

This statement, whilst often quoted, had remarkably little effect on children's school experience. Despite a directive from the Council of Europe requiring member states to promote mother tongue teaching for the children of migrant workers (Council of Europe, 1977), by 1984 only 2.2% of primary school pupils from different home language backgrounds were receiving such teaching in school (European Commission, 1984). The official attitude was encapsulated in the 1985 Swann Report from the Committee of Inquiry into the Education of Children from Minority Ethnic Groups, which recommended that mother tongue teaching should take place outside mainstream school in sessions run by ethnic minority communities themselves (Swann, 1985). Ironically, this report was entitled *Education for All*; it appears that the desired goal was education *in English* for all. Teaching minority languages in the mainstream was claimed to be potentially divisive, an argument that indicates the lack of political will to move towards an integrated multilingual society.

The monolingual assumptions that inform the Swann report were further reflected in the National Curriculum introduced several years later. No provision was made for the teaching of languages at primary level (other than Welsh and Gaelic, the status of which will be considered later in this chapter). At secondary level the possibility of teaching some minority languages was allowed but only on the condition that students also had the opportunity to study a European Union language. Inevitably, this gave rise to questions about language status and lent weight to arguments regarding the Eurocentric nature of the curriculum.

In this political climate, children were rarely able to use or develop their bilingual knowledge in mainstream school. Bilingual education was limited to small-scale research projects (Fitzpatrick, 1987; Jupp, 1990). Although such studies demonstrated the benefits of children being able to use their home language as well as English for classroom learning, no efforts were made at national level to build on the results. Pupils entering school with a language other than English were provided with support from 'bilingual assistants', where available, but the aim was to help them make the transition to English rather than to promote bilingual development (Bourne, 2001). Some secondary schools also included minority languages in their curriculum where there was perceived to be a demand from the particular school population.

Particular efforts to promote multilingualism were, however, made in London, under the auspices of the Inner London Education Authority (ILEA), which developed robust policies on anti-racism, equal opportunities and bilingualism. Tsow (1992: 3) comments that:

> Between 1983 to 1990, the ILEA offered the widest range of community languages within both the primary and secondary school curriculum, including the South Asian languages (Bengali, Gujarati, Panjabi, Urdu), Arabic, Chinese, Greek and Turkish. The languages were taught as subjects, as well as used in bilingual support accessing English.

There were inspection and advisory teams for heritage languages as well as for multicultural education. Biennial surveys were carried out between 1978 and 1989 by the authority's Research and Statistics Branch to identify (a) what languages were spoken by pupils across the different boroughs, (b) the number of speakers of each language and (c) levels of proficiency in English for those learning it as an additional language. Bodies such as the Centre for Urban Educational Studies and the Centre for Bilingualism were established and performed a key role in supporting the education of linguistic minority children by providing in-service training and an opportunity to share resources and expertise. The Inner London Educational Computing Centre developed the pioneering multilingual word processing program, Allwrite, which was made available free of charge to schools in the authority. Tragically, when the ILEA was abolished in 1989 (by the then Conservative government) and authority handed over to the separate boroughs, this support for multilingualism was substantially lost.

Against the prevailing monolingual ethos during the 1980s, teachers at grass-roots level tried to promote multilingualism through activities such as language awareness projects in the classroom (Hawkins, 1984). Projects coordinated by Anderson (1985, 1991) in two secondary schools demonstrated how drawing on the languages and cultures of the school and local community could serve to stimulate important insights about language, improve attitudes generally towards language learning and raise the status of bilingual learners. The introduction of a fragmented, narrowly conceived and highly prescriptive National Curriculum dealt a body blow to these developments (Brumfit, 1995), but the struggle between advocates of monolingual or multilingual approaches to education has continued until the present day.

Meanwhile, the political case for indigenous minority languages was being fought and partially won with respect to Welsh, Irish, Gaelic and Scots. The 1993 Welsh Language Act placed a duty on the public sector to treat Welsh and English on an equal basis, and proficiency in Welsh is now required for most Government and local authority employment. The Welsh Language Board has the power to request local authorities to prepare Welsh language education schemes, and bilingual schooling has been set up throughout Wales at primary and secondary level. Devolution of certain political powers to the Welsh Assembly, set up in 2000, has enabled further support for pro-Welsh initiatives.

The Scottish Parliament, also established in 2000, identified Gaelic education as a Priority Action Area and set up the Gaelic Development Agency to devise and implement a national plan. By 2004 there were 60 Gaelic units (schools or classes attached to English-medium schools) throughout the country (Edwards, 2004), and the Scots language could be studied as an option within the 5–14 curriculum in some schools. In 2005 the Gaelic Language (Scotland) Act was passed, recognising Gaelic as an official language of Scotland, commanding equal respect with English. The Act established *Bòrd na Gàidhlig* (Gaelic Language Board) as part of the framework of government in Scotland and required the creation of a National Plan for Gaelic.

Political changes in Northern Ireland in 1998/2000 also promoted language change. Following the Good Friday Agreement between the UK and Irish governments, the work of the Irish Language Board in the Republic of Ireland was extended to Northern Ireland through the creation of a new organisation called *Foras na Gaeilge.* Legislation places a duty on the Department for Education and Skills (DfES) to promote Irish language education, in recognition of the importance of the Irish language for 'the cultural identity and heritage of Northern Ireland's children' (DENI, 1998). Irish-medium primary and secondary schools are now being set up.

The status of indigenous minority languages remains fragile. There are still only small numbers of schools operating in Gaelic and Irish, and university education in these languages and in Welsh is restricted although growing. However, such schooling has demonstrated the success of bilingual education, and there are ongoing campaigns to extend it. Particularly in Wales, many English-speaking parents have chosen to send their children to bilingual schools, seeing the benefits of having access to two languages and cultures as well as increased employment opportunities (Baker, 1997). This raises the interesting prospect of Welsh switching status from a 'minority' to a 'prestige' language as defined by de Mejía (2002). But the switch is resisted by other sections of the English-speaking majority, and this may be why funding has not yet been provided for further growth in Welsh-medium schooling.

Contesting the Monolingual Ethos

The UK's 'deplorable monolingualism' was officially named as a problem by the Nuffield Languages Inquiry (Nuffield Inquiry Committee, 2000). Their report *Languages: The Next Generation* provided a trenchant critique of the state of language teaching and learning, making a strong link between lack of language skills and lack of economic competitiveness. The Inquiry discovered a chronic shortage of such skills in the UK workforce and the media took up the issue with headlines such as 'Monolingual workers cost Britain dear' (*The Guardian,* 2000). In a survey on *Europeans and Languages* (European Commission, 2001), Britain was revealed as the most monolingual country in Europe: 66% of UK citizens polled had no knowledge of any language apart from English, in comparison with only 2% of people questioned in Luxembourg, the most multilingual European country surveyed.

The message from the Nuffield report was therefore 'English is not enough', and it was recommended that a national languages strategy should be developed with particular emphasis on giving young children a flying start in language learning. *Languages: The Next Generation* grounded its argument in citizenship issues as well as economic ones. A manifesto arising from the Inquiry, the Agenda for Languages (CILT, 2001), contained the unambiguous headline 'Multilingualism is better'. The advantages of multicultural understanding linked to linguistic knowledge were further developed by the Languages National Steering Group, the task force appointed to plan a UK strategy.

The National Languages Strategy was launched in 2002 as *Languages for All: Languages for Life* (DfES, 2002), with separate policy documents for Wales, Scotland and Northern Ireland. The vision for language learning proposed in the National Languages Strategy recognises the importance in the modern world of thinking beyond traditional boundaries and of understanding how we are now more globally connected than ever before. It is a vision which looks outwards beyond Europe, but at the same time inwards so that the potential of the linguistic and cultural resources present in our own communities are seen as something to be valued and supported.

The Strategy maintains that languages are an essential part of being a citizen, and can be used for business, pleasure, communication and cultural understanding. In order to capitalise on young children's enthusiasm for language learning, primary school language teaching (still extremely limited in England) will expand considerably so that by 2010 every child aged seven to 11 will have an 'entitlement' to learn one or more languages in addition to their mother tongue.

At the same time, the Government allowed for languages to become optional at age 14, a change apparently founded on the hope that early learning would engender continuing enthusiasm and lead to positive choices being made in the teenage years. This move has been much criticised by language educationalists (Allford & Pachler, 2004) as likely to produce a decline in young people obtaining nationally recognised qualifications in languages at age 16. In two years there has in fact been such a dramatic fall in the number of pupils studying another language at Key Stage 4 that the government has written to schools requiring them to set a benchmark for the number of their pupils studying languages leading to a GCSE or other recognised qualification, with a minimum expectation of at least 50% of pupils ranging up to 90%.

A further apparent inconsistency in the Strategy is the total disregard of the recommendation in the Nuffield report (Nuffield Inquiry Committee, 2000: 92) to 'promote languages for the majority of 16–19 year-olds'. It is hard to see how there can be significant development of the UK's national capacity in languages, when less than 10% of students continue any form of language study beyond the age of 16 and when, as has also been happening recently, university language departments are being forced to close. It remains to be seen to what extent other measures within the National Languages Strategy, such as the expansion of primary school language learning and of Specialist Languages Colleges in the secondary sector, will make a positive impact on this situation.

Which Languages Count?

When the National Languages Strategy was unveiled, the key question for proponents of minority language teaching was 'which languages does the Strategy include?' At primary level, the DfES set up 19 pilot projects around the country, in local educational authorities designated as Pathfinder LEAs. These pilots mainly involved French, followed by Spanish and German, but seven Pathfinder LEAs included projects for community languages ranging from Panjabi to Turkish, and a consultant was appointed by the DfES to look at ways of encouraging LEAs to develop such languages as part of children's entitlement to language learning. The Pathfinder community languages projects included a 'family languages centre' based in a primary school in Richmond, London to offer Bengali classes in addition to existing Arabic classes. Enfield LEA in North London promised to 'include the teaching of Turkish alongside other modern foreign languages' and in Sheffield, Northern England, one secondary school aimed to support primary schools 'to provide community languages alongside modern foreign languages'.

These plans highlight the contradictory terminology employed to designate different languages in the UK. 'Modern foreign languages' or MFL was a term originally coined to differentiate languages such as French or German from classical ones such as Ancient Greek. With the advent of a wider range of languages from countries around the world, mainly former British colonies, MFL was retained to refer to languages from countries within Europe. Languages spoken by minority ethnic groups became known as 'community languages' or 'home languages', or 'mother tongue'. The inevitable implication was that these were not 'modern foreign languages' but 'traditional' ones with lesser status and currency.

In the statements from the Pathfinder projects referred to above, we see that Turkish in Enfield appears to have been assigned an equivalent status to 'other modern foreign languages'. However, in the information about Sheffield, 'community languages' remain differentiated from 'foreign languages'. This raises the fascinating possibility that some languages could become 'cross-over languages', switching status and nomenclature for a variety of reasons. If Turkey were to join the European Union, for example, it could become increasingly difficult to exclude Turkish from the 'modern foreign languages' category alongside French and German. Already, Spanish and Portuguese inhabit uneasy territory, as they are both languages of immigration and 'modern foreign languages'. Meanwhile, Mandarin Chinese (also a 'community language') is suddenly on the rise as a language of choice in secondary schools around the UK. This is particularly so in the private sector, where the economic benefits of studying Chinese are clearly perceived. A headteacher from a private school in Brighton recently announced that all his pupils would be learning the language, and he would be joining the classes himself (*The Times*, 2006).

Such political and economic changes have highlighted contradictions in the nomenclature applied to different languages, fuelling arguments for linguistic equality that have been pursued for decades by educational linguists and community groups.

The DfES has stated that all languages are to be considered as having equivalent status for the purposes of the National Languages Strategy. This gives an opening for the teaching of any language in primary or secondary school, but it remains to be seen whether and how it will be possible to implement this breadth of possibility, particularly for languages such as Bengali, Somali or Yoruba, which are not perceived as having economic or political power.

The prevailing ethos in the UK is still resolutely monolingual where community languages are concerned, as shown by a recent incident in which the new headteacher of a London secondary school decided to close down an innovative project teaching science bilingually in Turkish and English. The project was designed to help children of Turkish-speaking origin to understand scientific concepts in English through discussion in both languages, thus giving access to the science curriculum and enabling them to take nationally recognised examinations in English. Such teaching is based on the principle that academic skills learned in one language can be transferred to another language, as explained by Cummins (1984, 1991). This principle is also used in the currently expanding field of Content and Language Integrated Learning (CLIL), in which pupils in UK schools are now learning geography through French, for example. Not only does their French improve, but their geography knowledge is also of a high standard. Whilst CLIL is seen as the way forward in language learning in the 'modern foreign languages' field (CLIL Compendium, 2006; Euroclic, 2006; Grenfell, 2002; Marsh, 2002; Masih, 1999), bilingual teaching in community languages is constantly at risk. The question must be posed: would the bilingual science lessons have been closed down if they had been in French?

The London newspaper *The Evening Standard* used its editorial comment page to state that the headteacher was 'entirely right' to end the bilingual lessons (*Evening Standard*, 2006a). 'English is essential', insisted the *Standard*, and 'schools should use English as their medium of instruction because that is what their pupils need in order to live and work in this country'. The editorial showed a complete lack of knowledge of research findings on bilingual learning, but even more tellingly, invoked a monolingual discourse based on assimilation into an English-speaking UK: 'At a time when it has become obvious that some minority communities in Britain have become dangerously cut off from the mainstream, schools must give pupils every incentive to learn the language that will enable them to make the most of life in their new country.' The subtext is that continuing to develop their first language will turn young people into dissidents or terrorists, although research evidence demonstrates that multilingualism is beneficial both academically and for a secure sense of identity (Cummins, 1996; Kenner, 2004a). The effect of the editorial was only partially redressed by the headline a few days later on the Letters page, 'Mother tongues help pupils learn English' (*Evening Standard*, 2006b), where a London academic presented positive arguments for the bilingual science teaching project, based on research.

Blackledge (2006) points out that monolingual discourses lie just below the surface in the political as well as the educational arena, raising their head at key moments when politicians wish to emphasise their nationalist allegiance. The statement by David Blunkett in 2002 when Home Secretary, that Asian families should speak more English to their children at home, illustrates this. As with the bilingual science controversy, academics and community leaders contested his argument, and although Blunkett himself maintained that he was not against the learning of community languages (Blunkett, 2002), the original statement stemmed from and reinforced monolingualism. It is in this climate, where a continual struggle is taking place between monolingual and multilingual attitudes, that the National Languages Strategy will be put into operation.

'Incoherent Discourses' Around Multilingualism

The first evaluation of the 19 Pathfinder authorities participating in the National Languages Strategy at primary level (Muijs *et al.*, 2005) shows that only 1% of schools responding were teaching community languages. The evaluators commented: 'Where Pathfinders planned to introduce lesser taught languages (e.g. Arabic), these plans had frequently not borne fruit, although there were a few instances in the case study schools of successful community languages'. The report mentions one Pathfinder primary school that has succeeded in establishing a family learning centre for Arabic, but gives no further details. Meanwhile, 85% of the schools surveyed were teaching French, with a small percentage providing Spanish or German.

From the tiny percentage of minority languages being taught in this National Languages Strategy pilot, it could be surmised that there is a lack of fit between national policy and local practice. The current discourse of the DfES states that all languages are equal, and that schools can choose to teach the language best suited to their school community, depending on local circumstances. The DfES demonstrated its commitment to diversity by launching the Languages Ladder assessment framework in 2005, which will cover 26 languages including minority languages ranging from Arabic to Turkish, Urdu and Yoruba as well as the expected French, German and Spanish (DfES Languages website, 2006; Asset Languages website, 2006).

Why then do primary schools appear to be ignoring this range of possibilities and opting for the traditionally most privileged language, French? A closer inspection of policy discourse from a multisemiotic perspective reveals less coherence than the written commitment would suggest. Visuals in DfES documents encouraging language learning still show headlines of French or German newspapers, for example, rather than a variety of languages and scripts. The development of the language learning infrastructure, apart from the multilingual assessment scheme mentioned above, also tells its own tale. Schemes of work are produced in French, Spanish and German and the government supports primary teacher training courses for those languages, with pilots in Italian and Portuguese.

Meanwhile, at secondary level specialist language colleges have expanded to 275 in number, and are offering courses in some 15 languages other than French, German and Spanish, including a number of non-European languages. It is interesting to note how the choice of languages is made. Where languages such as Bengali, Panjabi and Urdu are offered, this is primarily because of demand from local communities and children studying the languages tend to come from a background where the language is spoken. Where languages such as Japanese and Mandarin are offered, economic factors are paramount and most learners have no background in the language. A division between 'community languages' and 'foreign languages' therefore tends to be maintained, with the associated danger of a hierarchy of language status. Furthermore, whilst approaches in Language Colleges may be viewed as relatively open and inclusive compared to the past, it should be remembered that such colleges represent a small proportion of state secondary schools. In other schools, diversification of the languages offer and support for minority languages tends to be much more limited.

Teachers of community languages in mainstream schools face considerable difficulties. Firstly, there has been an issue over the recognition of their qualifications and a lack of opportunity to gain qualified teacher status, with the result that they have frequently been employed as instructors rather than as fully qualified teachers. In an attempt to address this issue, some providers of initial teacher education have recently introduced Postgraduate Certification in Education courses for specialists in minority languages (CILT, The National Centre for Languages, 2005). Secondly, provision for professional development has been very limited in comparison with that aimed at teachers of the more widely taught European languages and this has had implications for promotion opportunities. Thirdly, there is a lack of clarity about where community languages should fit within the curriculum management structure. In some schools they come under the umbrella of Modern (Foreign) Languages, whilst in others they are given lesser status and placed within the English as an Additional Language and/or Special Needs Department. Fourthly, there has been a serious lack of resources for the teaching of community languages, in particular resources suitable for students growing up in this country. Thus the overall situation for minority languages in mainstream schools has been and remains one of marginalisation (Slattery, 2004).

A full-scale commitment by policymakers to an inclusive vision, integrating community languages into the National Languages Strategy, would require direct engagement and likely confrontation with the monolingual discourses discussed above. Amongst politicians and civil servants, local education authorities and headteachers, there are proponents of multilingualism and of monolingualism, with the latter holding greater power and often receiving support from the media, as shown in the case of the *Evening Standard*'s backing for a headteacher's decision to close down Turkish–English science lessons, quoted earlier. The struggle between these contradictory perspectives results in 'incoherent discourses' around multilingualism, as government policy gives to minority languages with one hand and takes away with the other. Similar struggles take place below the surface in local authorities and in schools, with few headteachers having a well developed understanding of the benefits of multilingualism and even fewer being prepared to make a stand against monolingualism by offering minority languages in the curriculum.

For all the government's rhetoric, the National Languages Strategy holds back from explicitly endorsing a truly integrated and inclusive language policy which would break down the barriers between 'foreign' and 'minority' languages and seriously challenge monocultural perspectives. A model for such a policy has been provided by Brumfit (1989, 1999). He urges institutions at all levels of education to embrace a language charter based on four elements:

(1) development of mother tongue or dialect;
(2) development of competence in a range of styles of English for educational, work-based, social and public-life purposes;
(3) development of knowledge of the nature of language in a multilingual society, including some basic acquaintance with at least two languages from the total range available in education or the community;
(4) development of a fairly extensive practical competence in at least one language other than their own.

(Brumfit, 1989: 13)

Brumfit sees these as being minimum requirements, adding that students who wish to specialise should be offered opportunities to develop further expertise in more than one language.

Research Findings on Learning in Community Language Contexts

Whilst the campaign to augment language teaching in mainstream schools goes on, thousands of children are learning languages in community contexts after school and at weekends throughout the UK. A survey by CILT (National Centre for Languages) and Scottish CILT on behalf of the Council of Europe's European Centre for Modern Languages, as part of the Valuing All Languages in Europe (VALEUR) project, aimed to map community language provision across Europe. Results for the UK were published in 2005 and showed that 61 languages are taught by ethnic minority communities (CILT/Scottish CILT, 2005). The UK Federation of Chinese Schools alone runs around 100 schools with over 13,000 pupils (UKFCS website, 2006).

Researchers have begun to conduct studies in community language classrooms, looking at pedagogies, how children learn, and the implications for identity and self-esteem. Observing in Gujarati classes in Leicester, Martin *et al.* (2006) analysed the bilingual teaching strategies used. Codeswitching between Gujarati and English allowed teachers and students to negotiate meanings and promoted the understanding of grammatical features of each language as compared to the other. Similar aspects were found by Robertson (2004) in her study of a lunchtime 'Urdu Club' at a primary school in Watford, north of London. The teacher drew attention to the different sounds of Urdu as compared to English, and discussed how to write words that appear in both languages such as 'icecream'. Many of these children also attended Qur'anic Arabic class and at the age of five took pride in their multilingual knowledge and were able to explain the different purposes for learning each of their three literacies.

Such metalinguistic awareness is likely to be contributing to children's mainstream learning as they bring to bear the skills they have acquired at community language class, for example by drawing on comprehension strategies from reading in Urdu when discussing literature in primary school (Sneddon, 2000). Although teaching and learning practices often differ between mainstream and community contexts, children are capable of 'syncretising' strategies from both contexts (Gregory & Williams, 2000) and can articulate the cumulative benefit of combining this variety of experience (Community Languages Research Group, 2006). If such benefits can be gained from a few hours a week in their 'other' classroom, often taught by dedicated volunteers with little access to space or resources, what would be the effects of integrating community language provision into the mainstream?

A research project examining how six year olds learnt English in London schools and Chinese, Arabic or Spanish at Saturday school (Kenner, 2004b) highlights young children's ability to comprehend different writing systems, the cognitive and cultural benefits to be gained from learning more than one language at a young age, and the children's desire to have their 'other language' recognised by their primary school. Some examples will be discussed here, together with the implications for extending the range of languages taught at mainstream school.

Selina, aged six, was already in her second year at Chinese Saturday school and was highly proficient at writing elegant and accurate Chinese characters (Figure 6.1). Her learning was supported by an hour's Chinese lesson every evening with her mother, and by practising informally with her 10-year-old sister Susannah – who let Selina use felt-tip pen instead of pencil for her writing and draw hearts to cover up her mistakes instead of rubbing them out and starting again. Susannah was generous with her marking, often giving Selina a hundred per cent instead of applying the stricter standards of her mother or her Saturday school teacher. Selina's mother discussed with her the meaning of different elements within Chinese writing, such as the symbol standing for 'female' which forms part of the character for 'big sister' or 'little sister'.

With the combined support of her family and her Chinese school, Selina was progressing well. She understood the system of building up a Chinese character through a specific sequence of strokes, each of which had to be exactly the right length and angle so that the character could not be confused with another that had a different meaning. She also showed that she understood how the Chinese writing system represented meanings in a very different way from English. She stated that Chinese did not have an alphabet and demonstrated how to find symbols within the characters that gave a clue to the meaning (Kenner *et al.*, 2004).

Selina was proud of her knowledge of Chinese and responded enthusiastically to the chance to teach her primary school classmates as part of the research project. Bringing her Saturday school books to mainstream school, she showed her peers how to write in Chinese, adapting her teaching to their needs as she realised how difficult it was for them to produce the complex characters she wrote with such ease. Her classmates rose to the challenge, quickly realising the accuracy required for writing in Chinese and trying to meet their young teacher's high standards. They began to discuss with Selina what the characters might mean. This interested reaction was also apparent when Ming, the six-year-old boy involved in the research project, taught Chinese to his entire primary school class for an hour and a half. Ming devised a series

Figure 6.1 Selina writing 'younger sister' in Chinese: learning the stroke sequence to build up the character (in the right hand column) and practising the whole character

of activities based on teaching methods at Chinese school and his classmates worked hard to tackle them (Kenner, 2004c).

The six-year-old research participants learning Arabic at Saturday school showed their knowledge of the different directionalities involved in Arabic and English (Kenner & Kress, 2003). When Tala was teaching Arabic to her primary school classmates, she pointed out that they were copying her writing incorrectly, from left to right. 'We don't start from there, we start from here!' she said, indicating the right-hand side of the page and drawing an arrow there to remind them, just as her teacher did at Saturday school (Figure 6.2). Yazan anticipated his classmates' monolingual approach to directionality when showing them his textbook from Arabic school. Pointing to the front cover, he stated 'Not the end'. Turning to the back cover of the book, he emphasised that 'This is the end', and returning to the front cover, 'This is the first'. Yazan was already aware that directionality could function differently in different scripts, and also realised that his classmates might not share this metalinguistic understanding.

Yazan and Tala, along with their peers at Arabic school, were learning another crucial aspect of the writing system: how letters join in order to produce Arabic script. Each Arabic letter can have up to four different forms: the form in which it appears as part of the alphabet, and the form taken when the letter is at the beginning, in the middle or at the end of a word. Children need to know these forms as soon as they begin Arabic literacy learning in order to read and write. Tala wrote her name in Arabic for her primary school classmates, then explained which alphabet letters she had used, and how the letters looked different 'because I joined them up'. Repeating the process, she showed them how the letters changed 'because Arabic is magic'. The shape-shifting characteristics of Arabic held special properties, seen through the eyes of a six year old.

The knowledge displayed by these young children, and the positive response of their classmates to the peer teaching sessions, demonstrates the potential for teaching a wide range of scripts in primary school in order to enhance language competence and metalinguistic awareness. By tapping into children's expertise from community language classes as an additional resource, the National Languages Strategy in mainstream school could benefit both monolingual and bilingual pupils.

Figure 6.2 Arrow used by Tala to remind her classmates to start on the right when writing in Arabic

Integrating Minority Languages into Mainstream Schools

However, certain key issues need to be considered when linking language teaching in the mainstream with 'funds of knowledge' (Moll, 1992) that children bring from community school. One is the need to tackle the monolingual ethos discussed above, to help mainstream teachers and parents understand the advantages of multilingualism. Another challenge is how to develop the skills of children who already speak the language alongside those of new learners, so that bilingual children's funds of knowledge are not merely exploited as a 'resource' in neocolonial terms (Martin-Jones & Saxena, 2003). Evidence from nursery settings in Ireland (Hickey, 1998) where Irish-speaking and English-speaking children were learning together in Irish showed that teachers tended to ignore the needs of first language speakers because they saw the needs of second language learners as more urgent. Comments from teachers included: 'Why would I give native speakers any special attention?' and 'I do not think it would be right to put native speakers together – in my opinion the beginners have greater need of attention.' Irish-speaking children therefore had little opportunity to develop vocabulary, styles and functions.

As several commentators (Broadbent, 1989; Tosi, 1986; Zaidi, 1996) have emphasised, to subsume community languages within teaching and assessment frameworks designed for MFL is problematic and fails among other things to take into account students' linguistic background and different cultural needs. It is worth pointing out in this regard that, in Wales, separate frameworks have been provided for those learning Welsh as a mother tongue as compared to those learning it as a second/foreign language.

A further issue is how to build the status of the community language so that English does not remain dominant in children's language learning interactions. Hickey's (1998) research in Ireland also demonstrated that where Irish-speaking and English-speaking children were supposed to work together in Irish, their conversations often reverted to English, due to the fragility of Irish in a society where English is culturally dominant.

A pilot project on Portuguese in primary schools in Stockwell, South London addressed the particular needs of native speakers by providing additional classes for them (CILT, 2004). Such an approach, however, raises questions as to whether mainstream provision will work in tandem with, or replace, community sector provision. Whilst mainstreaming of community language classes could improve status and give access to classroom space, funding and materials, are there risks here for the community sector as well as benefits to be gained? Some researchers have noted that the sector's independence, even though it arises from marginalisation, carries positive aspects. Community language schools are 'safe spaces' where children can develop their language and explore multilingual identities (Creese *et al.*, 2006; Robertson, 2005). If language provision is absorbed into the mainstream, will primary schools maintain the activities currently shared by parents, teachers and children that build the social and cultural base of each community?

We therefore conclude by observing that in this minority language context, where English has vastly more power and 'modern foreign languages' have higher status, the integration of community languages into mainstream classrooms will need to be approached sensitively and in ways that cater for bilingual children's needs as well as those of their monolingual classmates. To accomplish this will require a highly developed multilingual vision on the part of the mainstream school sector, constructed through a positive discourse towards minority languages with coherence at national and local level.

References

Allford, D. and Pachler, N. (2004) Editorial. *Language Learning Journal* 30, 2–4.

Anderson, J. (1985) A four-week interdisciplinary pilot scheme in Language Awareness. In National Congress on Languages in Education (NCLE) *Language Awareness Working Party Newsletter* 5, 8–14.

Anderson, J. (1991) The potential of Language Awareness as a focus for cross-curricular work in the secondary sector. In C. James and P. Garrett (eds) *Language Awareness in the Classroom* (pp. 133–139). London: Longman.

Asset Languages. On WWW at http://www.assetlanguages.org.uk/default.aspx. Accessed 10.3.06.

Baker, C. (1997) Bilingual education in Ireland, Scotland and Wales. In J. Cummins and D. Corson (eds) *Encyclopedia of Language and Education: Bilingual Education*. Dordrecht: Kluwer.

Baker, P. and Eversley, J. (2000) *Multilingual Capital*. London: Battlebridge.

Blackledge, A. (2006) The magical frontier between the dominant and the dominated: Sociolinguistics and social justice in a multilingual world. *Journal of Multilingual and Multicultural Development* 27 (1), 22–41.

Blunkett, D. (2002) Personal communication by letter to Charmian Kenner, 7 November, 2002.

Bourne, J. (2001) Doing 'what comes naturally': How the discourses and routines of teachers' practice constrain opportunities for bilingual support in UK primary schools. *Language and Education* 15 (4), 250–268.

Broadbent, J. (1989) Resources and materials for teaching a wider range of languages. In J. Geach and J. Broadbent (eds) *Coherence in Diversity: Britain's Multilingual Classroom* (pp. 114–128). London: CILT.

Brumfit, C. (1989) Towards a policy of multilingual secondary schools. In J. Geach and J. Broadbent (eds) *Coherence in Diversity: Britain's Multilingual Classroom* (pp. 7–19). London: CILT.

Brumfit, C. (1995) Language awareness. In C. Brumfit (ed.) *Language Education in the National Curriculum* (pp. 166–188). Oxford: Blackwell.

Brumfit, C. (1999) A policy for language in British education. In A. Tosi and C. Leung (eds) *Rethinking Language Education – from a Monolingual to a Multilingual Perspective* (pp. 30–35). London: CILT.

Bullock, S.A. (1975) *A Language for Life*. London: HMSO.

CILT (2001) *Agenda for Languages*. London: CILT.
CILT (2004) Early language learning – cornerstone of the National Languages Strategy. *Community Languages Bulletin* 15, Autumn. London: CILT.
CILT/Scottish CILT (2005) *Language Trends 2005: Community Language Learning in England, Scotland and Wales*. London: CILT.
CILT, The National Centre for Languages (2005) Qualify to teach in community languages. *Community Languages Bulletin* 16, 8–9.
CLIL Compendium (2006) On WWW at http://www.clilcompendium.com/. Accessed 10.3.06.
Community Languages Research Group (2006) On WWW at http://www.multiverse.ac.uk/viewArticle.aspx?contentId=10914&categoryId=0. Accessed 10.3.06.
Council of Europe (1977) *Council Directive on the Education of the Children of Migrant Workers* (77/48b/EEC, 25 July). Strasbourg: Council of Europe.
Creese, A., Bhatt, A., Bhojani, N. and Martin, P. (2006) Multicultural, heritage and learner identities in complementary schools. *Language and Education* 20 (1), 23–43.
Cummins, J. (1984) Language proficiency, bilingualism and academic achievement. In *Bilingualism and Special Education* (Chapter 6). Clevedon: Multilingual Matters.
Cummins, J. (1991) Interdependence of first and second language proficiency in bilingual children. In E. Bialystok (ed.) *Language Processing in Bilingual Children* (pp. 70–89). Cambridge: Cambridge University Press.
Cummins, J. (1996) *Negotiating Identities: Education for Empowerment in a Diverse Society*. Ontario, CA: California Association for Bilingual Education.
de Mejía, A.M. (2002) *Power, Prestige and Bilingualism: International Perspectives on Elite Bilingual Education*. Clevedon: Multilingual Matters.
DENI (Department of Education for Northern Ireland) (1998) *Education Reform in Northern Ireland: The Way Forward*. Bangor: DENI.
DfES (Department for Education and Skills) (2002) *Languages for All: Languages for Life*. Annesley, Notts: DfES.
DfES Languages. On WWW at http://www.dfes.gov.uk/languages/. Accessed: 10.3.06.
Edwards, V. (2004) *Multilingualism in the English-speaking World*. Oxford: Blackwell.
Euroclic (2006) On WWW at http://www.euroclic.net/. Accessed 10.3.06.
European Commission (1984) *Report on the Implementation of Directive 77/486/EEC on the Education of Children of Migrant Workers*. Brussels: EC.
European Commission (2001) *Eurobarometer* 54 (1). Brussels: EC.
Evening Standard (2006a) English is essential. 21 February.
Evening Standard (2006b) Mother tongues help pupils learn English. 27 February.
Fitzpatrick, F. (1987) *The Open Door*. Clevedon: Multilingual Matters.
Gregory, E. and Williams, A. (2000) *City Literacies: Learning to Read across Generations and Cultures*. London: Routledge.
Grenfell, M. (2002) *Modern Languages across the Curriculum*. London: Routledge, Falmer.
The Guardian (2000) Monolingual workers cost Britain dear. 10 May.
Hawkins, E. (1984) *Awareness of Language: An Introduction*. Cambridge: Cambridge University Press.
Hickey, T. (1998) Early immersion in Ireland. In V. Regan (ed.) *Contemporary Approaches to Second Language Acquisition*. Dublin: UCD Academic Press.

Jupp, C. (1990) *Bilingual Support Project 1988/9*. Hounslow: Hounslow Primary Language Service.
Kenner, C. (2004a) Living in simultaneous worlds: Difference and integration in bilingual script-learning. *International Journal of Bilingual Education and Bilingualism* 7 (1), 43–61.
Kenner, C. (2004b) *Becoming Biliterate: Young Children Learning Different Writing Systems*. Stoke-on-Trent: Trentham Books.
Kenner, C. (2004c) Community school pupils re-interpret their knowledge of Chinese and Arabic for primary school peers. In E. Gregory, S. Long and D. Volk (eds) *Many Pathways to Literacy: Young Children Learning with Siblings, Grandparents, Peers and Communities*. London: Routledge.
Kenner, C. and Kress, G. (2003) The multisemiotic resources of biliterate children. *Journal of Early Childhood Literacy* 3 (2), 179–202.
Kenner, C., Kress, G., Al-Khatib, H., Kam, R. and Tsai, K-C. (2004) Finding the keys to biliteracy: How young children interpret different writing systems. *Language and Education* 18 (2), 124–144.
Marsh, D. (2002) *CLIL/EMILE The European Dimension: Actions, Trends and Foresight Potential*. Jyvaskyla, Finland: UniCOM. On WWW at http://europa.eu.int/comm/education/policies/lang/doc/david_marsh-report.pdf. Accessed 10.3.06.
Martin, P., Bhatt, A., Bhojani, N. and Creese, A. (2004) *Final Report on Complementary Schools and their Communities in Leicester*. Leicester: University of Leicester.
Martin, P., Bhatt, A., Bhojani, N. and Creese, A. (2006) Managing bilingual interaction in a Gujarati complementary school in Leicester. *Language and Education* 20 (1), 5–22.
Martin-Jones, M. and Saxena, M. (2003) Bilingual resources and 'funds of knowledge' for teaching and learning in multi-ethnic classrooms in Britain. *International Journal of Bilingual Education and Bilingualism* 6 (3), 267–282.
Masih, J. (ed) (1999) *Learning through a Foreign Language: Models, Methods and Outcomes*. London: CILT.
Moll, L. (1992) Bilingual classroom studies and community analysis: some recent trends. *Educational Researcher* 21 (2), 20–24.
Muijs, D., Barnes, A., Hunt, M., Powell, B., Arweck, A., Lindsay, G. and Martin, C. (2005) *Evaluation of the Key Stage 2 Language Learning Pathfinders*. Annesley, Notts: DfES.
Nuffield Inquiry Committee (2000) *Languages: The Next Generation*. London: Nuffield Foundation.
Robertson, L.H. (2004) Multilingual flexibility and literacy learning in an Urdu community school. In E. Gregory, S. Long and D. Volk (eds) *Many Pathways to Literacy: Young Children Learning with Siblings, Grandparents, Peers and Communities*. London: RoutledgeFalmer.
Robertson, L.H. (2005) Teaching and learning in community language schools. *NALDIC Occasional Paper 19*. Herts, UK: National Association for Language Development in the Curriculum.
Slattery, S. (2004) *Multilingual Britain: Implications for MFL Teaching in Secondary School*. Community languages research on-line. On WWW at http://www.cilt.org.uk/commlangs/research/multilingualbritain.rtf. Accessed 20.4.06.
Sneddon, R. (2000) Language and literacy: Children's experiences in multilingual environments. *International Journal of Bilingual Education and Bilingualism* 3 (4), 265–282.
Swann, Lord (1985) *Education for all*. London: HMSO.

The Times (2006) School where Chinese is compulsory. 17 January.

Tosi, A. (1986) From wrong assumptions to ineffective teaching: Teaching bilinguals with a monolingual approach. *Language Issues* 1, 25–27.

Tsow, M. (1992) Community languages in Britain. *Bilingualism and Languages Network* 2 (5).

United Kingdom Federation of Chinese Schools (UKFCS) (2006) On WWW at http://www.ukfcs.info/. Accessed 10.3.06.

Zaidi, S. (1996) Community Languages Teaching: Some important issues. In C. Midwinter (ed.) *Global Perspectives in the National Curriculum: Guidance for Key Stages 3 and 4*. London: The Development Education Association.

Chapter 7

Bilingual Education in France: School Policies Versus Home Practices

CHRISTINE HÉLOT

Introduction

Despite a long tradition of foreign language teaching in France, the general feeling amongst civil society is that schools are failing to deliver the kind of competence needed for today's globalised world. Since 2000, the Ministry of Education has been involved in a major plan to 'renovate' the teaching of foreign languages. As part of this plan, several measures were implemented: in 2002, early foreign language teaching was fully integrated in the primary curriculum and from 2007–2008, all children aged seven will be taught a foreign language for three hours a week; several models of bilingual education were developed, in particular for regional minority languages, which have a very low level of family transmission; and at secondary level, Content and Language Integrated Learning[1] (CLIL) classes are being opened in European languages mostly. Thus, bilingual education in France has developed mainly as a means to find more efficient foreign language teaching approaches, and to a certain extent, to improve the status of regional minority languages. On the other hand, despite some measures taken to integrate the languages of immigration in the renovation plan, mother tongue education for minority language speakers remains marginal. Obliged by their circumstances to acquire the majority language, these pupils have little choice but to become bilingual, but their own bilingualism remains invisible; however, like their monolingual peers they can indeed be offered the chance to join bilingual education programmes, but not in their home language, these programmes being offered for the most part in dominant European languages.

Bilingual education is a fairly recent development in France, yet the issue is no less polemical than in many other countries. In a state known for its legislation on the national language as an instrument for the consolidation of centralised power and for its policies of vitiation towards minority languages, the development of bilingual education has taken a course which needs to be contextualised from different points of view. Deprez (2000), for example, suggests that the domain of bilingualism in France should be studied from three perspectives and distinguishes between 'dialectal bilingualism', 'migrant bilingualism' and 'educational bilingualism'. I have chosen a different approach based on analysing the development of bilingualism in two contexts: the family context and the school context and the relationship between them. I think that the development of bi/plurilingualism whether at home or at school and the conceptualisation of bilingual education should include all categorisation of languages and all kinds of linguistic experiences.

In this chapter, I would like to focus my analysis on the different models of bilingual education available at present and to question what seems to me to be a paradoxical situation: on the one hand the Ministry of Education has been involved in a major reform to improve foreign language learning and bilingual programmes are seen as one means to achieve this goal. In other words, education authorities are now very aware of the importance of plurilingualism and of the necessity for our school system to produce bilingual and multilingual citizens. On the other hand, more and more pupils grow up using a language at home which is different from the national language, but because of the low status of these languages, their bilingualism is being ignored or, worse, stigmatised.

It should be made clear that this situation is not unique to France, as most European countries are trying to reflect upon ways of developing more inclusive linguistic policies, particularly in relation to minority migrant languages. In other publications (Hélot, 2003, 2006; Hélot *et al.*, 2006), I have analysed the different perceptions of bilingualism in education in terms of a gap between the well known dichotomy of elite bilingualism and folk bilingualism. Within this framework I looked for means to bridge this gap at the level of the classroom: I tried to show how innovative pedagogical approaches can be developed where all forms of bilingualism are valued and linguistic and cultural diversity can become a collective resource for all children, monolinguals and bilinguals alike.

The basic point I would like to make here is that if we believe that bilingualism is an asset for the individual and for society, we cannot continue to think in terms of compensatory measures for minority pupils who become bilingual in the home context, and in terms of value added models of bilingual programmes for the monolingual elites. The situation at present in France is that there have been a lot of policies passed with a view to improving the foreign language skills of monolingual pupils and little has been done to support minority language speakers. Indeed, it has long been the case in France that assimilationist language policies in school have resulted in the loss of the home language, thus making bilingual pupils monolingual again. But today, paradoxically, schools are being asked, through the provision of bilingual education in regional languages in particular, to reverse the process of language loss that they have contributed to create.

I would like to argue in this chapter, that, on the whole, the ideology of bilingual education in France still reflects a monolingual bias (Benert, 2006; Hélot, 2003), and that despite the wide variety of programmes offered and the innovative pedagogical approaches being developed, the way bilingual education is being implemented at present creates a growing gap between pupils who have access to this and those who do not. Both these points can only be explained if one takes into account the historical context, particularly in relation to the history of the French language and the nature of the first bilingual programmes implemented in state schools in 1981, labelled as 'international sections'.

I would also like to point to an important distinction to be made between policy, provision and practice. Linguistic policies are decreed at national level, while provision can depend on local education authorities and practices are often slow to reflect the top-down decisions taken by a still very centralised Ministry of Education. In France, a gap can also been seen between the latest educational language policies on diversification of languages to be taught in schools and the actual choice of languages available in practice. The reasons for this are probably economic – it is costly to offer several languages in a school as it implies recruiting more teachers – but this is not the only reason. One should not forget the predominantly monolingual habitus of most French schools. In fact, the new policies make provision for rich and varied language learning, which could lead to possible improvement for minority languages. However, the organisation of the new provision is rather complex and it hides the fact that these new bilingual programmes remain discriminatory and favour dominant languages and monolingual pupils (Hélot, 2007).

It should be stressed that in this contribution the term 'bilingual education' is meant to refer to pupils who are educated in two languages, in other words, pupils who are given the opportunity to learn school subjects through two different languages, whatever the amount of time devoted to each language, or the organisation of schooling through the two languages. Thus, learning a foreign language for three hours per week will not be considered bilingual education (it is known as a model of language learning usually called extensive), but learning physics in German three hours per week is indeed a form of bilingual education. Particular attention will be given to the terms used for the different models being implemented, because the terminology used to classify the various languages (other than French) in the curricula is not only confusing, it also reveals the ideology at work when languages are labelled. Indeed, one of the reasons why the labels are difficult to understand is that they tend to reflect linguistic policy rather than actual practice. Readers should also be reminded that, strictly speaking, it is difficult to speak of minority languages in a country which, according to its constitution, does not recognise minority groups.

The Conceptualisation of Bilingual Education in France

To understand the political and educational context of bilingual education in France, we must first bear in mind the central position of the French language.

The hegemony of the French language

In France, the debate on how one should handle linguistic diversity goes back a long way, and language policies have been highly coherent. From as far back as the 15th century with the Ordonnance de Villers-Cotterets (1539), through the Revolution, up to the law of 1975 on the use of the French language, and to the amendment of Article II of the Constitution in 1992 which made the French language the sole language of the Republic, the hegemony of the French language has been thought of as an instrument to consolidate central power and later on, the State. Considered as an institution which guarantees national unity through various societal structures, such as schools, laws, political discourses and even the media, the central position of the French language has made it difficult to allow for the growing linguistic diversity of French society at large, not to mention the great variety of practices within the French language itself.

However, this does not mean that there has not been any discussion in France on the question of linguistic diversity. On the contrary, there have been many debates on the status of 'regional languages'. Presidential candidates and ministers of education have made various declarations of intent and several reports have been published (Carcassonne, 1998; Poignant Report, 1998) on the compatibility between the European Charter on Regional and Minority languages and the French Constitution, not forgetting Cerquiglini (2003), who proposed a list of the possible 70 or so languages that could be included in the Charter.

Regional languages are the languages spoken in various regions of France, such as Brittany, the Basque Country, Corsica, Alsace, the South of France and the overseas territories, such as Martinique and Guadeloupe, La Reunion or New Caledonia. The education system has always been the main domain of intervention for the implementation of policies towards regional languages. These were strictly forbidden, for example, with the 1881–1884 laws of Jules Ferry, which made schooling obligatory, free and secular and imposed French as the sole language of teaching and learning. The use of a regional language or of a 'patois' was severely punished in the classroom and the playground alike. It was not until 1951 that the Dexonne law was passed allowing Breton, Basque, Catalan and Occitan to figure in the curriculum,[2] although actual implementation of the law took another 20 years, with Corsican being added to the list in 1974 and Alsatian in 1982.

Today, regional languages are spoken by a tiny minority; there are no monolingual speakers left and the rate of transmission is very low. Under the influence of European policies designed to protect linguistic and cultural diversity, the regional languages of France have acquired a new visibility, particularly in 2002, when they were included in the new primary curriculum alongside modern foreign languages. But despite this new legitimacy, the provision is offered in such a way that regional languages are in fact in competition with foreign languages, as pupils must choose between one foreign language and one regional language. It is clear that only very committed parents will choose Breton instead of English, for example, but at least there is now some provision for the learning of regional languages and their related culture for those who want it. However, one should add that the latest education bill (Fillon law, 2005) has reduced the number of languages on offer in the new 'Socle commun de connaissances et de compétences' (2006), the basic curriculum which must be acquired by the end of compulsory schooling.

Bilingual education in regional languages

Thirty years ago, bilingual education in regional languages started in the private sector under the initiative of regional associations and parental groups who wanted their children to be educated through the medium of a language they felt needed to be supported in schools as well as at home. In 1969 the Basque Schools, Seaska, were created, then in 1977 the Diwan schools in Brittany. In 1979 the Calendretas for Occitan in the South of France appeared, followed in 1991 by the ABCM in Alsace. Based on the example of Canada, these private schools chose the immersion model of bilingual education and because of their success, regularly asked the Ministry of Education to integrate them into the State sector. They have not been successful for two reasons: one due to the 1994 amendment to the Constitution (referred to as the Toubon law[3]), which stressed the central role of the French language in the education system, and the other owing to the immersion model chosen. Total immersion in the regional language is seen as not giving enough learning space to the French language.

However, in 2001, when the first official texts describing bilingual programmes in regional languages came out, two models were proposed, one called 'immersion' and the other one 'paritaire', meaning there must be parity of time allocated to the French language and to the regional language.[4] The immersion model was declared unconstitutional on two occasions; thus, provision for full immersion is only available in private schools.

Although the 'paritaire' model is not called immersion in the French official texts, it can be considered partial immersion (Baker, 1996; Coste, 2002): school subjects can be taught either in the regional language or in French or in both languages. Each language is distributed on either a half daily or daily basis. In some cases (Alsace) two teachers are involved and in others (Corsica) one bilingual teacher is in charge. Pupils join the programme at kindergarten level and can continue at elementary and secondary levels. According to Colinet and Morgen (2004), approximately 25,000 pupils were studying in bilingual programmes at primary level and 3500 at secondary in 2002/2003. In Alsace, this represents almost 6% of primary pupils; in the Basque country 21%; whereas Occitan only has 2% of primary school pupils. In Brittany, 10,406 pupils[5] study in the bilingual programme French Breton (3851 in the public sector, 3659 in private catholic schools and 2896 in the Diwan schools). In Alsace, the programme is developing at secondary level where there are 72 classes with a total of 1437 students who will be taking a special baccalaureate called ABIBAC, a combination of the French exam and its equivalent in Germany, the Abitur. The reason why the bilingual programmes in Alsace are more developed than in other regions (apart from Corsica) needs to be explained.

Bilingual education in Alsace

The context of bilingual education in Alsace is unique in France because the regional language is German, rather than the local spoken varieties still in use called Alemanic dialects or Alsatian. In 1982, education authorities in Alsace (Deyon, see Huck, 1999) decided that German was the written form of the Alsatian dialects, as well as being the language of its neighbours on the other side of the border; thus in a sense, and for educational purpose, German acquired the status of a regional language of France. This decision was clearly a political move to legitimise the teaching of German in Alsace, which means, as Huck (1999) argues, that pupils learn standard oral and written German at school. The situation is paradoxical because standard oral German is seldom spoken in Alsace, so that the great majority of children enrolled in bilingual programmes in Alsace never hear German at home, and even fewer hear or speak the Alsatian dialect, which has an extremely low rate of transmission. However, bilingual education in French and German is all the more attractive to parents who want their children to become competent in a widely spoken European language.

The situation in Alsace is an example of how language policies can be interpreted at the local level and make the provision for bilingual education possible in a European language, in this case German. The proximity of Germany is also used as an argument to justify this choice and German in Alsace is often referred to as 'the language of our neighbours'. Such criteria obviously cannot be applied to a language like English. Apart from the support for German by local education authorities in Alsace, the central ministry in Paris also has its own motives to support such a policy: the hegemony of the English language in the education system is most prevalent from the primary level up to secondary, in universities and even in teacher education. The main strategy chosen at policy level has been to insist on the diversification of foreign language learning. However, in practice, this has not worked. English has remained the favoured choice of most parents and students. By making the provision for bilingual education possible in German, the central Ministry in Paris is seen to be taking measures to implement diversification. It is also trying to remedy the sharp decline in the number of pupils who choose German at a time when closer links between France and Germany are being established at European level. Indeed, the Fillon law (2005) stipulates that the teaching of German must be increased by 20% in the next few years.

The example of German in Alsace is another illustration of the way bilingual education is always linked to political and ideological considerations (Heller, 2002). It also shows how the use of categorisations like regional language or foreign language is ambiguous and can serve to support some languages and to ignore others, in other words to erect barriers between languages. In the case of Alsace, the educational policies chosen favour a dominant language at the expense of its local variety and bilingual education in this case will accentuate the loss of the Alsatian language, which seems counterproductive. Furthermore, it is difficult for parents and teachers to see the logic at work in the various provisions made possible by policies where the rationale has more to do with questions of political and economic power than with educational matters.

This said, it is clear that there is a social demand for the teaching of regional languages which are seen to have a historical and cultural dimension linked to a region and to be part of the regional identity. This is the reason why, at the educational level, the demand for the inclusion of regional languages in the curriculum came from the regions rather than from the traditional centralised ministry in Paris, even if decision makers in the capital are also influenced by European measures in favour of minority languages,[6] particularly within the development of regional links across Europe. Regional languages are also envisaged as the languages of our neighbours in a European space where the notion of borders is changing. Thus, the decision to develop bilingual education in these languages can be seen as a positive step. However, in view of the very low rate of family transmission, the total immersion model would no doubt be far more effective and could better support parents who wish to pass on their language to their children. But, as explained above, the French state is not prepared to relent on the education of its future citizens being dispensed predominantly in a regional language at the expense of the national language, even if regional languages are now recognised as part of the country's heritage.

Foreign[7] languages and Content and Language Integrated Learning (CLIL)

Strictly speaking, the term *enseignement bilingue* is used only for regional languages. Other languages in the curriculum cannot be taught according to the partial immersion model for the same reasons as explained above: partial immersion allows for half the curriculum to be taught through the foreign language and such provision would give it far too much space in the curriculum, or rather would restrict the place of French. This would be particularly worrying in the case of English, the most popular foreign language taught in France, as in other non-English-speaking European countries.

For this reason, a different kind of provision has been made available following the same principle as in immersion; the foreign language is used as a medium of instruction for nonlinguistic subjects but to a lesser extent than in partial immersion. These models are based on the idea that more time should be devoted to foreign language learning but as the timetable cannot be extended, using the foreign language as a medium of instruction means increased exposure to the language. CLIL, or in French EMILE (*Enseignement d'une matière intégrée à une langue étrangère*[8]) are the labels used to refer to such provision in the literature on bilingual education. The foreign language becomes more than just an object of study; it is used as a medium to learn different school subjects and the pedagogical rationale is that such an approach is more efficient.

There are various types of CLIL provision in France referred to under differing denominations which reflect the context of their development. In 1981, 20 years before partial immersion in regional languages was available, 'international sections' were created and implemented at kindergarten, primary and secondary levels; they were followed in 1992 by 'European and Oriental sections'; and in 1999 by 'Latin and romance programmes' in the region of Toulouse. There are major differences between 'international sections' and 'European sections', which I would like to explain.

International sections

International sections can only be found in a few schools in big cities where they were created to educate the children of an 'international' elite and few of them can be found in the public sector. On the whole, they are meant for bilingual and plurilingual pupils who speak dominant languages[9] at home. Their home language is supported through classes in literature and history, which are offered on top of the regular French curriculum. Pupils are assessed before joining the programme. There are many beneficial aspects to this provision: the subjects taught in the language other than French follow the curriculum of the relevant country and this enables pupils to enter foreign universities easily; most teachers recruited for these sections are native speakers, which means the pupils experience varied pedagogical approaches; and they can also benefit from extra support in French as a foreign language if needed. Legendre (2004) gives the figure of 10,000 pupils attending international sections in 2002, half of them in English and only 61 in Arabic.

I have explained in other articles (Hélot, 2003) that international sections are a well known form of elite bilingual education (de Mejía, 2002). This does not means the model itself is elitist, but rather that because of the way it is implemented it is not available for everybody. Groux (2006), describing international and bilingual schools in and around Paris, shows clearly that the part of the city where they are situated works as a discriminating factor and that there is a correlation between the three levels – social, spatial and educational – at which segregation develops. She points to the fact that most pupils attending these sections belong to families with a high socioeconomic status, that they are very high achievers used to travelling and to having numerous contacts with other plurilingual speakers and thus are not just bilingual but often also trilingual. In other words, these pupils are in a very privileged situation: they are the recipients of the best multilingual education possible; the education system supports both their home language and the school language and ensures bi/multiliteracy at a high level. It is clear this type of language education extends their already large linguistic capital.

European sections

Based on the acknowledged success of international sections, the Ministry of Education decided to develop the model and to offer it more widely. In 1992, European sections were created as explained above to find more efficient ways of teaching foreign languages. The introduction of foreign language learning at the primary level also meant that new pedagogical approaches needed to be developed in order to maintain learners' motivation through their 10 years of schooling.

European sections are different from international sections; they do not cater for bilingual pupils but are designed to offer all pupils a more intensive and efficient approach to foreign language learning. But because they were based on the model adopted for international sections, the provision is organised according to the same model: one or two subjects are taught through the foreign language, from the third grade of secondary education; prior to this, the foreign language is taught more intensively in the first two years so that pupils can acquire a sufficient level of linguistic competence to learn history or physics or any other nonlinguistic subject through the foreign language.

The languages concerned are dominant European languages such as English, German, Spanish, Italian, Czech and Dutch and the European dimension is very much present in the objectives which are not only linguistic but also cultural. From 500 in 1994, European sections have grown to 2500 in 2002; a majority of pupils choosing English (50,127 out of a total of 101,110 pupils registered in 2002, according to Legendre, 2004).

Oriental sections

At the same time as the European sections were created for European languages, 'oriental sections' were also included in the official texts[10] to cater for other languages, such as Arabic, Japanese, Chinese, Russian and Vietnamese. Legendre (2004) gives the figure of 644 pupils attending these sections in 2002: 55 for Arabic, 331 for Chinese and 150 for Japanese. Theoretically, there are two criteria for such sections to be opened: a sufficient number of parents need to make a request, and teaching staff should be available. However, oriental sections remain mostly unknown to the public and even to teachers, therefore very few children choose these languages instead of English, for example.

I would like to point out the gap between policies designed to make bilingual education available in a wide choice of languages and the lack of implementation at the ground level. I am not convinced the dominance of English is the only reason. Traditional centralised top-down policies as well as the high number of official documents sent to heads of schools almost daily, plus the complexity of the different models available for language learning do not help to translate these policies into actual practice. But another reason must be mentioned. These sections, whether European or oriental, are based on the principle of continuity. In other words, pupils must have studied Arabic at primary school if they want to join the oriental section in Arabic at secondary level. The figures speak for themselves, as only 0.2% of children (RERS, 2007) have been able to take Arabic as a first foreign language at primary level.

Bilingual Education and Elitism

Interestingly, European sections were created on the basis of the success of international sections,[11] without, it seems, any awareness of the importance of taking the sociolinguistic context into account when measuring the effectiveness of any form of education, not just bilingual education. It is not surprising that 'international sections' are successful when we take into account all the positive factors involved, and it is increasingly obvious that European sections cannot achieve the same level of language competence with basically monolingual pupils.

Another point should be explained at this stage. Throughout this discussion, I have used the term 'section' to describe the various CLIL models of bilingual education available in the context of language education in France. This refers to the way these programmes have been implemented within the schools. Indeed, it is important to understand that the Ministry of Education did not want to develop bilingual schools *per se*, because of the principle of equality that is central to public education. In other words, the Ministry was well aware that bilingual education could give rise to some form of elitism and, in order to avoid this, decided to implant international, European or oriental sections within mainstream schools. Thus, for example, a child enrolled in a European section will be attached to a regular class, but for language learning she will be attached to her language section (the English section for example). This means that for nonlinguistic subjects all children are together, but that those enrolled in bilingual sections leave the regular class for their language learning. This system is thought to prevent elitism.

The same principle is at work as far as regional bilingual education is concerned. Bilingual sites are opened within mainstream primary schools, so that no public school in France is a totally bilingual school. At primary level, however, a particular school becomes a 'bilingual site' when in some classes children are taught in two languages and not in French only. This means that within one school some children attend the regular programme with extensive foreign language learning (from 2 to 3 hours weekly) and others are lucky enough to have been accepted in the bilingual class or at secondary level in the European section.

In other words, bilingual education is not available for all pupils. Those who want to enter European or oriental sections at secondary level are evaluated. Marks in French and Math are taken into account, the reasoning being that bilingual education implies a heavier workload, and thus only the high achievers will be able to cope. We are referring here to practice rather than official documents, which are silent about this form of selection.

It is easy to imagine the consequences of such policies. Heads of schools and parents alike were very quick to notice the many advantages of bilingual programmes: better status for the school (and often increased funding), better students in the classes and increased chances of success for pupils. The General Inspectorate's report[12] admits this and recognises that the selection put in place in some schools 'resembles a ritual reserved for a social and intellectual elite' (my translation). The same report advises heads of schools to recruit pupils from all social classes but this is followed up only on a very small scale. However, one should not deny that European sections are available in some vocational schools, even if in relatively small numbers.[13]

The 2005 statistics from the Ministry of Education (RERS, 2005) give the figure of 3.2% of pupils registered in European and international sections. European sections, in particular, are very popular and show a 12% increase between 2003 and 2004. But it is still only a minority of selected children who can avail themselves of bilingual education, therefore who benefit from pedagogical innovations and more competent teachers. These pupils (or their parents) are also aware of the better professional chances it gives them. Heads of schools cannot ignore the fact that such programmes give better status to their schools, attract better students and lead to higher overall results in final state examinations.

However, it should be made clear that the models of bilingual education in place in public schools are not elitist by nature; on the pedagogical level they are innovative, and they meet a very strong demand amongst French parents to improve language education. It is the way they are implemented, the way education authorities choose some schools rather than others and the way pupils are selected that make these programmes elitist. Moreover, the various means devised by education authorities to prevent the creation of elitist schools have not worked. For example, in schools where international sections have been implanted, no more than 50% of pupils can be registered in these sections. However, this measure does not prevent the school from being seen as 'international', and thus more attractive.

While some French authors demand bilingual education for all pupils (Groux, 2006; Hagège, 1996), rather than early foreign language teaching (according to the extensive model), a major hurdle would need to be overcome to implement this, and that is teacher education. At present, there are not enough teachers for early foreign language learning at primary level; at secondary level, teachers are required to pass a state exam in only one subject and they are refusing the various proposals from the government to teach two subjects like in many other European countries. It is obvious that teaching academic subjects in a foreign language demands a high level of competence in that language and if the Ministry were to make bilingual education available to every pupil it would mean investing a substantial amount of effort and money in teacher education. In other words, it would demand clear political will.

Consequently, private schools are cashing in on this situation, offering mainly English bilingual education, recruiting native teachers and attracting more and more pupils whose parents can afford high fees, study trips abroad, etc. This is the reason why foreign language has become a discriminating discipline and not only within the private sector.

To summarise, while bilingual education is rather new in France, one should not forget the long tradition of foreign language teaching. But precisely because foreign language teaching as it has existed all these years has not been felt to be very effective, it has been necessary to find new ways of teaching foreign languages. Bilingual education grew out of this demand, yet within the existing constraints, such as the battle against the hegemony of the English language and the priority given to the French language. This last factor is very important and justifies Benert's (2006) remark that bilingual education in France is gallocentric. Indeed, it is the French curriculum that is taught in the bilingual programmes (in regional languages and in European and oriental sections), according to French pedagogical approaches and by French teachers. This means that a lot of pedagogical materials must be newly designed, whereas at present many teachers simply translate French materials into the target language. Thus, the notion of bilingualism and bilingual education in France is still marked by a vision of two parallel monolingualisms, rather than by the idea that learners can develop a plurilingual competence. As will be explained in more detailed in the next section, a plurilingual competence encompasses knowledge of different languages at different levels, for different purposes and working in a complementary fashion. It does not necessarily mean that the aim of language learning should be bilingualism, or reaching native speaker competence in all of the student's languages.

Language Education Provision for 'Newly Arrived' Children and for Pupils who Speak a Language of Immigration

In previous articles (Hélot, 2003, 2006), I have described children who speak a language other than French as bilinguals, for even 'newly arrived' pupils (as they are referred to in French official documents) should, in my opinion, be considered bilingual or at the very least as incipient bilinguals. However, this is not the terminology used in France, and this has an influence on teachers' attitudes towards these children's linguistic competences. This is not surprising, in view of the long policy of assimilation in France, the reluctance of dealing with its colonial past, and the denial of the positive contribution of immigration to French society. The analysis is not made easy by the fact that two types of pupils need to be considered when studying the languages of immigration. On the one hand, there are foreign children arriving in our schools needing support for the acquisition of the French language, and on the other, children who were born in France but who speak the language of their immigrant parents at home, or if they don't speak it, who are in contact with a language and culture linked to former French colonies.

Policies for 'newly arrived children'

According to a recent text dealing with the integration of foreign children in the education system, the objectives of the Ministry of Education are very clear. While they insist on the respect which must be shown towards the pupils' 'languages of origin', they also state that the harmonious integration of foreign pupils depends first and foremost on the learning of the French language. Zirotti's analysis (2006) of 40 years of policies towards migrant and foreign pupils comes to the conclusion that public policies have largely ignored the linguistic and cultural diversity of ethnic minority pupils in schools.

In the 1970s, several measures were decided on, to support foreign children, such as 'integration classes' (CLIN[14]) in primary schools, 'adaptation classes' (CLA[15]) in secondary schools, heritage language classes (ELCO[16]) in mother tongues and the establishment of special centres dedicated to producing pedagogical materials for migrant children (CEFISEM[17]). In the 1990s, because there were fewer foreign children arriving in our schools, these centres decided to target the children of more established immigrants. However, in 2000, the trend was reversed, as many older foreign pupils entered French schools having often had only limited schooling in their own country. CEFISEM were changed into CASNAV,[18] aimed at ensuring schools teach the French language and culture as well as the values of the French Republic, because these are seen as the basic conditions for social integration (Forestier, 2002). Nowhere in these new directives is respect for the home languages of the foreign pupils mentioned.

In 2002, a new ministerial directive (de Gaudemar, 2002) addressed the needs of 'newly arrived foreign pupils without sufficient knowledge of French or without basic education'. The five-page document contains only one paragraph about the home languages of these pupils. It states that newly arrived children should be taught a foreign language as soon as they arrive, and that they should be encouraged to study their first language as a foreign language in their regular class or within the ELCO programme. Pupils in secondary school can have free access to a distance education course in their L1 if this language is not taught in their school.

One might conclude that from the point of view of policy, an integrated approach to the children's languages is offered, but in reality the same hierarchy still prevails. The school language predominates, the foreign language will be taught three hours per week and lastly, and on an optional basis, the home language is offered, if it is available in the school. As to the support for the acquisition of the school language, in 2000 there were 372,268 foreign pupils in primary schools, representing

5.9% of the total number of children in public and private schools, but only 1519 were in integration classes (CLIN). At secondary school level, there were 257,000 pupils, or 4.8% of the total (RERS, 2005), and according to Lacerda and Ameline (2001) only 3500 pupils were attending adaptation classes (CLA), the main reason being that there is a shortage of courses catering for foreign pupils.

The ELCO programme or classes in so-called 'languages of origin'

The teaching of the mother tongue of migrant children was started in the 1970s with two official objectives: to help integrate the languages of immigration into the school curriculum by giving them the status of school subjects and to make sure children kept a link with their country of origin, in case of a possible return to that country.

In fact, the ELCO programme was never really integrated into the curriculum. The teaching rarely takes place within the regular timetable but after school hours. In both cases, the programme distinguishes pupils according to their supposed origin, which is contradictory to the principles of equality of the French education system. The teachers are recruited in the country of origin and basically all the school does is to lend a room. Many French teachers resent these classes, because they have no control over the lessons and perhaps mainly because they see them as contradictory to the lay principles so central to our education system.

Since 2001, the Ministry of Education has tried to integrate the languages of immigration into the regular curriculum. Arabic, for example, was added to the list of foreign languages which could be taught at primary level as early as 1995. But 11 years later, only two or three schools (one in Montpellier and two in Paris) offer the language within the regular foreign language teaching provision. The RERS statistics (2007) speak for themselves. Only 0.20% of pupils studied Arabic at primary school in 2006/2007. In secondary schools, since 2001/2002, only 6000 pupils have studied Arabic (Caubet, 2001).

If one remembers that there are approximately two million Arabic and Berber speakers in France (Chaker, 1997) and that Magrebi Arabic was recognised as one of the languages of France (Cerquiglini, 2003), one might ask why so few schools offer the language. Furthermore, if one looks closely at the curriculum, the fact that Arabic has been included alongside foreign languages means that the implementation and objectives are the same for Arabic as for English or German. It is clear that at primary level the objectives for the teaching of so-called 'foreign' languages can consider all learners as beginners, but such an assumption is rather inexact in the case of Arabic speakers. It is also surprising that in the pedagogical booklet dealing with the Arabic language there is no reference made to the knowledge the pupils might already have of this language. Thus, the text is silent about the possible bilingualism of some pupils and treats all as beginners.

There are other measures concerning Arabic which separate the language from its speakers. The Baccalaureate exam is based on classical Arabic, when most young people who know the language speak one of the dialects. There is, however, an optional exam which can be taken in Arabic dialects, but the courses given in schools do not prepare for this exam, because only classical Arabic is taught. So, I think it is fair to say that the integration of Arabic in the curriculum, while proposed at policy level, is not effective at the level of provision and as far as practices are concerned, the hierarchy between classical Arabic and its local varieties is reinforced.

The integration of former languages of immigration like Spanish, Italian and Portuguese has been less problematic because these languages changed status when the respective countries joined the European Union. Today, there is a major difference in attitude towards former immigrants from European countries (Spain, Italy and Portugal) and immigrants from non-European countries (North Africa and Turkey, for example). However, one new measure is worth noting. The classes in languages of origin are now open to all pupils and no longer reserved for the children who belong to a particular national origin. In theory, this is a good measure (albeit for majority language speakers), but in practice it does not change anything for minority language speakers, because these languages are rarely offered by schools in the first place. It is also interesting that the justification given by Lang (2001) for such a change is focused on the varied linguistic needs of the nation, and the economic potential such knowledge represents. Nowhere is the knowledge of immigration languages referred to as a resource or a form of wealth brought to France by its speakers.

Moreover, in official documents, immigration languages are still envisaged in terms of linguistic handicap, rather than in terms of resources for linguistic and cultural diversity. For the first time ever, in 2002, the primary curriculum included one page on 'the case of children who do not have French as a mother tongue'. There is, thus, a clearly observable tendency to formulate these directives in negative terms. I mentioned above the case of 'Newly arrived children *without sufficient knowledge of French*', and here we have 'the case of children *who do not have French as a mother tongue*', as if these pupils have been robbed of a privilege. This text is short, very ambiguous, full of negative structures and, as I have argued elsewhere (Hélot, 2006), probably reinforces teachers' negative attitudes towards the linguistic practices of ethnic minority children. Indeed, nowhere is the term 'bilingual' used to describe them, no doubt because the authors of the official texts are thinking of immigration languages, even if they are not clearly mentioned. This is particularly worrying when school failure and violence is associated with the linguistic deficit of minority speakers and teachers receive little training on how to deal with the growing pluralism in our society.

One must stress again that language policies in France are part of wider policies where the relationship to the national language is inscribed within the cultural model of our society. The main aim of these policies is the maintenance of a single national community. As Zirotti (2006: 89) explains, 'the model of successful social insertion is the "Frenchisation" of immigrants, their assimilation in a social and homogeneous totality, and if the threat of heterogeneity arose, it could entail the end of society. Such a conception feeds a certain suspicion towards the languages of immigrants, whose persistence is seen as an obstacle to assimilation' (my translation).

Within such a context, it is clear that political priorities are not going to be very encouraging towards the development of a form of bilingualism acquired in the family or in a local community context, and the valuing of the linguistic and cultural diversity it brings is not part of the political agenda. Paradoxically, insisting on improving the teaching of foreign languages is a very high priority, particularly in the European context, and politicians need to address the strong criticism of most parents in relation to the perceived inefficiency of language teaching in general. Another paradox is that the foreign language teaching curriculum includes very clear objectives about education for 'otherness', and at the same time, many languages and cultures present in our classrooms remain invisible. It seems to me that the diversity present in the pupils' linguistic repertoires could be a better source of education on alterity and learning to live together than discovering 'the' culture associated with one foreign language; 'a' culture which is so often presented in a monolithic and stereotyped approach, particularly in textbooks.

Bridging the Gap, Some Proposals for the Future

In the face of such paradoxes, it is necessary to move beyond a dichotomous conception of bilingualism in terms of elite bilingualism and minority bilingualism and propose different approaches which can help us to think of bilingualism from a more integrated perspective. I shall argue for ways to bridge the gap at the different levels of policy and practice and will base my analysis around the notion of plurilingual competence, as well as using Hornberger's (2003) Continua of Biliteracy model to show how power relationships between languages of different status can be reversed at the level of classroom practices.

The notion of plurilingual competence

In 2003, the Council of Europe published a useful guide for the development of language policies in Europe. The authors (Beacco & Byram, 2003) explain that the notion of plurilingualism is at the heart of the common approach to language policies for Europe and that this is the central value to be supported and developed at economic, social and cultural levels. Indeed, plurilingualism is seen as the main characteristic of European citizenship and a key factor in the construction of a European identity. It is also linked to the notion of democratic citizenship, which means that protecting linguistic and cultural diversity is not an end in itself but that it is working at the same level as the construction of a more tolerant society based on solidarity.

While the term 'plurilingualism' is not free of ambiguity, it can be interpreted as a principle that aims to increase the offer of languages by education systems. In a sense, this is what the Ministry of Education in France is trying to do, if only to combat the hegemony of the English language. But as the authors of the guide warn us: 'diversifying the number of languages is a necessary but insufficient condition for acting on motivation to undertake plurilingual education' (Beacco & Byram, 2003: 36). For plurilingualism can also be interpreted as a principle for preserving the linguistic diversity of European people. This means looking at linguistic diversity as heritage, protecting minority languages which are in danger of disappearing and valuing family transmission of lesser spoken languages. Thus, political and educational institutions should make sure people understand the intrinsic value of linguistic varieties and plurilingualism being conceived as a form of contact with others: 'this means embracing the teaching of all languages in the same educational project and no longer placing the teaching of the national language, regional or minority languages and the languages of newly arrived communities in water tight compartments' (Beacco & Byram, 2003: 37).

Such an approach obviously questions the hierarchy at work in most language curricula. It also questions the notion of competence, because plurilingualism is seen as an unexceptional ability shared by all speakers. Plurilingualism is therefore a competence that can be acquired and which is within everyone's grasp. It is not synonymous with mastering a great number of languages at high level but with acquiring the ability to use more than one linguistic variety to differing degrees and for different purposes. Moreover, a plurilingual repertoire is not necessarily homogenous. It is a changing repertoire in time and in composition; rather, it is a repertoire of communicative resources that speakers use according to their needs.

As the authors of the guide explain, when implementing language education based on plurilingualism one should remember that plurilingualism is plural: 'It is not a matter of advocating a single plurilingualism for Europeans, a sort of standard repertoire, identical everywhere... Teaching of, or teaching in several languages may take many forms according to the languages used in a given national and international context, to national and interregional needs, to the affiliation of each citizen and to their needs and wishes' (Beacco & Byram, 2003: 38). Finally the authors conclude that the question of languages needs to be reformulated: 'It is less a matter of deciding which and how many foreign languages should be taught in education systems than of directing the goals of language education towards the acquisition of a competence in fact unique, encompassing the mother tongue, the national language(s), regional and minority languages, European and non European languages etc.' (Beacco & Byram, 2003: 39).

The European Centre for Modern Languages in Graz,[19] whose activities are meant to put into practice the recommendations of the Language Policy Division of the Council of Europe, also state in their 2004–2007 project *Languages for Social Cohesion* that totally different attitudes towards language learning are necessary, i.e. that a global approach must be adopted, integrating all the languages of speakers as well as valuing linguistic diversity, varied competences and speakers of any language.

What is slowly emerging is a much wider vision of language education, where teaching and learning foreign languages take place in a multilingual context rather than in the traditional monolingual context, where the choice of languages is more diversified, envisaged within the perspective of life-long learning, rather than solely within the school context. In a multilingual context, the objective is not just to learn languages but also to value language and cultural diversity and to become aware of plurilingualism as a resource. This entails respecting speakers' competence in all the languages they have been in contact with.

Although the expression is not mentioned in the European documents we are quoting, this different perspective echoes the various ecological models described by several researchers (Creese & Martin, 2003; Hornberger, 2003) who are interested in the interrelationships between an individual and her/his languages and how these interrelationships are negotiated in particular in the classroom, and underpinned by ideological, cultural and political histories.

Hornberger's Continua of Biliteracy Model

I have described above the paradoxical attitudes towards bilingualism in the French educational context: on the one hand bilingualism can give advantages, prestige and power, and on the other it can be the source of problems and disadvantages, disempowering individuals who happen to speak minority languages. Alleman-Ghionda (1999: 3) talks of the same phenomenon in terms 'of an imaginary wall, often unconscious, which separates the two domains'. Therefore, I think it is important to go beyond the differences that separate these two forms of bilingualism and work within an adequate conceptual framework that integrates the two dimensions in a convergent analysis.

Hornberger's model of the Continua of Biliteracy, first developed in 1989 and revisited in collaboration with Skilton Sylvester (2003), provides such a framework. The model is original because it 'recognises the numerous shifting and interwoven factors through which biliteracy develops in linguistically diverse settings' (Hancock, 2005: 17). These factors are organised in a dynamic framework that allows for possible changes and in which relations of power play a central part. The strength of the framework lies in the visibility of the multiple dimensions and complex relationships between them and the clear identification of how policymakers and practitioners can bring about change. By making it possible to examine in detail instances of biliteracy practices or policies in relation to contexts, development, media and content, and by locating them within a multidimensional space, Hornberger helps us to understand that prestigious and minority forms of bilingualism are not rigid polar opposites. On the contrary, the difference between the two is not fixed and one-dimensional but must be understood across a variety of dimensions and disciplinary perspectives.

Most interestingly, from the point of view of practice, the model helps to clarify the reasons for the unequal balance of power across languages and literacies, why some of them are supported by education systems and why others are not. Thus, it confronts educators with the question of whether they want to reinforce the traditionally more powerful monolingual end of the continua or emphasise the less powerful bi(multi)lingual end in order to promote biliteracy. As Hancock (2005: 18) suggests, teachers 'can make choices and exercise power by encouraging children to write and publish dual language books within the classroom or invite parents to read stories in their home language'.

In the Didenheim project (Hélot & Young, 2003, 2006; Young & Hélot, 2003), parents were invited to a small primary school to present their language and culture to the pupils. Over three years the children encountered 18 different languages and their associated cultures and discovered many different systems of writing. This model of language education, known as language awareness, challenges the traditional linguistic hierarchy and legitimises the languages of immigration, by focusing on the languages of the pupils or their family and putting all languages on an equal basis. It also illustrates that home language knowledge is an educationally significant component of pupils' cultural capital. When a little girl wrote in Arabic on the blackboard in front of her peers and translated what she had written for her teacher, her biliteracy was not only revealed but looked upon in a positive light. In other words, her knowledge of Arabic had become a teaching resource to be shared by her peers and her teacher. This is an example of how reflective practitioners, as in the case of the Didenheim teachers, can overturn traditional relations of power, by sharing their classroom with parents, by not fearing to deal with languages they do not know, and by valuing knowledge developed in the family context.

However, I would argue that while language awareness is certainly a good basis to start building an education for plurilingual awareness, linked to education for democratic citizenship, one needs to find models of interactions in the mainstream classroom where pupils can make full use of their linguistic repertoires and negotiate their multiple identities (Cummins, 2006). Thus, it is necessary, for example, to go beyond bilingual language programmes that keep the two languages strictly apart, or foreign language classes which separate the different languages so that pupils can never make links in the classroom between the school language and the foreign languages they learn, not to mention, in some cases, their home language. As Cummins explains (2006: 68), 'when the languages of instruction are left in isolation from each other, monolingual instructional strategies are applied rather than potentially much more powerful bilingual strategies'.

Conclusion

As clearly argued by Zirotti (2006), there is political priority given in France to bilingualism developed within the school context at the expense of bilingualism developed in the home or community contexts. The examples of Alsatian or Arabic show that provision in these languages is not aimed at their speakers but favours the more powerful language variety of German or classical Arabic. The minority, contextualised, vernacular use is ignored, in the same way as acquisition that takes place in the home. In other words, despite what might look like advances at the level of policies towards regional languages or immigration languages, the way their provision is implemented shows that any prior knowledge of these languages is not envisaged as a potential social resource or as valuable linguistic capital. Thus, including Arabic in the curriculum alongside dominant foreign languages does not give more power to its speakers; on the contrary, it highlights the more powerful value of the classical variety.

On the other hand, bilingual education programmes that are developed for majority dominant languages are being used to discriminate amongst pupils. In some cases, they have changed the social make up of the school, and they can even create negative attitudes amongst teachers who see these new bilingual programmes being favoured by educational authorities at the expense of pupils who need special education, for example.

Thus, the ideology at work in the management of languages in the French education system is responsible for the widening gap between, on one hand, a form of elitist bilingualism supported and encouraged by the education system, and on the other the ignored bilingualism of minority speakers of migrant background. Speakers of regional languages are in a somewhat better position because they can avail themselves of immersion education in their regional languages (as in Corsica, for example), but it is doubtful whether bilingual education will help to redress the very low rate of family transmission. What one needs to do is to go beyond a very hierarchical vision of languages which erects barriers between its speakers and which makes it so difficult for French schools to move away from their monolingual habitus. In the words of Hornberger (2002: 30), 'multilingual language policies are essentially about opening up ideological and implementational space in the environment for as many languages as possible', which means that the official discourse of diversification in France must be challenged because it does not change the perceived language orders and it does not question the ideological line construed by the national language. It also means that teachers must be made aware of their own underlying ideologies in order to create different policies of their own, which allow for their linguistically diverse pupils to find their own multilingual voices.

Notes

1. Content and Language Integrated Learning is a model of bilingual education where some school subjects are being taught through the medium of the foreign or second language.
2. The law Dexonne, no. 51-46 of 11/1/51.
3. It is somewhat ironic that the Toubon law was passed mainly to protect the French language from English and that it ended up having a negative impact on the teaching of regional languages.
4. Which also means that for French policymakers the term immersion education is synonymous with total immersion.
5. Figures for 2005 from www.diwanbreizh.org.
6. Although France still has not ratified the European Charter for the Protection of Minority Languages.
7. We use the term 'foreign language' here as this is the term used in language education in France. The terms 'modern' or 'second' are not used.
8. According to Gajo (2001), quoting Stern (1984), these models correspond to a minimal definition of bilingual education. Gajo also explains the different didactic approaches used in CLIL And EMILE models. Another very confusing acronym is used in French: DNL for 'disciplines non linguistiques', implying that nonlinguistic subjetcs can be taught through the foreign language, as if the learning of any school subject did not involve some language learning as well.

9. The languages concerned are English (US and UK), German, Spanish, Italian, Danish, Portuguese, Norwegian, Swedish, Dutch, Polish, Japanese and Arabic.
10. BO no. 33 September 1992, and Circular 92234 of 19 August 1992.
11. This analysis is based on the official texts which explain the objectives of European sections, and how they should be implemented: BO no. 33, September 1992.
12. Available at http://www.education.gouv.fr/cid1971/les-sections-europeennes-et-de-langues-orientales.html. No date is given.
13. The numbers of pupils in European sections in 2002/2003 are as follows: 79,443 in lower secondary schools, 42,320 in lycées and 2698 in vocational schools (Legendre, 2004).
14. CLIN: classes of 'initiation' to the French language.
15. CLA: classes of 'adaptation'.
16. ELCO classes: 'enseignement des langues et cultures d'origine', or extensive teaching of the home language outside of the regular curriculum.
17. Centre de formation et d'information et d'information pour la scolarisation des enfants de migrants.
18. Centre académique pour la scolarisation des nouveaux arrivants et des enfants du voyage.
19. http://www.ecml.at.

References

Alleman-Ghionda, C. (ed.) (1999) *Education et diversité socio-culturelle*. Paris: L'Harmattan.

Baker, C. (1996) *Foundations of Bilingual Education and Bilingualism*. Clevedon: Multilingual Matters.

Beacco, J.C. and Byram, M. (2003) *Guide for the Development of Language Education Policies in Europe*. Strasbourg: Language Policy Division, Council of Europe.

Benert, B. (2006) Quels sont les obstacles à l'enseignement de la langue allemande en Alsace? In J. Aden (ed.) *De Babel à la mondialisation. Apports des Sciences Humaines à la didactique des langues* (pp. 197–210). Dijon: CRDP Bourgogne.

Carcassonne, G. (1998) Etude sur la compatibilité entre la Charte européenne des langues régionales ou minoritaires et la Constitution, Rapport au Premier Ministre, La Documentation française, October, 130 p. On WWW at http://www.admifrance.gouv.fr and then on http://larecherche.service-public.fr/df/oxide?criteriaContent=CArcassonne&x=12&y=8&page=resultatsrapports&action=launchsearch&DynRubrique=&DynCorpus=&DynDomain=BRP. Accessed 5.02.08.

Caubet, D. (2001) L'arabe dialectal en France. *Les Cahiers de la Francophonie. Arabofrancophonie* no. 10, Paris: L' Harmattan.

Cerquiglini, B. (2003) *Les langues de France*. Paris: PUF.

Chaker, S. (1997) La langue berbère en France, situations actuelles et perspectives de développement. In M. Tilmatine (ed.) *Enseignement des langues d 'origine et immigration nord-africaine en Europe: langue maternelle ou langue d'Etat*? Document pédagogique, Paris: ERASMUS, INALCO/CEDREA CRB.

Colinet, J.C. and Morgen, D. (2004) Les langues régionales de France: Etats des lieux à l'automne 2002. In Ministère de l' Education Nationale de l'enseignement supérieur et de la Recherche, Direction de l' Enseignement Scolaire, *Enseigner en Classe Bilingue* (pp. 261–275). Paris: Direction de l' Enseignement Scolaire.

Coste, D. (2002) Compétence à communiquer et compétence plurilingue. In V. Castellotti and B. Py (eds) *La notion de compétence en langue* (pp. 115–123). Notion en Question no. 6. Lyon: ENS Editions.
Creese, A. and Martin, P. (eds) (2003) Multilingual classroom ecologies: Interrelationships, interactions, and ideologies. *International Journal of Bilingual Education and Bilingualism* 6 (3&4).
Cummins, J. (2006) Identity texts: The imaginative construction of self through multiliteracies policies. In O. Garcia, T. Skutnabb-Kangas and M. Torres-Guzman (eds) *Imagining Multilingual Schools. Languages in Education and Glocalization* (pp. 51–68). Clevedon: Multilingual Matters.
de Gaudemar, J.P. (2002) Organisation de la scolarité des élèves nouvellement arrivés en France sans maîtrise suffisante de la langue française ou des apprentissages. Circulaire no. 2002-100 du 25-04-2002, Bulletin Officiel de l' Education Nationale, no. 10 (no. spécial), 25 avril 2002. On WWW at http://www.education.gouv.fr/bo/2002/special10/texte.htm#organisation.
de Mejía, A.M. (2002) *Power, Prestige and Bilingualism. International Perspectives on Elite Bilingual Education*. Clevedon: Multilingual Matters.
Deprez, C. (2000) Le jeu des langues dans les familles bilingues d'origine étrangère. *Estudios de Sociolingüistica* 1 (1), 59–74.
Fillon law (2005) Loi no. 2005-380 du 23 avril 2005 d'orientation et de programme pour l'avenir de l'école (1). On WWW at http://www.legifrance.gouv.fr/affichTexte.do?cidTexte=JORFTEXT000000259787&dateTexte=.
Forestier, C. (2002) Missions et organisation des centres académiques pour la scolarisation des nouveaux arrivants et des enfants du voyage (CASNAV). Ministère de l'éducation nationale-DESCOA1, circulaire n°2002-102 du 24.4.02.
Gajo, L. (2001) *Immersion, bilinguisme et interaction en classe*. Collection LAL. Paris: Didier.
Groux, D. (2006) L'apprentissage précoce des langues: des pratiques sociologiquement et politiquement marquées. *International Review of Education* 52 (1–2), 107–123.
Hagège, C. (1996) *L'enfant aux deux langues*. Paris: Odile Jacob.
Hancock, A. (2005) Review of 'Continua of Biliteracy: An Ecological Framework for Educational Policy, Research and Practice in Multilingual Settings' by N.H. Hornberger (ed.) Clevedon: Multilingual Matters. *NALDIC Quarterly* 3 (1), 17–18.
Heller, M. (2002) *Eléments d'une sociolinguistique critique*. Paris: Hatier.
Hélot, C. (2003) Language policy and the ideology of bilingual education in France. *Language Policy* 2 (3), 255–277.
Hélot, C. (2006) Bridging the gap between prestigious bilingualism and the bilingualism of minorities: Towards an integrated perspective of multilingualism in the French education context. In M. O'Laoire (ed.) *Multilingualism in Educational Settings* (pp. 49–72). Tübingen: Stauffenburg Verlag.
Hélot, C. (2007) *Du bilinguisme en famille au plurilinguisme à l'école*, Paris: L'Harmattan, collection Espaces Discursifs.
Hélot, C. and Young, A. (2003) Education à la diversité linguistique et culturelle: le rôle des parents dans un projet d'éveil aux langues en cycle 2. In *Numéro spécial de la revue* LIDIL (Linguistique et Didactique des Langues), D.L. Simon and C. Sabatier (eds) *Le plurilinguisme en construction dans le système éducatif: contextes, dispositifs, acteurs en situation formelle d'apprentissage* (pp. 187–200). Grenoble: Université Stendhal.
Hélot, C. and Young, A. (2006) Imagining multilingual education in France: A language and cultural awareness project at primary school. In O. Garcia, T.

Skutnabb-Kangas and M. Torres-Guzman (eds) *Imagining Multilingual Schools. Languages in Education and Glocalization* (pp. 69–90). Clevedon: Multilingual Matters.

Hélot, C., Hoffmann, E., Scheidhauer, M.L. and Young, A. (eds) (2006) *Ecarts de langues, écarts de cultures. A l'école de l'Autre.* Frankfurt: Peter Lang.

Hornberger, N. (2002) Multilingual language policy and the continua of biliteracy. *Language Policy* 1, 27–51.

Hornberger, N.H. (ed.) (2003) *Continua of Biliteracy. An Ecological Framework for Educational Policy, Research, and Practice in Multilingual Settings.* Clevedon: Multilingual Matters.

Huck, D. (1999) Quelle langue régionale en Alsace? In L. Dabène (ed.) *Les langues régionales: Enjeux sociolinguistiques et didactiques* (pp. 43–60). LIDIL no. 20, Université Stendhal, Grenoble: LIDILEM.

Lacerda, E. and Ameline, L. (2001) Les élèves de nationalité étrangère scolarisés dans les prmeiers et seconds degrees. *VIE Enjeux-migrants-formation* 25, CNDP.

Lang, J. (2001) *Discours d'ouverture de M. Jack Lang, ministre de l'éducation nationale, aux journées nationales d'étude et de réflexion sur la scolarisation des élèves nouvellement arrivés en France,* 29 May 2001. On WWW at http://cravie.ac-strasbourg.fr/primo/primo.htm.

Legendre, J. (2004) Rapport Sénat, no. 63. On WWW at http://www.culture.gouv.fr/culture/dglf/lang-reg/langreg7.htm.

Poignant Report (1998) On WWW at http://portalcat.univ-perp.fr/ftp/Rapport Poignant.pdf.

RERS (2005) Repères et Références Statistiques sur les Enseignements, la Formation et la Recherche. Ministère de l' Education Nationale, Enseignement supérieur et Recherche, Division de l'évaluation et de la prospective. Paris. On WWW at www.education.gouv.fr/stateval.

RERS (2007) Repères et Références Statistiques sur les Enseignements, la Formation et la Recherche. Ministère Education Nationale, Enseignement et Recherche. Paris: Direction de l' évaluation et de la prospective.

Socle Commun de Compétences pour l'Ecole. On WWW at http://www.education.gouv.fr/cid2770/le-socle-commun-de-connaissances-et-de-competences.html.

Stern, H.H. (1984) L'immersion: une experience singulière. *Langue et Société* 12.

Young, A. and Hélot, C. (2003) Language awareness and/or language learning in French primary schools today. *Journal of Language Awareness* 12 (3 and 4), 236–246.

Zirotti, J.P. (2006) Enjeux sociaux du bilinguisme à l'école. In *Langages et Sociétés,* no. 116, *Le scandale du bilinguisme. Langues en contact et plurilinguismes* (pp. 73–92). Paris: Maison des Sciences de l'Homme.

Chapter 8

Languages and Language Learning in Catalan Schools: From the Bilingual to the Multilingual Challenge

CRISTINA ESCOBAR URMENETA and VIRGINIA UNAMUNO

Introduction

The Spanish Constitution presently in force was enacted in 1978[1] and it granted regional languages a co-official status alongside Spanish in the territories where such languages were spoken. In Catalonia, a bilingual community,[2] this resulted in the progressive return of Catalan to schools, where it had been absent for the previous 40 years. Soon afterwards, the Act on Linguistic Normalisation (Generalitat de Catalunya, 1983[3]), emanating from the Statute of Autonomy (Estatut d'Autonomia de Catalunya, 1979[4]), generalised the use of the regional language as the medium of instruction for content subjects in kindergarten, primary and secondary education. Twenty-two years later, some of the main objectives set by the Act on Linguistic Normalisation have been successfully achieved, whereas a few remain elusive.

In the interim, a more complex linguistic scenario has emerged as a consequence of globalisation and new realities are progressively making their way into schools. On one hand, society demands that schools raise their standards in international languages, which, for the moment, has resulted in (a) lowering the compulsory starting point for foreign language learning from the sixth grade (12-year-olds) to the third grade (eight-year-olds) (1990) and, more recently (2004), from the third to the first grade (six-year-olds); and (b) a slow-paced but steady growth of Content and Language Integrated Learning courses offered in primary and secondary schools.

On the other hand, increasing numbers of immigrant people from all over the world are coming to Europe and settling in Catalonia, as well as in other regions. Their offspring bring their languages and cultures to schools; meaning that schools are not only bilingual, but rather become multilingual learning environments.

Aware of the new challenges and in an attempt to provide a response, the education authorities have designed specific linguistic programmes for schools. These programmes aim at three major goals: (a) to move forward in the process of Catalan normalisation; (b) to improve school leavers' competence levels in the international foreign languages taught in schools[5]; and (c) to cater for the linguistic needs of immigrant children so as to favour their progressive integration into mainstream education.

This paper aims to describe and analyse these programmes as they appear in the documents which define them, as well as the tensions created by the implementation of multilingual practices in schools. The tension between official plurilingualism for immigrants, official plurilingualism for mainstream students and 'backstage' plurilingualism shows how difficult it is to overcome the conditions that favour the reproduction of social differences.

The challenge of harmonising local policies with policies that affect populations on a global scale is one of the most interesting aspects of globalisation. It gives rise to the question of how to overcome the apparent contradiction between the need to reassert local identities at the same time as developing emerging transcultural identities.

Catalonia is an interesting case in this respect as it faces tensions due to its political determination to preserve its unique language and culture, whilst it also takes an active part in the symbolic and economic construction of Europe, which includes its role as a region which attracts immigrant populations. In the field of languages and language teaching, this involves the coexistence of linguistic policies aiming at (apparently) opposing targets. Indeed, promoting a vernacular language and adopting global policies which favour the free circulation of workers and goods across Europe are two objectives which may seem hard to reconcile.

This chapter aims to provide an analysis, through both the official discourse of the education authorities and through the specific practices implemented in Catalan schools, of how Catalan society attempts to resolve the tensions caused by the friction between local, regional and global policies at the beginning of the 21st century.

Historical Background

The journey of Catalan from prohibition to normalisation

During Franco's regime (1939–1975) all Spanish regional languages – Catalan being the one with the highest number of speakers – remained confined to family use. It was not until 1970–71 that Catalan was allowed to be taught in schools for a few hours a week. Since then, three major political events have determined a dramatic shift in the status of Catalan in society and, more particularly, in education. They are (a) the passing of The Statute of Autonomy of Catalonia, approved by State Law 4/1979, which in Article 3 stated that (our translation):

1. La llengua pròpia de Catalunya és el català.	1. Catalonia's own language is Catalan.
2. L'idioma català és l'oficial de Catalunya, així com també ho és el castellà, oficial a tot l'Estat espanyol.	2. Catalan is an official language of Catalonia, together with Castilian, the official language of the Spanish State.

(b) The transfer of all competencies in the field of education from the central to the regional government in 1980, which favoured policies to ensure not only the teaching of Catalan, but also the use of Catalan as a means of instruction. (c) The Act on Linguistic Normalisation (Generalitat de Catalunya, 1983), which stated that:

- Catalan is[6] Catalonia's *own* (vernacular) language, therefore it is the language of education, at all levels.
- Children below six have the right to be educated in their family language, be it Catalan or Spanish.[7] The authorities are obliged to guarantee this right.
- Catalan and Spanish are to be compulsory subjects in kindergarten, primary, secondary and vocational education.
- In order to be able to comply with their teaching demands, teachers must be proficient in both co-official languages.
- The language of the Catalan Education Authority shall be Catalan.

From Catalan immersion programmes to the generalisation of Catalan as a working language

After passing the Statute of Autonomy of Catalonia, the Autonomous Government implemented an optional Linguistic Immersion Programme to guarantee generalised competence in Catalan and Spanish. The programme was originally addressed to 3–7-year-old children, but was soon extended to include children up to the age of 12. Early total immersion implies that all instruction, including literacy, is provided in Catalan whereas content subjects in Spanish are introduced gradually from Grade 3 (eight-year-old children) onwards.

In the 1992–1993 academic year, new educational legislation was implemented in Catalonia for non-university levels. Decree 75/1992 stipulates that the Catalan language is to be generalised as a working language in infant and compulsory education. The regulations in the Decree were also made official by the Catalan Act on Linguistic Policy 1/1998 (Generalitat de Catalunya, 1998). Catalan immersion was the basis for the consolidation of a unique network of schools, from the linguistic point of view, which adopted Catalan as their main working language for the whole school community, at the same time as guaranteeing adequate exit levels in Spanish for all students. This is an option which differs greatly from the strategies implemented, for example, in the Basque Country or Andorra, where students are streamed according to the linguistic option chosen by their parents.[8] The extension of the use of the vernacular language in the school system was objected to by minority groups on two basic premises: (a) Catalan schooling for all would imply the discrimination of Spanish speaking children, who would be disadvantaged in relation to their Catalan speaking peers, and (b) Catalan-speaking children would be disadvantaged because they would be denied the opportunity to reach native-like competence levels in Spanish. One more argument, kept to private circles, was the assumption that students aiming at low qualification positions would not need Catalan in their future jobs.

These arguments were soon counteracted by majority support for generalised schooling in the minority language. This tendency can be explained by two factors: (a) the widespread perception that Catalan was undergoing a process of minorisation, mainly due to unequal competition with Spanish, the official language of the state and a language used on the international stage, and (b) the public debate about linguistic issues which engaged Catalan society at the beginning of the eighties and the high level of consensus which emerged from it: one single school network for all learners, regardless of their linguistic origin, was to be preferred. This demand was based on the principle of non-discrimination and on the desire to avoid internal divisions in Catalan society. Social cohesion would be achieved through the learning of Catalan by *all* Catalan children, meaning all children who lived in Catalonia. In terms of learners' opportunities to develop competencies in Spanish, it was assumed that the pervasive presence of this language outside the school premises and the variety of contexts where Spanish is the habitual language would guarantee the acquisition of bilingual competences by all students. Soon, Catalan schooling was generalised to all primary schools, regardless of the context and the student population, whereas secondary schools presented – and still do – much less well defined linguistic profiles.

The concern for social equity which informed some of the decisions stated above coexisted with and was influenced by a political discourse and practices which aimed at associating the advantages of knowing Catalan with economic and social benefits (Junyent & Unamuno, 2002). As a result, Catalan was also presented as a resource of undeniable material value. This instrumental vision of language focused on changing the local markets, in order to try and increase the price of the knowledge of Catalan, so as to extend the number of speakers of that language.

Evaluating the impact of the generalisation of Catalan as the main language of instruction

The use of Catalan as the main language of instruction has largely come of age and many studies and reports have evaluated its impact. According to the Committee of Experts who monitor the implementation of the European Charter for Regional or Minority Languages (ECRML) (Council of Europe, 1992), immersion is a well established practice. Their report, issued in September 2005, states

> ... this (policy) has led, for example, to 88.9% of primary school classes in Catalonia being taught in Catalan during the school-year 1999/2000, whereas 7.3% followed a bilingual education model. At secondary school level, 51.2% of the classes were in Catalan and the rest received most of the teaching in Catalan plus a number of subjects in Castilian. (Council of Europe, 2005: 31)

In the same document, the Committee of Experts also remarks that the system adopted in Catalonia has succeeded in achieving an impressive reversal of the previous trend: a regional/minority language that was still oppressed just 30 years ago has become the 'default language' in the educational system and the first language of instruction. The Committee concluded that the undertakings listed in the ECRML for minority languages had been fulfilled in Catalonia (Council of Europe, 2005: 31–32).

Other studies have attempted to evaluate the impact of these programmes on students' linguistic development. These studies cover two main areas: (1) the patterns of language use at school, in order to measure the impact of the school system on the sociolinguistic profile of the community, and (2) the possible negative consequences that the language switch from home to school might have on Spanish-speaking children. In the first case, the studies demonstrate that the decision made in favour of Catalan as the working language at school does not necessarily entail a change in the patterns of language choice and language use in peer interaction (Consell assessor de la llengua a l'escola, 2006; Nussbaum, 2003; Nussbaum & Unamuno, 2006; Vallcorba, 2005), or even in the patterns of interaction between learners and teachers in informal settings, such as break or lunch time. Such interactions tend to mean that Spanish takes on the role of the preferred language in schools, especially in schools located in urban and semi-urban neighbourhoods (Unamuno, 2000, 2005; Vila, 2005; Vila Moreno & Vial, 2003; Vila Moreno, 2004).

The second type of study showed that there were no significant differences between Spanish- and Catalan-speaking children with respect to their school results (OECD, 2001, 2003; INCE, 1999, 2000). This finding has been attributed to two relevant facts: (a) Spanish has an important presence at school and is the predominant language in many out-of-school milieus; and (b) all teachers are highly competent in Spanish, a language which is commonly used in order to avoid communication breakdowns and guarantee the understanding of school content (Arnau, 1985; Arnau *et al.*, 1992; Vila Moreno & Vila Mendiburu, 1998). Competencies in Spanish[9] are also obviously influenced by the significant proportion of secondary school teachers who opt for Spanish as the working language in their teaching and, of course, by the formal Spanish tuition that students receive throughout their entire school life.

This is the bilingual environment in which immigrant students integrate, and their arrival revives age-old questions of how immigration may affect the sociolinguistic dynamics of a region or a country, and how linguistic and educational policies must be defined in the near future.

Emergent Discourses, Policies and Practices

Growing numbers of migrant families come and settle down in Catalonia, as well as in other regions of Western countries. Migrant children bring their languages and cultures to schools and the previously bilingual schools that receive them become, all of a sudden, multilingual learning environments.[10]

In a way, the arrival of these students has reopened the debate about Catalan, not only as part of an ethnic heritage, but mainly as to its survival as an effective and efficient means of communication in all areas of Catalan society (Junyent & Unamuno, 2002; Nussbaum, 2003). It has also generated different reactions in public institutions and in civil society, but the official discourse that places Catalan at the centre of the education process is still in force.[11]

The Pla d'acollida[12] or Insertion Scheme for immigrant pupils

The government organisation in charge of designing, executing and monitoring the policies to favour the reception and incorporation of newly immigrated pupils was recently named *Secretariat per la llengua i la cohesion social* (Secretary for *Language* and *Social Cohesion*; our emphasis). The name of this organisation indicates that the relationship between immigration and social cohesion is mediated or influenced by language. This interpretation is coherent with the idea stated above, given that the Catalan language is one, or *the* main, identity trait, and it must therefore continue to be the focal point of the new society that is being created.

This Secretary is in charge of the education policy for the reception of migrant pupils in schools and also for the promotion of the use of Catalan within the education system. The coordination of functions of such a different nature is based on two general assumptions: on one hand, as stated above, Catalan must play a key role in contributing to the integration of migrant students into Catalan society, so as to guarantee social cohesion; on the other hand, it is perceived that the arrival of migrants with diverse linguistic origins, who are likely to adopt Spanish as a lingua franca among them (Nussbaum & Unamuno, 2006), may contribute to increasing the fragility of Catalan.

One of the major outcomes of the Secretary for Language and Social Cohesion has been the design of the Language and Social Cohesion Plan (*Pla per la llengua i la cohesion social or LIC Plan*), which was released by the Catalan Department of Education in 2004 (Departament d'Educació, 2004). This 36-page document specifies the measures to be implemented in schools to favour the insertion of recent immigrant pupils.

Plurilingualism[13] as the core of the LIC Plan

The LIC Plan is the reference document that guides the implementation of insertion actions for newly arrived students. Its guidelines refer to the educational and linguistic measures to be adopted by schools in order to ease the incorporation of pupils who may lack basic linguistic competencies and/or previous school experience. The notion of plurilingualism established as an educational goal by the LIC Plan must be interpreted starting from the two fundamental elements on which it is based; namely, the avoidance of the social exclusion of the immigrant population, and the promotion of Catalan.

Excerpt 1[14]

> There are three areas that require special attention: the rising number of immigrant children in schools, the emergence of new causes of social exclusion and the shortfall in the extent to which the Catalan language has been standardised in social life. It is necessary to raise awareness, promote and consolidate Catalan as the mainstay of a multilingual and intercultural education policy in order to achieve greater social cohesion. (LIC Plan: 4)

In Excerpt 1, the phrase 'multilingual and intercultural education policy' could be interpreted as integrating the family languages that migrant children bring to school. This interpretation may be reinforced by the text reproduced in Excerpt 2, which also declares that optional courses in these languages will be offered and that they are to be open to *all* pupils (our emphasis) as part of the after-school activities programmed by the school.

Excerpt 2

> [In after-school hours and] In accordance with criteria laid down by the Department of Education and the PLC, all pupils will be offered

> classes in the languages spoken by new immigrants as part of the extra-curricular timetable (Arabic, Amazig, Chinese and so on). (LIC Plan: 28–29)

Interestingly, the wording in Excerpt 2 hints at recognition of the fact that the knowledge of these languages is also pertinent for pupils with different family languages. However, the fact that these courses are planned as part of after-school activities implies that the educational authorities are not obliged to supply schools with the necessary resources to implement this policy, and, consequently, that schools are not obliged to offer them.

The LIC Plan displays a number of organisational structures and resources to achieve the educational intentions stated above. The most relevant is the *aula d'acollida* [*Reception Classroom*, literally translated], officially translated into English as 'Insertion Scheme'.[15] The Reception Classroom is an environment where newly arrived pupils spend up to 12 hours a week and where they can find tailor-made attention aimed at helping their integration into mainstream classes. This includes intensive exposure to Catalan (Excerpt 3).

Excerpt 3

> The insertion scheme is a point of reference and an open working environment in the school which gives immediate, tailor-made attention to new pupils and provides support for teachers in the new challenges to teaching. It is an organisational structure that enables the school to draw up a series of curricular and methodological measures, teaching materials, and so forth which guarantee intensive language learning and progressive incorporation of pupils into mainstream classes. (LIC Plan: 30)

Summing up, in the above section we have tried to present how the LIC Plan approaches the relationship between policies relating to immigration as well as the promotion and strengthening of the Catalan language. The role that foreign languages play in this plurilingual project is analysed in the following section.

The Status of Foreign Languages

The European Commission *White Paper on Education and Training* [WPET], in its fourth general objective, emphasised the importance of democratising access to foreign language learning: 'It is no longer possible to reserve proficiency in foreign languages for an elite or for those who acquire it on account of their geographical mobility'[16] (European Commission, 1995: 51). The participation of Spain and Catalonia in the European space, the free circulation of workers, student mobility and the development of the information and knowledge society have made citizens aware of the need to improve the traditionally low standards in international languages shown by school leavers in Catalonia, a handicap shared with the rest of Spain (Bonnet, 2004).

Effective access to the plurilingualism promoted by the EU is affected by social factors which determine to a great extent the levels of proficiency in foreign languages of international status (English mainly, but also French or German) reached by students. In recent years, the Catalan authorities have promoted and implemented a range of strategies[17] that aim at equipping students with a reasonable command of, at least, one international language[18] – English in the majority of cases. Recently, efforts have been made to start up a network of plurilingual state-run schools that offer Content and Language Integrated Courses (CLIL) courses (CRLE, 2006) in line with the European Commission recommendation.[19] The network is not a large one and the majority of CLIL courses offered are optional, but they have shown the great attraction that these types of approaches have for middle-class families. Nevertheless, recent reports (Consell superior d'avaluació de Catalunya, 2005) show that these reforms are by no means sufficient and the general standards reached by students in English continue to be lower than desirable.

This situation drives middle and upper class families to turn to private tuition in after-school centres specialised in teaching foreign languages to children and adolescents. At the same time, primary and secondary schools are also aware that offering special foreign language programmes in their curricula is a very effective means to recruit students, at a time when very low birth rates are emptying schools. This strategy is especially visible in the two networks of private schools[20] that recruit their students mainly among the middle, professional and upper classes. All this confirms the high symbolic and practical value that Catalan society places on international foreign languages in general and English in particular.

The majority of families, however, do not have the resources to afford private foreign language tuition or are not prepared to do so. In the medium term, the inadequate capacity to function in English that school leavers from lower social or sociocultural status show limits their access to the qualified labour market and to the assumed advantages of the free circulation of workers within Europe. This underprivileged state of affairs affects native and immigrant pupils alike. In line with this aspiration towards a multilingual society, the LIC Plan echoes (Excerpt 4) European principles on this matter:

Excerpt 4

> By the end of primary education pupils must be able to understand and express simple messages in a given context in one foreign

> language. By the end of secondary education they must be able to understand and *produce oral and written messages in one foreign language* (...) In addition, (...) have a *basic level in understanding and speaking a second foreign language.* (LIC plan, Appendix 2: 28; our emphasis)

However, it is worth noting that no specific guidelines are provided in the document on how schools are to tackle this task.

Implementation of Regional Language Policies in Schools: A Case Study

El Port is a primary school in the old district of Barcelona, committed to providing learners with high-quality educational experiences of an integrative nature, such as learning projects which take advantage of and involve the community.[21] All the staff participate in the discussion, design and implementation of the school's insertion scheme (*aula d'acollida*), which is extremely flexible so as to adapt to the particular characteristics and needs of every learner (Nussbaum & Unamuno, 2006). For over three years, we have carried out a joint research project in El Port, where a team of university researchers and school teachers have been collaborating in an attempt to describe, understand and improve the language practices implemented in the school in the context of the current language policies.

Within the framework of this ethnographic study, different types of data collection procedures have been implemented: classroom participant observation and field notes in mainstream and reception classrooms; interviews and discussions with the board of directors and staff members; and semi-experimental work, which aimed at assessing the learners' competencies in the different languages taught at school in order to identify variables which could explain individual or group differences. Full access to this exemplary school and the readiness of the teachers to discuss with the researchers on an equal-to-equal basis have allowed us to detect the practices described below, selected precisely because of their problematic nature.[22] The tensions and gaps identified in El Port may give us some clues as to what may be happening in less dedicated schools, where we would be denied access. More specifically, the ethnographic data have allowed us to reconstruct the effects that the official discourse has on the specific practices in the classrooms, the ways in which this discourse is accepted or rejected by educational agents and, ultimately, to illustrate with empirical data the social and linguistic practices in relation to the official discourses.[23]

Using Carrasco and Soto's (2000) terminology, El Port School is a *concentration* institution [*institución de concentración*], that is, a school that has undergone a process of transformation concurrent with the changes that have taken place in its neighbourhood in the last few years: a school traditionally made up of pupils who came from local families of humble background, which now admits pupils from all five continents who have just arrived in Barcelona, and therefore may suffer from the consequences of a late arrival into the local education system. The board of directors and the teachers have made substantial efforts to accommodate to the new situation and have searched for teaching strategies, material and personal resources to better cater for the emerging and ever changing needs of their school population.

As in virtually all primary schools in Catalonia, Catalan is the official language, the language for signs, announcements, letters to parents, etc. and the working language in content subjects. This implies that in the majority of public spaces, Catalan, either oral or written, is by far the preferred language. Spanish, on the other hand, also plays a major role. Hafi[24] (HAF), who was born in Pakistan and joined El Port one year ago, explains this in a very effective way in his conversation with the researcher (CEC) (Transcript 1[25]):

Transcript 1 Interview with Hafi

CEC: mm| i aquí així _ eh-| fora de casa\ no/|	CEC: Mm. here you do. Outside home. don't you?
HAF: sí|	HAF: Yes.
CEC: quina llengua parles?|	CEC: Which language do you speak?
HAF: fora de casa/| doncs castellà|	HAF: Outside home? Spanish, of course.
CEC: normalment| i català/| [s'acaba la cara A del cassette]	CEC: Usually. And Catalan? [End of side A.]
CEC: estàvem parlant de que_ de que tu parles català solament a l'escola|	CEC: We were saying that you only speak Catalan at school.
HAF: sí|	HAF: Yes.
CEC: i per què?|	CEC: Why?
HAF: perquè fora ningú parla en cas_ català| tots parlen en castellà XXX|	HAF: because outside nobody speaks Sp_ Catalan. Everybody speaks Spanish XXX.
CEC: mm|	CEC: Mm.
HAF: sí|	HAF: Yes.
CEC: i aquí a l'escola amb qui parles català?|	CEC: And here, at school who do you speak Catalan with?

HAF: amb la mestra|	HAF: With the teacher.
CEC: amb la mestra| amb totes les mestres/|	CEC: With the teacher. With all the teachers?
HAF: sí|	HAF: Yes.
CEC: sí| i amb els companys/|	CEC: Yes. And with your classmates?
HAF: castellà|	HAF: Spanish.
CEC: sí/|	CEC: Really?
HAF: sí|	HAF: Yes.
CEC: i a classe també-| quan esteu treballant així|	CEC: Also in the classroom, when you are at work, like this?
HAF: sí| en castellà també|	HAF: Yes. In Spanish too.
CEC: sí/| i al pati/|	CEC: Really? What about break time?
HAF: castellà|	*HAF: Spanish.*

According to Hafi, the presence of Spanish is pervasive not only outside school, but also inside, where it functions as the usual means of communication among students. Jony (JON), a Philippine boy, adds one more variable to the description of the linguistic uses in El Port (Transcript 2).

Transcript 2 Interview with Jony

CEC: ah-| amb els monitors\ és clar| mm| i amb els mestres-| que parles?|	CEC: Ah. With the [canteen] monitors. Of course. Mm. How about the teachers? What language do you speak?
JON: cat_ català|	JON: Cat_ Catalan
CEC: amb tots/|	CEC: With all of them?
JON: mm-| no| amb tots no| amb_ amb la Montse sí [la tutora de curs]|	JON: Mm. No. Not all of them. With, with Montse [class teacher] I do.
CEC: mm||	CEC: Mm.
JON: perquè ella ensenya llengua Catalana| és per això|	JON: Because she teaches Catalan. That's why.
CEC: mm| i amb la directora/|	CEC: Mm. How about the Headmistress?

JON: sí també|	JON: Yes. Also with her.
CEC: i amb la Isabel parles anglès [és la professora d'anglès]/|	CEC: And with Isabel [English teacher] do you speak English?
JON: sí | amb la Isabel {@ parlo anglès \}|	JON: Yes. With Isabel {(laughing) I speak English\}|
CEC: [riu]	CEC: [laughs]
JON: però a vegades també ca_ castellà |	JON: but sometimes also Spanish.
CEC: ah sí /|	CEC: Really?
JON: quan estem al pati o a baix | només parlem anglès quan estem en la classe [+ klasa +]|	JON: When we are in the schoolyard or downstairs. We only speak English when we are in the classroom.
CEC: a la classe/|	CEC: In the classroom?
JON: sí|	JON: Yes.
CEC: així no:_ així_ per_ per xarrar així no/|	CEC: Like this you don't'. Chatting like this you don't?
JON: no|	*JON: No.*

According to Jony, informal interactions with the teachers are also accepted in Spanish if they take place outside the classroom (downstairs, in the schoolyard). In the same way as Hafi and Jony, the majority of immigrant pupils in El Port use Spanish and Catalan in their everyday life. They can make language choices according to the communicative context and can also switch from one language to another (Unamuno, 2005).

It is in this context that El Port teachers defend the priority given to Catalan during the reception of newly arrived children, even to the exclusion of any other language. Coherent with the LIC Plan, they consider that the current position of Catalan is that of a minorised language and, consequently, the school should guarantee the opportunities to learn this language, precisely because such opportunities may be scarce in the pupils' social milieu. This is to be carried out through spaces which favour monolingual practices, with reception classrooms being one of the very few spaces of this kind.

In spite of the *monolingual* discourse articulated by the teachers, classroom observation shows that plurilingualism is present in the classroom at various levels. Family languages are used by the students of the same linguistic origin in their private conversations. With time, family languages tend to be replaced by the use of Spanish, which progressively becomes the default language for communication among learners. They also begin to mix Spanish and Catalan in their contributions to the development of lessons. This hybrid use of the languages is not considered pertinent by the teacher and, in general, is gently redirected by means of retakes which translate the students' words into the target language or through questions which hint at the return to Catalan. Any languages other than Catalan or Spanish have an exclusively symbolic presence in this classroom, in the form of posters or labels that decorate the walls.

Following the recommendations in the LIC Plan, in addition to their stay in the reception classroom, the newly arrived learners in El Port School are assigned to a standard classroom made up of either pupils their own age or pupils who are up to one year younger. In the standard classroom,[26] newly arrived immigrant learners participate in a variety of activities that do not require advanced linguistic competencies in Catalan, i.e. Music, PE or Art and Crafts, which are progressively extended to other areas of the curriculum.[27] In content subjects, control over the teachers' linguistic use is lower and, as pointed out by Hafi, the habitual language used among pupils is Spanish, which alternates with other languages according to the repertoire available to the learners in each situation. In these lessons, Catalan is often restricted to pupil–teacher interaction and teachers may sometimes resort to Spanish in different situations, especially when they consider that bilingual practices may contribute to a better understanding of school activities.

Although the only provision made for the learning of Spanish either in the LIC Plan or in the El Port School in formal contexts are the compulsory Spanish language lessons, the immigrant learners monitored in El Port made very fast progress in this language (Nussbaum & Unamuno, 2006). It was also observed that Spanish was the default language used between autochthonous children and newcomers, especially in informal settings such as the playground and, eventually, the default language that immigrant children use among themselves. On average, in about 18 months, the majority of immigrant children observed in El Port show competencies in Spanish that match those of their autochthonous peers (Nussbaum & Unamuno, 2006). It is to be concluded, then, that the proficiency reached in such a short time span is due mainly to peer interaction among learners in informal settings.

This shows that learners soon acquire a multilingual repertoire in family and school languages, which they accommodate to different settings and communicative goals. Coherent with the official language policy, the institution prioritises the use of Catalan in their interactions with learners, while students switch from Catalan to Spanish, depending on whether they address the teacher or a peer learner. Family languages other than Catalan or Spanish are present in the playground or in peer-to-peer conversations.

El Port does not offer any courses or special activities aimed at promoting family languages. As stated by the Deputy Head of the school, the school focuses on curricular aspects which are common to all learners and may help them feel that they belong to one common community, whereas highlighting differential aspects is consciously avoided. In her view, multicultural proposals have the undesirable side effect of fragmenting the school community, whereas an integrated project must be built around the characteristics that are common to the different ethnic, cultural and social groups, and the core of such a project must be the teaching and learning of Catalan.

Teachers in El Port usually justify this project and insist that the learners should have the opportunity to speak and learn Catalan within the school premises, on the grounds that the chances of hearing and speaking Catalan off the school premises for children who live in the old district of Barcelona are extremely rare. Our ethnographic research confirms this perception: in this area, Spanish, Arab, Punjabi or Tagalog are much more frequently heard than Catalan. Hafi, our Pakistani pupil, sees it like this (Transcript 3):

Transcript 3 Conference with Hafi

CEC: i qui parla català aquí?|	CEC: Who speaks Catalan here?
HAF: en_en l'escola/|	HAF: At at school?
CEC: en el_ en general\\|	CEC: in the.. in general.
HAF: ah-| bueno\\| no ho sé\\| en_ el cole_ en el cole són les mestres i ja està\\| ningú més\\|	HAF: Ah. Well. I don't know. At school it's the teachers and that's all. Nobody else.
CEC: mm\\| i per què és important saber català?|	CEC: Mm. And why is it important to be able to speak Catalan?
HAF: perquè és {(¿) les paraules} en català_ perquè socials i naturals totes són en català\\| i_	HAF: Because it's {(¿) the words} in Catalan. Because Social Studies and Science are in Catalan.
CEC: però a_ a més a més de l'escola/|	CEC: But apart from school?
HAF: no lo sé\\| porquè fora de l'escola mai he parlat català\\|	HAF: I don't know. Because outside school I've never spoken Catalan.
CEC: mm\\| i-| aquí la gent que parla català així-| hi ha gent que parla català normalment així fora de l'escola/|	CEC: Mm. And here are there people who speak Catalan like this? are there people who usually speak Catalan like this outside school?

HAF: sí| però jo no conec|	HAF: Yes, but I don't know anyone.
CEC: mm|	CEC: Mm.
HAF: jo no conec ningú|	HAF: I don't know anyone.
CEC: i qui són aquests?|	CEC: And who are these?
HAF: los que són catalans| els que han nascut aquí | ells sí que parlen català|	HAF: Those who are [native born] Catalan. Those who were born here. They do speak Catalan.
CEC: però tu coneixes gent que ha nascut aquí|	CEC: Do you happen to know people who were born here?
HAF: què?|	HAF: What?|
CEC: tu coneixes gent que ha nascut aquí|	CEC: Do you know people who were born here?
HAF: no· |	HAF: No.
CEC: i la Carla|	CEC: How about Carla?
HAF: sí\ però-| ella mai parla català|	HAF: Yes. But she never speaks Catalan.
CEC: mm|	CEC: Mm.
HAF: sempre parla en castellà|	*HAF: She always speaks Spanish.*

In Hafi's view, Catalan is a language of restricted use, limited to school practices and, more specifically, to interactions with teachers (Transcript 1). The importance of this language lies in its functions as a vehicle for the transmission of curricular content. Beyond the school's boundaries, he claims not to be acquainted with anyone who speaks that language. The only people that speak Catalan outside the school, according to Hafi, is a social group labelled 'the Catalans', which is made up of the native-born population, but which, interestingly enough, does not include his classmates with whom he usually interacts in Spanish.

In order to deal with this state of affairs, the teachers consider that the teaching of Catalan and their insistence that immigrant learners become proficient in Catalan is in itself a strategy to fight possible discrimination, as it allows learners to equip themselves with an asset which is highly valued by Catalan society. Two types of arguments consistently appear in their discourses: (a) its symbolic value, as the language opens the doors to being accepted as a full member of the Catalan society and (b) its material value, as access to many jobs, as well as to university education, requires a high command of Catalan.

The first type of argument is related to the identity traits (see above) that are prioritised in the symbolic construction of 'being Catalan' (Pujolar, 1997, 2001; Woolard, 1989, 1992). The defensive stance that the teachers and the board of directives take regarding Catalan as the insertion language is even more striking if we consider that the majority of them are from other regions of Spain and that they learned Catalan in their youth or adulthood, as a second language. The second type of argument is related to the increased value that Catalan has obtained in the past few years, especially in the field of education and services. The teachers in El Port argue that to deprive these children of the use of Catalan would imply limiting them in their future careers.

We shall now explore the role that the foreign language plays in this plurilingual context, first looking at practices related to the reception classroom, and later examining a mainstream English lesson. Carme, the insertion tutor in 2003–2004, used English in a flexible way as an aid to mutual understanding with the children that had just joined her class. Carme improvised English tests which were administered in order to identify the pupils' strengths in that language. She also encouraged the learners' participation in the English lessons, if the children showed some knowledge of the language. In contrast, Pilar, the insertion tutor in 2004–2005, had very limited command of English, which might have been the cause of the absence of reference to this language in her lessons.

The case of Brenda, a newly arrived Philippine girl, is also interesting. After initial exploration, Brenda was considered a timid girl with below average school abilities for her age, and a learning plan was designed for her on this basis. In a conversation with one of the researchers[28] Brenda showed unusually high competencies in English, through which she could comfortably display some previous knowledge of different school subjects, which had remained hidden up till then. The finding led to the reconsideration of the learning path designed for Brenda.

As for the mainstream classroom, Transcript 4 exemplifies the multilingual practices that take place in standard English classrooms in El Port.

Transcript 4 An English lesson

Mestra: is pakistan listen please| is pakistan {(DC)(F) bigger}than bangladesh/\ or is bangladesh {(DC) (F) bigger} than pakistan|	Teacher: is Pakistan listen please. Is Pakistan {(DC)(F) bigger}than Bangladesh? Or is Bangladesh {(DC) (F) bigger} than Pakistan?
Noia1: pakistan {(AC) es más grande\}|	Girl1: Pakistan {(AC) is bigger\}|

<table>
<tr><td>Mestra: {(FF) in english\}| {(F) home\nen\}|</td><td>Teacher: {(FF) in English\}. {(F) home\boy\}|</td></tr>
<tr><td>Noia1: {(P) ay vale\}|</td><td>Girl1: {(P) Oh. OK. \}|</td></tr>
<tr><td>Mestra: XXX patatera\ tu\|</td><td>Teacher: XXX patatera\ tu\|</td></tr>
<tr><td>EEE: XXX</td><td>EEE: XXX</td></tr>
<tr><td>Mestra > xxxx espera\| què?|</td><td>Teacher > xxxx wait. What?|</td></tr>
<tr><td>Noi1: {(PP) pakistan\} < 3 > is bigger_</td><td>Boy1: {(PP) Pakistan\} < 3 > is bigger_</td></tr>
<tr><td>Mestra: bigger than\|</td><td>Teacher: bigger than...</td></tr>
<tr><td>Noi1: {(PP) than bangladesh\} < 0 ></td><td>Boy1: {(PP) than Bangladesh\} < 0 ></td></tr>
<tr><td>Mestra: {(F) bangladesh\}| very well\ eh/| ok\| then you write now\| venga\| tu XXX XXX\| vamos a escribir\| venga\| very well\| can you repeat Yanina\| can you repeat\| is bigger que-| who is bigger\ < 0 ></td><td>Teacher: {(F) Bangladesh. \}very well. Eh? Ok. Then you write now Come on. You XXX XXX. We are going to write. Come on. Very well. Can you repeat Yanina? Can you repeat? Is bigger than-| who is bigger\ < 0 ></td></tr>
<tr><td>yanina: pakistan\|</td><td>Yanina: Pakistan.</td></tr>
<tr><td>Mestra: is bigger than blangladesh or bangladesh is bigger than pakistan/|</td><td>Teacher: is bigger than Bangladesh or Bangladesh is bigger than Pakistan?</td></tr>
<tr><td>yanina: pakistan\|</td><td>Yanina: Pakistan.</td></tr>
<tr><td>Noi2: pakistan is bigger the bangla_</td><td>Boy2: Pakistan is bigger the Bangla_</td></tr>
<tr><td>Mestra: than \|</td><td>Teacher: than...</td></tr>
<tr><td>Noi2: than banglades\</td><td>Boy2: than Banglades.</td></tr>
<tr><td>Mestra: desh\|</td><td>Teacher: desh.</td></tr>
<tr><td>Noi2: blangladesh\|</td><td>Boy2: Bangladesh.</td></tr>
<tr><td>Mestra: where are you from?|where are you from?| pakistan or bangladesh/|</td><td>Teacher: where are you from? Where are you from? Pakistan or Bangladesh?</td></tr>
<tr><td>Noi3: pakistan\|</td><td>Boy3: Pakistan?</td></tr>
</table>

The foreign language alternates with Spanish (Turn 5) and Catalan (Turn 6) in a way that a three-language tapestry is progressively woven. According to the teachers, the presence of other languages on such occasions is justified by the students' low competence in English, and its use by the teacher is justified as a strategy to facilitate comprehension and production in English. Unlike in the reception classroom, multilingual practices do not cause tensions in the English classroom. Here, it is the teachers themselves who codeswitch, as shown in Transcript 4.

In short, in El Port School, English is a language some students and some teachers refer to in order to aid comprehension and to ask for help in production activities, but its presence within the reception classrooms depends to a great extent on the teacher's command of the language. It is necessary to add that foreign languages are not a requirement for teachers in charge of reception classrooms, as they are not for primary teachers in general.

As has been pointed out above, teachers in El Port expressed the view that English is not a priority for *all* their pupils. In their own words, the children who attend this school probably will not need English in their future academic or professional lives. That is why the emphasis is placed on teaching content which is considered, in this case, more basic and relevant than a foreign language. This would also explain why the pupils' knowledge of English had not – up to the time we collected the data – been explored on a regular basis on their arrival at the school.

This interpretation is consistent with reports from teachers and observations made in other schools, which seem to suggest that, in the case of immigrant students, this deficit is worsened by an unofficial but apparently common practice,[29] which consists of their partial or total exemption from foreign language classrooms. This practice is usually justified by the need to fix priorities for the newcomers – many of them with little or even no previous school experience – who would not be able to cope with so many languages and so much content at a time. Thus, the foreign language periods are spent on what are considered 'core subjects'. A first consequence of this policy, as put forward by a primary teacher, is that when removed from the English classroom, the immigrant pupils are withdrawn from the one classroom in which they are more or less on equal footing to local children in terms of communicative competence in the official classroom language. This might also contribute to undermining or at least not helping to build up the pupils' self-esteem. Meanwhile, without denying the importance of establishing priorities, it is clear that the young immigrants who are treated in this way are deprived of opportunities to access knowledge which (a) sooner or later is to be assessed by the institution and (b) provides high potential for social promotion.

As in Brenda's case, it is interesting to note that this segregation may happen without taking into consideration whether the immigrant has some degree of competence in the foreign language taught at the school, as may be the case for English for some of the students coming from Pakistan, or French for some of the Moroccan students. Being an immigrant entails, in some observed practices, being someone who lacks any assets to which school, and society in general, attach high symbolic or practical value (Unamuno & Nussbaum, 2006). The study carried out by Codó (2003) in non-school settings on the attention provided to immigrants by the Spanish central government also came to the same conclusion.

To Conclude

Discourses and specific practices show heterogeneous ways of defining the notion of plurilingualism, the goal of the current linguistic policies in Catalonia. Among El Port teachers, there is a high degree of consensus as to the importance of learning Catalan, independently of students' cultural origins, owing to a range of symbolic and practical reasons, and the discourse elaborated by the board of directors and teachers is in agreement with that of the official documents. More specifically, with regard to the need for monolingual practices in Catalan, the official documents seem to be an accurate reflection of the arguments provided by the teachers sustaining this approach. Nevertheless, these ideal notions of plurilingualism are not clearly reflected in the practices at El Port School.

On the other hand, it is apparent that there exists tension in the assumptions and the system of priorities that underlie the participants' linguistic practices. The development of monolingual spaces which favour the learning of Catalan is limited to a few moments of the day to day of the school, where teachers can exert control over participation and linguistic practices. The Reception Classroom is one of these spaces, due to its reduced number of pupils and to the interactive dynamics that take place there. As for the remaining school activities, plurilingualism is the norm and not the exception. However, what we observe in El Port is not the plurilingual project drawn up in the official regional documents (i.e. LIC Plan). It is also not the sort of plurilingualism presented in European documents (i.e. WPET) or in the middle-class schools that offer CLIL courses.

It is rather a different kind, a 'backstage' plurilingualism (Goffman, 1971; Heller, 2000), which emerges from the social conditions, the tensions among opposing goals and the contradictions shown by the agents when they define institutional educational and social aims. In the observed practices, plurilingualism is defined in relation to the physical and symbolic distribution of Spanish, the majority language, and Catalan, the language of the institution. The learners' native language/s, which are almost absent in the school's official discourse and therefore pushed into the background, occupy diverse contexts of learning and use. The foreign language – English, in this case – appears as an isolated element, not integrated in the school practices and the value attributed to it remains somewhat diffuse. Although English could become a useful tool when welcoming children from some Asian countries, this role is not officially recognised. This type of assumption applies even in the case of children who come from Pakistan or the Philippines, whose competencies in English are not systematically assessed on arrival, and therefore may, in some cases, be overlooked. Also, contrary to the official Catalan policy for foreign languages stated in the LIC Plan, Appendix 2 (see Excerpt 4), the foreign language is not promoted on an equal basis among all the foreign pupils enrolled in this school, which is probably due to the lack of specific orientation provided in the LIC Plan to succeed in this venture.

The tension between official plurilingualism for immigrants, official plurilingualism for mainstream students and 'backstage' plurilingualism shows the difficulties in overcoming conditions that favour the reproduction of social differences. Twenty years ago, Catalonia was a pioneer region in the implementation of a single bilingual education network for children coming from two different language backgrounds, which adopted the minority language as the main working language. The accomplishments of this policy have gained international recognition (Council of Europe, 2005). Nowadays, Catalonia faces the challenge of integrating students from many different linguistic and cultural backgrounds who may, in time, become citizens of the European Union.

It is well known that the use that societies make of languages may promote or hinder social mobility. In this respect, it is essential that newly arrived children in Catalonia find a school that helps them become full members of the community which welcomes them, while the doors towards social promotion and mobility remain open to everyone. From our standpoint, this twofold challenge can only be faced with policies aiming at (a) supporting newcomers in the process of learning the two co-official languages, which implies guaranteeing rich educational experiences in Catalan for those pupils who would otherwise have very limited access to this language; (b) making provision for measures which guarantee that, by the end of their compulsory education, all learners – regardless of their linguistic origin – possess a sound knowledge of at least a third language of international use; and (c) establishing a solid framework for initiatives leading to the appreciation and promotion of the languages brought by immigrant families.

These three general guiding principles could materialise into actions such as (i) the generalisation in schools of teaching strategies which link the school to the community, in the way that, for example, El Port does in their radio station project. (ii) The dissemination of teacher training modules which guarantee the teachers' ability to, at least, understand one or more foreign languages of international use, such as English, French or Arabic. (iii) Raising teachers' awareness of the linguistic wealth that migrant families bring with them. (iv) Helping practitioners identify the characteristics of interaction in multilingual contexts and equipping them with specific teaching strategies and language management skills which can be used to the benefit of migrant pupils and of the whole school community. (v) Providing clear, unprejudiced guidelines on the role that the official foreign languages in the school should play in the adapted curriculum offered to the newly arrived learners. (vi) Finally, the progressive inclusion in the school curriculum – as languages with academic value – of the languages brought by these new learners cannot be postponed. This process would involve the progressive inclusion of the 'new' languages in the University Entrance Examination.[30] The joint use of these policies may, in our view, contribute to bridging the gap between the different conceptions of plurilingualism present today in the Catalan society.

It is clear that society and schools must establish an order of priority in relation to their educational goals, but in our view, these priorities need to be set, not so much according to the social, cultural or linguistic characteristics of the students, as to the individual needs that learners present. The risk of the former is prejudging learners' capacities according to social or cultural stereotypes. El Port is a school where tailoring the curriculum to learners' individual needs is the norm and not the exception. Precisely for this reason, the mismatches observed in this outstanding learning environment between official discourses, school discourses and school practices are especially revealing.

Overcoming the conditions that favour the reproduction of social differences is a complex undertaking that needs to be tackled. We believe that the critical examination of discourses and practices may provide an important contribution to this endeavour.

Acknowledgements

Our gratitude to the editors and the anonymous reviewer for their comments and dedication. Special thanks are due to our colleague Luci Nussbaum for her feedback and support. The gathering and processing of the data used in this paper was financed by the following research projects: 'The category of 'foreigner' in insertion schemes for immigrant learners' (PNL2004-38); 'Collaborative tasks for CLIL classrooms' ARIE 210060 & 10056; and 'Multilingual Competencies in the teaching and learning of content areas in primary education' (SEJ2004-06723.CO2-01/ EDUC). The research project in El Port has been financed by the Ministry of Education and Science, and the Ministry of Science and Technology: BSO2001-20030, SEJ 2004-06723-C02-00 and SEJ2004-06723-C02-01.

Notes

1. This Constitution brought a 42-year period of political abnormality, beginning with a civil war (1936–39), a dictatorship (1939–1976) and a transition period to democracy, to an end.
2. Roughly speaking 50% of the population state that they have a Catalan-speaking background and 50% a Spanish-speaking one.
3. The Act on Linguistic Normalisation 7/1983 was later reformed by the Act on Linguistic Policy 1/1998 (Generalitat de Catalunya, 1998).
4. A new Statute of Autonomy is presently in force (Estatut d'Autonomia de Catalunya, 2006). This new law has not introduced any major changes in relation to the statute of languages in education.
5. Mainly English. French is usually offered as an optional second foreign language, with German slowly gaining ground. Other European languages, such as Italian, Greek or Portuguese, have a much smaller presence and play a minor role.
6. The present tense is used, as these principles were integrated into the 1998 law and, therefore, are still in force.
7. In the 1960s and 1970s, many families from other areas of Spain moved to the more industrialised Catalonia in search of new opportunities. It has only been in the late 1990s onward when Catalonia has become a destination for non-Spanish people.
8. Since 1983, three linguistic models have been present in Basque schools. In Model A, all subjects are taught in Spanish except the Basque language. In Model B, half of the subjects are taught in Basque and half in Spanish. In Model D, all subjects except Spanish are taught in Basque. (Note: Letter 'C' does not exist in Basque.)
9. PISA 2003 average score for Spanish (a) in Spain: Primary Ed. 65%; Secondary Ed. 64%; (b) in Catalonia: Primary Ed. 65%; Secondary Ed. 63%. *Source:* Departament d'Educació (2006: 53).
10. The specificity of the Catalan case does not lie in the proportion of population of non-European origin – 8% of the total, 75% of which are concentrated in Barcelona and its industrial belt – but in the increasing rate of the migratory process in the last few years, which is having an important impact on society and the school system in particular. Since 2001 there has been an increase of 300% in the presence of foreign students in Catalan schools and in 2006 the percentage of students born abroad grew to 9.6% of the total of the school population.
11. The importance attached to Catalan in the construction of a new society must be understood in the light of the role that this language has played in the shaping of the Catalan identity and in the processes of social inclusion and exclusion in Catalonia. If being a Catalan equals being able to speak Catalan, promoting Catalan among the newly arrived population will surely imply opening the gates for them to social belonging and Catalan identity. See Woolard (1992), for example.
12. 'Welcome Plan', in literal translation. In the official English translation of the document the term 'Insertion Scheme' is used with two different meanings: (a) as it is used in this paragraph, to refer to the whole set of actions planned and implemented by a school, and (b) to refer to the classroom where newly arrived immigrant children receive special attention. In this second meaning, the literal translation *Reception Classroom* (see the final section) is preferred by the authors of this paper, as it better reflects the practices we have observed in schools. Thus, it is the term that will be used from now on for

the words we are authoring. In this second meaning, the official translation *Insertion Scheme* is reserved for literal quotations from the official documents.

13. In this paper 'plurilingualism' and 'multilingualism' are used indistinctly.
14. All excerpts from the LIC Plan are quoted following the official translation available on the Internet.
15. In the official English translation of the document the term 'Insertion Scheme' is used to refer to the whole set of actions planned and implemented by a school and also to the reception classroom where newly arrived immigrant children receive special attention. In this second meaning, the literal translation *Reception Classroom* is preferred by the authors of this paper as it reflects better the practices we have observed in schools. Thus it is the term that will be used from now on for the words we are authoring. The official translation *Insertion Scheme* is reserved for literal quotations from the official documents.
16. Paradoxically, it might be interesting to note that the use of singular when referring to the mother tongue ('in addition to their mother tongue') used to describe this fourth objective failed to take into account the existence of bilingual and plurilingual families and societies within Europe, and their trend towards expansion, revealing, thus, a vision of society deeply rooted in monolingualism. Catalonia, an almost completely bilingualised society in Spanish and Catalan, with a high proportion of bilingual families, is a good example of the limiting effects of the use of the singular to refer to one's native language(s).
17. Among those strategies, three are to be highlighted: (a) the implementation of an aural component to be added to the reading and writing sections, in the compulsory foreign language test which provides access to tertiary education; (b) the lowering of the compulsory starting point for foreign language learning from the sixth grade (12-year-olds) to the third (eight-year-olds) grade in 1990 and, more recently (2004), from the third to the first (six-year-olds) grade, and (c) the offer of financial support and in-service teacher development courses to schools that implement innovative approaches in foreign language teaching.
18. A second foreign language, usually French or German, must be offered by all secondary schools, but is optional for students.
19. 'It could even be argued that secondary school pupils should study certain subjects in the first foreign language learned, as is the case in the European Schools' (European Commission, 1995: 47).
20. The school system is Spain is made up of three separate networks: (a) the network or state schools, (b) a network of private schools, which are financed by the state and (c) a network of costly private schools. The schools in (b) complain that the funding they obtain from the administration does not cover all the expenses, thus justifying the charging of fees to families. Up to now this policy has left out children from families that would not or could not afford those fees. An agreement between social forces and the educational authorities [Departament d'educació], aimed at progressively overcoming any discrimination between the two state-funded networks, was reached in March 2006. The outcomes of this agreement are still to be seen.
21. One example of this, among the many available, is the school radio station, where the pupils interview *interesting* people who live in the neighbourhood, following scripts previously elaborated in the classroom.

22. It is important to note that the selection of incidents must not be taken as a representative sample of the school practices, but of the problems that the school faces.
23. In order to avoid any anecdotic account, we have made a selection of incidents that exemplify and support the reports provided from teachers in schools we do not have access to.
24. Original names have been substituted by aliases.
25. The transcriptions belong to the GREIP-UAB research group [http://dewey.uab.es/didllengua/inicillengua.htm]. Transcripts 1 and 2 were carried out and/or supervised by V. Unamuno and T. Díaz. Transcript 3 was carried out by L. Nussbaum. See symbols in Appendix.
26. It must be understood that this is done following tailor-made insertion programmes that are constantly re-examined.
27. This is mostly done through projects that integrate different content areas in a *Language Across the Curriculum* approach. One of the aims of these projects is to favour the joint work of newly arrived children, less recent immigrants and autochthonous pupils.
28. The difficulties many primary school teachers have communicating in English can partly explain why the pupils are not systematically assessed in this language.
29. At least, as reported by a number of practitioners we have talked to. Some of these teachers position themselves in favour of this practice as a facilitating strategy, whereas others position themselves against, arguing the potential discriminatory effects that this practice may bring about.
30. At the moment, the Catalan students who take the University Entrance Test can only choose English, French, German or Italian. This is a similar situation to that in the other Spanish Autonomous Regions.

References

Arnau, J. (1985) Educación en la segunda lenguas y rendimiento escolar: una revisión de la problemática general. In M. Siguan (ed.) *Enseñanza en Dos Lenguas y Resultados Escolares* (pp. 7–20). Barcelona: ICE-Publicacions de la Universitat de Barcelona.

Arnau, J., Comet, C., Serra, J.M. and Vila, I. (1992) *La Educación Bilingüe.* Barcelona: ICE-Horsori.

Bonnet, G. (2004) The assessment of pupils' skills in English in eight European countries 2002. European network of policy makers for the evaluation of education systems. On WWW at http://cisad.adc.education.fr/. Accessed 4.07.

Carrasco, S. and Soto, J. (2000) Estrategias de concentración y movilidad escolares de los hijos de inmigrantes extranjeros y de minorías étnico-culturales en Barcelona. Ponencia presentado en ell II Congreso sobre la inmigración en España. Madrid, 5–7 October.

Codó, E. (2003) The struggle for meaning: Immigration and multilingual talk in an institutional setting. Unpublished Doctoral Thesis, Filologia Anglesa, Universitat Autònoma de Barcelona.

Committee of Experts ECRML (2005) Report of the Committee of Experts on the Charter. Application of the Charter in Spain. Initial monitoring cycle. Council of Europe. On WWW at http://www.coe.int/. Accessed 3.07.

Consell assessor de la llengua a l'escola (2006) *Conclusions.* Barcelona: Generalitat de Catalunya.

Consell Superior d'avaluació de Catalunya (2005) *La Situació de la Llengua Anglesa al Batxillerat a Catalunya 2000–2004*. Barcelona: Generalitat de Catalunya, Departament d'Educació.

Council of Europe (1992) *European Charter for Regional or Minority Languages (ECRML)*. On WWW at http://www.coe.int/. Accessed 7.07.

Council of Europe (2005) Monitoring the implementation of the European Charter for Regional or Minority Languages. Reports and Recommendations: Application of the Charter in Spain. On WWW at http://www.coe.int/. Accessed 7.07.

CRLE (2006) CLIL in Catalonia. In N. Figueras (ed.) *CLIL in Catalonia, From Theory to Practice*. Barcelona, APAC Monographs 6, 31–37.

Departament d'Educació (2004) *Language and Social Cohesion Plan*. On WWW at http://www.xtec.es/lic/documents.htm. Accessed 2.08.

Departament d'Educació (2006) *Quaderns d'Avaluació, 6. Consell Superior d'Avaluació del Sistema Educatiu* (p. 53). Barcelona: Departament d'Educació i Universitats.

Estatut d'Autonomia de Catalunya (1979) Organic Law 4/1979 of the 18 December (DOGC 38 – 31 December 1979). On WWW at http://www.gencat.cat/generalitat/cat/estatut1979/index.htm. Accessed 2.08.

Estatut d'Autonomia de Catalunya (2006) Organic Law 6/2006 of the 19 July (DOGC 4680 – 20 July 2006 on the Reform of the Statute of Autonomy of Catalonia). On WWW in English at http://www.gencat.net/generalitat/cat/estatut/index.htm. Accessed 2.08.

European Commission (1995) *White Paper on Education and Training*. On WWW at http://aei.pitt.edu/1132/.

Generalitat de Catalunya (1983) Act on Linguistic Normalisation 7/1983, of the 18 April. DOGC No. 322 of 22 April 1983.

Generalitat de Catalunya (1998) Act on Linguistic Policy 1/1998, of 7 January 1998, DOGC No. 2553, of 9 January 1998.

Goffman, E. (1971) *The Presentation of Self in Everyday Life*. Harmondsworth: Penguin.

Heller, M. (2000) Bilingualism and identity in the post-modern world. *Estudios de Sociolingüística* 1 (2), 9–24.

Instituto Nacional de Calidad y Evaluación (INCE) (1999) *Evaluación de la Educación Primaria*. Madrid: MECD.

Instituto Nacional de Calidad y Evaluación (INCE) (2000) *Evaluación de la Educación Secundaria*. Madrid: MECD.

Junyent, C. and Unamuno, V. (eds) (2002) *El Català: Mirades de Futuro*. Barcelona: Octaedro.

Nussbaum, L. (2003) Immigration et dynamiques polyglossiques en Catalogne. In L. Mondada and S. Pekarek (eds) *Plurilinguisme, Mehrsprachigkeit, Plurilingualism* (pp. 15–28). Tubingen: Francke.

Nussbaum, L. and Unamuno, V. (eds) (2006) *Usos i Competències Multilingües d'Escolars d'Origen Immigrant*. Bellaterra: Servei de Publicacions de la Universitat Autònoma de Barcelona.

Organisation for Economic Cooperation and Development (OECD) (2001) Programme for International Student Assessment (PISA 2001).

Organisation for Economic Cooperation and Development (OECD) (2003) Programme for International Student Assessment (PISA 2003).

Pujolar, J. (1997) *De què vas, tio? Gènere i Llengua en la Cultura Juvenil*. Barcelona: Empúries.

Pujolar, J. (2001) *Gender, Heteroglossia and Power: A Sociolinguistic Study of Youth Culture*. Berlin/New York: Mouton de Gruyter.

Unamuno, V. (2000) Frente a frente: lenguas, diversidad y escuela. *Grenzgänge* 7, 37–49.

Unamuno, V. (2005) *L'Entorn Sociolingüístic i la Construcció dels Repertoris Lingüístics de l'Alumnat Immigrat a Catalunya*. Noves SL, Primavera.

Unamuno, V. and Nussbaum, L. (2006) De la casa al aula: ámbitos y prácticas de transmisión y aprendizaje de lenguas. ***Textos** de Didáctica de la Lengua y la Literatura* 42, 43–51.

Vallcorba, J. (2005) La situació de la llengua als centres educatius: Accions per consolidar-la i potenciar-la. Ponencia presentada en Jornades de llengua i ensenyament. Barcelona, Octobre.

Vila, I. (2005) Els programes de canvi de llengua de la llar a l'escola: El repte de la catalanització escolar. Ponencia presentada en Jornades de llengua i ensenyament. Barcelona, Octobre.

Vila Moreno, F.X. (2004) Hem guanyat l'escola, però hem perdut el pati? *Llengua, Societat i Comunicació* 1, 8–15. On WWW at http://www.ub.edu/cusc. Accessed 2.08.

Vila Moreno, F.X. and Vial, S. (2003) Models lingüístics escolars i usos entre iguals: Alguns resultats des de Catalunya. In J. Perera (ed.) *Plurilingüisme i Educació: els Reptes del Segle XXI. Ensenyar Llengües en la Diversitat i per a la Diversitat* (pp. 207–226). Barcelona: Institut de Ciències de l'Educació, Universitat de Barcelona.

Vila Moreno, F.X. and Vila Mendiburu, I. (eds) (1998) *Bilingüismo i Educació*. Barcelona: Proa-UOC.

Woolard, K.A. (1989) *Doubletalk: Bilingualism and the Politics of Ethnicity in Catalonia*. Stanford, CA: Stanford University Press.

Woolard, K.A. (1992) *Identitat i Contacte de Llengües a Barcelona*. Barcelona: La Magrana (Els Orígens; 32).

Appendix

Symbols used in the original transcripts

Initials in upper case: Participants
Initials in upper case > Same participant continues the turn
Tone: lowering: **** raising: **/** wh-question**?** sustained **-**
Pauses: short | medium || long <**number of seconds** > no pause <**0** >
Syllable stretching, according to length · ·· ···
Overlaps:
= speaker A's text =
= speaker A's text =
Interruptions: **text_**
Intensity:
piano {(P)text} pianissimo {(PP)text}
forte {(F)text} fortissimo {(FF)text}
High Pitch **{(A) text}** Low pitch **{(B) text}**
Accelerated tempo **{(AC)text}** Decelerated tempo **{(DC)text}**
Utterance while laughing **{(@) text}**

Non alphabetic transcription **[+text+]**
Comments **[text]**
Incomprehensible fragments, according to length **XXX** | **XXX XXX** | **XXX XXX XXX**
Doubtful fragments **{(?) text}**

Chapter 9

Educating for Participation in a Bilingual or a Multilingual Society? Challenging the Power Balance between English and Irish (Gaelic) and Other Minority Languages in Ireland

MUIRIS Ó LAOIRE

Introduction

Language as we know can be viewed as a form of cultural or symbolic capital (Bourdieu, 1991) or as a symbolic resource which becomes a source of power and prestige. Languages symbolise and are vehicles for different value systems within communities. The fields of bilingual and multilingual education that are being investigated in this chapter are fields of multidisciplinary investigation, theory building and policy development. As Cummins (2003) has argued, bilingual educational research alone is 'voluminous' as well as 'controversial' and 'confusing'. Furthermore, it has, over the years, produced contradictory results; it may have oversimplified problems and asked unhelpful questions and has been driven, perhaps, by the need to be policy relevant. In broad terms, there is a large body of literature that is discipline bound, in terms of the research questions that are being addressed, context bound, in terms of the language context the research seeks to describe, programme bound, in terms of the educational intervention being described, and politically bound, in terms of the other factors that are associated with bilingualism, such as ethnicity, indigeneity, issues of power and social class.

Context plays a significant role in research on bilingual education. The programmes, the status of the languages, and the social, cultural and political contexts are important factors in shaping policies, in provision and expected outcomes of bilingual education.

It is against the background of these considerations that I would like to explore certain issues in the background to bilingual education (i.e. immersion-type) in Ireland and discuss how future expansions, particularly in language education provision to linguistic and cultural minorities, may need to bridge the gap between elite and folk bilingualism.

A Brief Overview: Irish Language Revitalisation in Education

Ireland has a considerably long history in the promotion of bilingualism through education. Until very recently, bilingualism in Irish schools always referred to the promotion of the official languages Irish and English. The Irish language, even though it is the official language, is spoken as first language by approximately 4% of the population located in the Irish language speech communities along the western seaboard. Intensive efforts have always been made, however, to teach the language to the entire population as part of the process of language revitalisation.

From the 1920s onwards, not only were schools in Ireland expected to teach the Irish language as a subject, they were asked to use it as a medium of instruction in immersion-type programmes in primary schools.[1] A strong political stance on the language was being taken by the State in an effort to revitalise it. In fact, state language planning efforts to restore Irish devolved primarily on the education system in the hope that the language would become the language of work and play in schools. From the schools, it was expected that the revitalised language would extend to the home. An influential Professor of Education in the National University of Ireland at the beginning of the State believed that the Irish language could be revived through the agency of the school alone and without reference to the home (Corcoran, 1925) in the same way that English had supplanted Irish in the schools in the 19th century.

Perhaps the most salient feature of the teaching of Irish in primary schools at this time was the 'immersion' approach. The immersion programme had a number of characteristics of the home–school language switch programmes in North America where additive bilingualism was promoted (Cummins, 1978), but differed from these programmes, of course, in that Irish was not a prestige language of wider communication. A new programme early in the 1930s laid down that Irish be the sole medium of instruction and activities during the first three years of schooling. This meant that English-speaking children throughout Ireland on commencing in primary schools were immersed in an Irish language environment for all classroom interactions in infant and early classes (grades). The intensive promotion of bilingualism through the schools was largely unsuccessful, however, and towards the end of the 1940s, the immersion schools waned in number.

A new 'grassroots' movement of Irish immersion began to emerge in the 1970s. Growing out of an earlier unfavourable climate, the campaigners for these schools took on the struggle typical of schools in a prestige/elite–minority power imbalance context, i.e. the schools had to try doubly hard, as it were, to convince parents that education through the non-elite language would not constrain children's progress – given that

English is a prestigious international language of upward mobility and of gaining access to employment opportunities in the global marketplace. In some ways, the new type immersion programmes tried to challenge the power imbalance between English and Irish.

In 1974 about 53% of the students enrolled in these schools were from English-speaking homes (Coady, 2001). The schools were established as a result of parental demand for Irish-medium education as distinct from top-down, government policy-imposed schools. They have been described as being part of a new trend rather than a reconstructed version of the existing schools (Ó Riagáin, 1997). A study conducted in 1979 revealed that 51% of the fathers of children enrolled in Irish-medium schools were government or semi-state employees whose jobs required Irish (Ó Riagáin & Ó Gliasáin, 1979). Cummins (1978) described these schools as qualitatively different from their predecessors. He noted that the new wave of schools consisted of a large degree of parental participation and support, as well as participation in Irish national cultural events.

Since the early 1970s, the number of *Gaelscoileanna* has continued to increase. Concerns linger, however, over the extent to which education in the immersion schools might be a disadvantage in the context of the global importance of English. Two concerns dominate in particular:

(1) Parents are concerned that their children's progress will be delayed in English.
(2) Parents, in choosing all-Irish immersion programmes for their children, are often torn between knowledge of the powerful certainty of the English language as a gateway to particular forms of social and economic access and Irish as a minority subordinated language that (mainly) gives access to cultural identities.

In the Gaeltacht regions, on the other hand, where Irish is a living language, parents also have considerable concerns. According to a recent report (COGG, 2004), Gaeltacht (Irish language speech communities) students' home language is not supported in schools, in that almost one fifth of them leave school with only a reasonable level of language competence, with a further 10% reported to have little or no Irish at all.

While one may argue that the duality referred to above is a consequence of colonisation or unequal power relations, the reality is that ideas, perceptions and tensions around this dilemma influence perceptions of language status and inform decision making about Irish-medium education. Parents are particularly susceptible to doubts about the capacity of Irish immersion education as a vehicle to develop and sustain academic skills. Here, we must not only think of parents who send their children to Irish-medium schools, but also parents who are potentially able to enrol their children in all-Irish-medium schools. This raises the crucial issues involved in parents' choice of education for their children.

What makes Ireland interesting is the way in which the disjunction between Irish and English has been replicated, as it were, by a new struggle between English or Irish or both languages and the minority languages of immigrant communities.

Bilingualism, Multilingualism and Immigrant Communities

Immigration is a relatively new phenomenon for Ireland, a country more familiar with the departure of its population over the centuries than with the arrival of newcomers. Since the mid-1990s increasing numbers of non-national children in Irish classrooms in Ireland, whose first language is neither Irish nor English, have posed a challenge to schools and have initiated a small-scale debate on bilingualism and/versus multilingualism. Recent 2006 census figures show that there are currently 167 languages being used in Ireland, ranging from Acholi to Zulu (www.cso.ie).

The Council of Europe in a recent language education profile on Ireland (CoE, forthcoming) referred to growing concern about the treatment of language issues for this increasing number of immigrants. Limited efforts are being made to adapt to the linguistic demands of these new populations. Primary schools in Dublin, which has the largest number of immigrant communities, are reported to be endeavouring to cope over recent years with the challenge of teaching students whose L1 is neither English nor Irish. The issues debated so far have mainly surrounded the provision of English classes. There are no support classes offered in Irish. An English language support teacher is made available if a minimum of 14 non-English-speaking children is present. It is reported that while the support teachers are qualified, they nonetheless lack specific training for the sensitive task of developing English language skills, drawing on immigrant learners' reservoir of multilingual metalinguistic awareness.

It is interesting to note that recent immigrants are given instruction in English only with no offers of extra instruction in Irish, a situation that contrasts strikingly with Catalonia, for example, where newcomers receive instruction in both Catalan and Castilian (Huguet & Janés, 2005). One hears little reference, however, to the fact that the vast majority of these learners are already bilingual, trilingual or multilingual. It is worth noting in this context that recent research conducted by Martí *et al.* (2005) on behalf of UNESCO showed that at least a third of world languages are not represented in educational institutions. The authors claim,

> When the population goes to school but their own language is not present, it is difficult to imagine what benefit these children can obtain from these schools. The negation of identity involved in a situation of this sort is unimaginable for the majority of the citizens belonging to communities with a dominant language. These citizens have grown up thinking that education can only be transmitted in certain languages or that it is best if it is done only in the dominant language. In many cases, this is also the opinion deliberately instilled into citizens belonging to communities with minorised languages that are not reflected in the educational system... The right to an education in one's mother tongue constitutes a fundamental right recognised by UNESCO since 1953. Nevertheless most linguistic communities cannot exercise it. (Martí *et al.*, 2005: 153)

A recent survey (Ó Laoire, 2002) revealed that principals in schools are often unaware of the languages being spoken by immigrant children in their schools, with some principals listing ' Nigerian' as a home language of some of their students, rather than Igbo or Youruba. The research identified that learners were withdrawn from the classroom for these 'special' English lessons. It is particularly important to ascertain the longer-term effects of learning the majority language, English or Irish for the non English-speaking immigrant learners. Will the situation lead to considerable levels of subtractive bilingualism, for example, as these learners become separated from their own linguistic community from which they inherit not only linguistic identity, but also, and significantly, their sense of ethnicity and personal identity?

The bilingualism or multilingualism that immigrant children may bring with them to the language classroom appears often to be ignored or sidelined. The home languages of these children remain silent. There is, however, a debate in the National Council for Curriculum and Assessment (NCCA)[2] on the extent to which 'other' languages can be included in the curriculum, in order to cater for the needs of new communities and their linguistic heritages. There is reference in the Council of Europe language education profile report (CoE, forthcoming) to the benefit to be derived from the 'imported' languages as a national resource for Ireland. So, the uneasy relationship between Irish and English bilingualism has been replicated, as it were, in the tacit, quiet subtractive bilingualism taking place among our new Irish immigrant communities.

Parental Concerns

In language revitalisation initiatives, parents are a significant interest group and a very different interest group from the 'language speaking community' because it is their children who are enrolled in language programmes and it is usually the parents who then bear the burden of the educational work required to support language development and academic achievement.

In talking about efforts in Aotearoa–New Zealand, Hohepa (1998) has argued that parents have played a pivotal role in initiating, implementing and supporting educationally located language regeneration attempts. Parental expectations and attitudes are also seen as a significant factor in determining the outcomes of bilingual education. Lyon (1996) also says, for example, that those parents who wish their children to be bilingual are more likely to encourage their child's bilingual education, and children may be more motivated to become bilingual in a society that values bilingualism. Hohepa's (1998) study group of parents had overlapping motivations, which included a sense of belonging and cultural identification through to practical advantages seen to be gained from being able to speak Māori, such as the development of enhanced employment prospects.

Parents who choose bilingual education are, by definition, supportive of language education and of bilingualism. However, parental choices or decision making are complicated by many other factors, such as social class, ethnicity, access to choices, transport, school loyalty, specific family circumstances, etc. The assumption underlying this model of schooling is that parents will choose schools that offer the most cognitive opportunities, that is, the higher quality programmes. Experience over two decades of reform however has shown that parents are now choosing immersion-type bilingual education as a pathway to securing elitism and prestige for their children.

The evidence emerging from bilingual and immersion education programmes is that bilingualism, given the right conditions, can confer and bestow intellectual, psychological, social and cultural benefits on the individual. Bialystok's (1991) research, for example, shows that bilingual children develop processing mechanisms, executive functions (attention, switching, memory) and abilities for selective attention in input earlier than their monolingual peers. Such enhanced abilities emerge, for example, in problem solving. Evidence corroborated in research emanating from bilingual contexts such as Canada, Switzerland and Belgium is not necessarily readily available to all the partners in bilingual education programmes.

When parents make pragmatic decisions about their children's education in contexts like Ireland and elsewhere where economic and social accesses to mobility are predominantly linked to English, the import of research may be lost, if it is not translated into the compelling discourse of economic and social power and prestige. Policymakers, teachers and researchers who are involved with bilingual programmes in international languages often have little contact with researchers and practitioners are concerned with bilingual education programmes in minority communities. This separation leads to a necessarily limited view of the progress of bilingualism and bilingual education, and means that linguistic and pedagogical insights and perceptions from each tradition are often not available to inform future general developments in the field.

There is often considerable investment by relevant authorities to promote a highly visible bilingualism involving languages of prestige. Bilingualism, involving a minority or lesser-used languages, on the other hand, as Hélot (2006) argues, leads, in many cases, to an 'invisible' form of bilingualism in which the language of the home or community is undervalued and associated with underdevelopment, poverty and backwardness. So while bilingualism may well confer prestige and power (de Mejia, 2002), it can often give rise to problems and disadvantages, disempowering individuals who happen to speak languages considered of limited value in the global marketplace.

Thus the contribution of bilingualism and bilingual education to general language development (metalinguistic awareness)/multilingual development/communication/social and economic development/plurilingual education, etc., needs to be emphasised over political concerns.

The new wave of immersion schools in Ireland in the 1990s is the result of a large degree of parental participation. In a recent study, qualitative data obtained from parents as to why they enrol their children in Irish-medium education revealed that in addition to language and education related reasons, parents cited additional reasons that were neither linguistic nor educational. Parents, for example, stated that they sought non-traditional educational options such as co-education and a non-Catholic (or multidenominational) educational option (Coady & Ó Laoire, 2002). Parents further stated that they sought an educational environment in which they themselves could actively participate in the organisation and management of the schools.

Conclusion

Two conclusions are immediately apparent. While much emphasis is justifiably placed on the growth of immersion programmes in recent years, Irish-medium education is precarious (the vast majority of parents do not choose it as an option). The fear that students may not do as well in the all-Irish schools as they would in English mainstream schools is a reflection of the power imbalance between English and Irish that Irish bilingual education must constantly confront.

The changing sociolinguistic map of Ireland raises new questions about bilingual education in the country. It has been shown here that since the mid-1990s immigration continues to contribute to language change in Ireland. In recent years increasing numbers of non-national children whose first language is neither Irish nor English have been arriving in Ireland. This poses a challenge for schools in second-language learning and teaching. As it stands, language education in Ireland, while promoting Irish–English bilingualism, takes little or no account of the home or heritage languages of these new immigrant students. This situation echoes and reflects in many ways the tensions and struggles surrounding the establishment of Irish–English bilingualism. This new linguistic and cultural diversity calls for educators and policymakers to legitimise the bilingualism of minority speakers, including speakers of Irish in the *Gaeltachtaí*, which is not recognised at present, in order to transform this diversity into a cultural resource for all. The lack of recognition is ironic, given the postcolonial power struggle to extend the minority but national language through education. Such power imbalance affects people at the individual level through the language chosen for them in which they must learn or the perceptions they have of their own language(s) – and at the macro level, in language education policies implemented by education systems. Thus, ironically, there is a growing disjunction between an official bilingualism and a personal bi/multilingualism that disempowers. A recent review of languages conducted by the NCCA (www.ncca.ie) is beginning to address the rationale for diversification in the language curriculum. The identification and establishment of a range of criteria for the inclusion of languages must have as its starting point the need to address the unequal relations of power that affect, afflict and disaffect. Thus, this new context has the potential for a new interplay and a new model of language education in Ireland.

Notes

1. For full account of Irish language revitalisation, see Ó Laoire (2005).
2. The NCCA, a statutory body set up to advise the Minister in areas of curriculum reform, are currently involved in setting up guidelines for teachers of English to all primary students. Integrate Ireland, Trinity College Dublin has already put in place a range of supports for non-national children with English language deficit. These include the development of English language proficiency benchmarks for non-English-speaking pupils at both primary and post-primary level.

References

Bialystok, E. (1991) *Language Processing in Bilingual Children*. Cambridge: Cambridge University Press.

Bourdieu, P. (1991) *Language and Symbolic Power*. Cambridge: Polity Press.

Coady, M. (2001) Policy and practice in bilingual education: Gaelscoileanna in the Republic of Ireland. Unpublished doctoral dissertation, University of Colorado, Boulder.

Coady, M. and Ó Laoire, M. (2002) Dilemmas of language policy and practice in education: Gaelscoileanna in the Republic of Ireland. *Language Policy* 1 (2), 143–158.
COGG (An Chomhairle um Oideachas Gaeltachta agus Gaelscolaíochta) (2004) *A Study of Gaeltacht Schools 2004.* Dublin: An Chomhairle um Oideachas Gaeltachta agus Gaelscolaíochta.
Corcoran, T. (1925) The Irish language in the Irish schools. *Studies* 14, 277–88.
Council of Europe (CoE) (forthcoming) *Language Education Profile. Experts' Report.* Strasbourg: Council of Europe.
Cummins, J. (1978) Immersion programs: The Irish experience. *International Review of Education* 24, 273–282.
Cummins, J. (2003) Bilingual education. In J. Bourne and E. Reid (eds) *World Yearbook of Education: Language Education* (pp. 3–20). London: Kogan Page.
de Mejia, A-M. (2002) *Power, Prestige and Bilingualism. International Perspectives on Elite Bilingual Education.* Clevedon: Multilingual Matters.
Hélot, C. (2006) Bridging the gap between prestigious bilingualism and the bilingualism of minorities: Towards an integrated perspective of multilingualism in the French education context. In M. Ó Laoire (ed.) *Multilingualism in Educational Settings* (pp. 49–72). Hohengehren: Schneider Verlag.
Hohepa, M.K. (1998) Hai Tautoko I te Reo. Māori language regeneration and Whānau bookreading practices. Unpublished PhD thesis, University of Auckland.
Huguet, A. and Janés, J. (2005) Immigrant children in bilingual societies. Attitudes towards languages by newcomers to Catalonia. *Cultura y Education* 17 (4), 309–321.
Lyon, J. (1996) *Becoming Bilingual. Language Acquisition in a Bilingual Community.* Clevedon: Multilingual Matters.
Martí, F., Ortega, P., Idiazabal, I., Barrena, A., Juaristi, P., Junyent, C., Uranga, B. and Amorrotu, E. (2005) *Words and Worlds. World Languages Review.* Clevedon: Multilingual Matters. UNESCO Etxea.
Ó Laoire, M. (2002) Immigration and language resources in Ireland. Paper presented at Sociolinguistics Symposium 15 Gent.
Ó Laoire, M. (2005) The language planning situation in Ireland. *Current Issues in Language Planning* 6 (3), 251–314.
Ó Riagáin, P. (1997) *Language Policy and Social Reproduction.* Oxford: Clarendon Press.
Ó Riagáin, P. and Ó Gliasáin, M. (1979) *All Irish Primary Schools in the Dublin Area.* Dublin: Institiúid Teangeolaíochta Éireann.

Websites

National Council for Curriculum and Assessment. Review of Languages at www.ncca.ie. Accessed 13.1.06.
Central Statistics Office. www.cso.ie. Accessed 1.07.